HENRY WILLIAMSON
A BIBLIOGRAPHY

Hugoe Matthews

HALSGROVE

First published in Great Britain in 2004

British Library Cataloguing-in-Publication Data.
A CIP record for this title is available from the British Library.

ISBN 1 84114 364 2

HALSGROVE

Halsgrove House
Lower Moor Way
Tiverton, Devon EX16 6SS
Tel: 01884 243242
Fax: 01884 243325
email: sales@halsgrove.com
website: www.halsgrove.com

Printed and bound in Great Britain by
The Cromwell Press, Trowbridge

Dedicated to Nurse Thain

CONTENTS

INTRODUCTION TO THE ENTRIES

From 1921 to 1972 Henry Williamson published 53 books and since his death in 1977 there have been 12 volumes of collected writings and two of transcripts of his radio broadcasts. He also contributed to more than 40 books by other authors and published over 800 items of various sorts in the newspapers and magazines of his time. Efforts to document this material, however, have been limited to the book by Waveney Girvan (D 1931) which was published just ten years after Williamson started writing, and two articles by John Homan in *The Henry Williamson Society Journal* which list the printings of *Tarka* (HWSJ 16, 1987) and *The Flax of Dream* (HWSJ 20, 1989).

The concept behind this work, therefore, was that it should document all Williamson's known publications in a single volume which would be practical rather than academic, affordable rather than out-of-reach, and broad rather than deep in its coverage of the material. In general the approach has been to focus on what readers might want to know, rather than what a bibliographer thinks they ought to know, and to adapt the methods of bibliography to the form of Williamson's writings (which are sometimes unorthodox) rather than the other way round. The hope is that it will serve not just as a manual for the identification of Williamson's books, but also as a tool for further research into the whole range of his work.

Throughout the book items are arranged in chronological order whenever possible, except for Section C where the periodicals are first listed alphabetically by title. Cross-references are either to a numbered item (A1), a particular title (BY), a particular printing (BY 1921), or an entry in one of the later sections (B 1928). Square brackets [ ] denote supplied data.

In Section A, which forms the main part of the book, the objectives have been:

1. To identify and describe, at least in outline, all the UK and American printings of Williamson's books, which up to the present time amount to over 400 items. Foreign-language editions have been noted where they have been encountered or reported, but not actively sought. Provided they have not been tampered with, all these printings can be identified reliably on the basis of the title, the year, the publish-

er's imprint (or lack of it) on the title-page, and a part of the edition statement on verso of the title-page or elsewhere in the book. To accommodate the data in one volume bibliographical description is limited to that which is necessary to determine that a book is complete and in its original casing and jacket (if one was issued) and is less for reprints than for new and first editions.

2. To document the contents of each item with reference to quotations, dedications, illustrations, the main text, dates and end-notes, and indicate whether any important material, such as introductions, prefaces etc., has been added or taken out compared to previous printings.

3. To determine where each printing has come from, in relation to both the type-setting and the text. With most authors this would be relatively straightforward, but with Williamson it is not. Most works of fiction are never revised, but with Williamson it was standard practice (there are five versions of *Dandelion Days* and six of *Tarka*) and to complicate matters further these changes were often made within a previous type-setting (ie without creating a new edition) and sometimes without any indication (eg *The Pathway* 1929a).

For this analysis, therefore, it has been been necessary not only to make a detailed comparison of a large number of texts, but also to devise a specific category of book, namely a 'Reprint with Revisions', which if not bibliographically unique in fiction is certainly uncommon. It is for this reason also that throughout Section A the textual and printing origins of each book have had to be treated as two distinct and independent strands.

In describing the printing origins of each item the term 'Edition' is defined strictly as a work derived wholly or mainly from a new setting of type, and 'Reprint' as a work derived wholly or mainly from a previous setting of type (whether by type-press, lithography or photographic reproduction). The term 'Issue' refers to the way in which all or part of a printing is marketed or presented (eg signed issue, cheaper issue etc.), and 'Reissue', though it occurs rarely, to a situation in which sheets from a previous printing have been bound up in a different format and remarketed after an interval of time.

Sections B and D are essentially lists with notes but no bibliographical description, with the criteria for inclusion given at the start of each Section. Section C represents the first attempt that has been made to compile a list of all Williamson's contributions to periodicals, though some of the data is incomplete and there is little doubt that more items will be found in the future. To describe all these items fully and determine their complex connections with his published books would require another volume.

Methods used in Section A:
'1930': the year of publication, usually from the book itself but occasionally from other sources; also used to identify a particular printing (eg BY 1930).

'Faber & Faber Limited': a transcription of the publisher's imprint as given on the title-page or elsewhere in the book, printed in bold type when the item has been seen and documented by this author; published in the UK unless otherwise stated.

'Reprint of 1929; the second text': a summary of the source of the type-setting and the text (see part 3 of the Introduction above).

'First published in Mcmxxx': a transcript of the critical part of the edition statement, from verso of the title-page unless otherwise stated, followed by additional statements of limitation etc. if present.

'Printed by ...': the printer's imprint as given in the book; confined to first and new editions; printed in the UK unless otherwise stated.

'Puffin Story Book No.60': where the item is part of a designated series.

'Pp': the total number of pages between the free endpapers, including blanks and integral advertisements, given as a single number (pp.100) where the preliminaries are included in the pagination, and as two numbers (pp.x + 100) where they are not; plates and illustrations are included if they are reckoned, and identified if they are not.

'Illustrations': black and white unless otherwise stated.

'190 x 125mm': the approximate size of the front cover measured first from the top to the bottom edge and then from the hinge to the fore-edge.

'Covers': all items are cased in boards unless otherwise stated.

'Edges': all are trimmed (to varying degrees) unless otherwise stated.

'Endpapers': white or cream and unprinted unless otherwise stated.

'Dust jacket white': indicates that the underlying paper is white (not coloured) even if overprinted with a background colour; as jackets can be moved inappropriately from one book to another, particularly within a sequence of impressions, they are described in some detail, with the emphasis on significant points of difference.

Abbreviations: for book titles see 'Contents' page; others used in the text are:

ad/s	advertisement/s
bib note	bibliographical note
chap/s	chapter/s
b/w	black and white
ed/s	edition/s
HW or W	Henry Williamson
HWS	The Henry Williamson Society
HWSJ	The Henry Williamson Society Journal
ms/s	manuscript/s

Acknowledgements:
The two people without whom this work would not have been completed are first, my wife, who not only tolerated the project but actively supported it, and second, Stephen Francis Clarke, bookseller, who has provided access to many rare items, the results of his own past researches, and much of the motivation. I am indebted also to John Gregory for important contributions to the periodicals section and for reading the proofs, and to Dr Tony Boakes, Mr Tony Evans and Mr Ted Wood for unrestricted access to specimens that I would not otherwise have seen. Finally my thanks are due to the Trustees of the Henry Williamson Literary Estate for their kind and prompt permission to quote from copyright material, and to Anne Williamson personally for the indispensable and detailed records of Henry's life (D 1995, 1998) that have provided most of the background for this study.

A: BOOKS AND PAMPHLETS BY WILLIAMSON

Included in this section are all the printings of Williamson's books and pamphlets that have been identified or reported up to the time of writing (December 2003). Items are arranged in their correct chronological order whenever possible, given the limitation of our knowledge of publication dates, with each of the main titles followed by all the known subsequent printings of that title.

A1 THE BEAUTIFUL YEARS A Tale of Childhood

In the spring of 1921 Henry Williamson (aged 25) left the family home in Lewisham and went to a cottage at Georgeham in North Devon to make his living as a writer. His first book was already finished and had been accepted for publication but was not yet in print.

Published six months later *The Beautiful Years* was just the first of four books in which he set out to tell the story of 'one human unit of Europe immediately before and after the War'. The books were to be subtitled 'A Tale of Childhood', 'A Tale of Boyhood', 'A Tale of Youth' and 'A Tale of Life', though only the first of these was actually used, and the 'human unit' would be William (Willie) Maddison, who appears in the first book at the age of seven, motherless, mischievous and misunderstood. By 1928 *Dandelion Days, The Dream of Fair Women* and *The Pathway* had been published and in 1936 the whole work was brought together in one volume under the title *The Flax of Dream* (A24).

In an early copy of *The Beautiful Years* presented to Gwendoline Rendle ('Spica Virginis') Williamson wrote: 'if as you read, it seems a little rough, a little wild, a little awkward, remember that its lone parent at least did all he could for it. If too, its clothes are wrong; if its ears are dirty; if it is gauche; do not judge harshly ...', but sales were poor and the first edition was never reprinted. Later printings derive either from the revisions of 1929a and 1929b or the final text of 1936.

1921. W. Collins Sons & Co. Ltd. *First edition.*
'Copyright, 1921'. No printer's imprint. Collins' 'First Novel' Library. Pp.viii + 256. 193 x 124mm. Blue cloth, orangestamped on the front and

spine. Dust jacket white, printed in blue and red, with a colour illustration of three figures round a bonfire (from a scene in the book), signed 'Lendon', on the front panel. Price 7/6. Published October 1921. 750 copies; some remaindered at 10d each (Girvan, D 1931).

Contents:
- quotation from Richard Jefferies on title-page, Francis Thompson p.162;
- dedication: 'In deep affection to my Mother and my Father, this story of far away and long ago is given';
- 'Note' explaining that this is Book I of *The Flax of Dream*, that Book II is 'being spun' and that the characters 'have no existence in the world of reality';
- text (pp.1–252) in 5 sections, headed, with subheadings in the text, ending 'Brockley, June - November 1920', with the barn-owl device that Williamson had designed and was to use in most of his books:

Paternity	
One Year	13 subheadings
Another Year	14 subheadings (the last with 4 numbered parts)
The Broken Year	10 subheadings
Paternity	

1929a. Faber & Faber Limited. *New edition, revised; the second text.*
i) 'First published in Mcmxxix'. Printed by Trend and Company. Pp.248. 198 x 125mm. Red cloth, goldstamped on the spine. Dust jacket white, printed in red and black, with a scroll device on the spine panel; some with a wraparound advertisement band, green, printed in black, quoting a review by Frank Swinnerton. Girvan states that a few jackets, probably on review copies, had 'Awarded the Hawthornden Prize' (ie the author, not this book) on the front panel. Price 7/6. Published October 1929 (letter from Faber 1966). 2580 copies (Girvan).

Some advance review copies have an error on p.62 where lines 5 and 6 are transposed so that line 5 begins 'neither' and line 6 begins 'keepers'; corrected in the published edition.

ii) Signed, large-paper issue: as i) except: 'This edition printed on English hand-made paper is limited to two hundred copies. This is number ...' followed by the number and author's signature in ink, on recto of the first leaf. 235 x 150mm. Blue buckram, goldstamped on the front and spine;

top edge gilt, others untrimmed (uniform in style with the signed issues of DD, DFW, PW). No jacket. Price 2 guineas. 200 copies, but additional copies are known: one signed but unnumbered and another inscribed to the artist C.R.W. Nevinson dated New Year's Day 1930 (in return for an etching that Nevinson had sent for Christmas 1929).

In this edition the subtitle and Note are omitted, the dedication reads 'To the Mother and To the Father' (a curious change), and the quotation from Francis Thompson is reduced to a sentence. At the end 'Brockley' is omitted and a new 'Note' added listing the titles in *The Flax of Dream* and *The Star-Born* (not then published).

In the text the three middle sections have headings to indicate Willie Maddison's age and are divided into 30 conventional chapters, unheaded: 'Seven Years Old' (chaps. 1–10), 'Eight Years Old' (chaps. 11–22), 'Nine Years Old' (chaps. 23–30). Words or lines are changed on over half the pages and in the later chapters passages of narrative or dialogue amounting to full pages are omitted or rewritten.

It was the critical interest generated by *The Pathway* that prompted Williamson to revise the earlier books in *The Flax of Dream*, but neither Collins nor Cape would agree to publish them so they went to Faber. In the bibliographical note in FOD Williamson says: 'During the rewriting ... it was always the author's determination that the spirit of each book should remain as in the original version. Therefore the humour of Book One was not refined from its twenty-two-year-old crudity and inexperience ...'

1929b. E.P. Dutton & Co., Inc. New York. *American edition of the second text, with further revisions; the third text.*
'Copyright, 1929 ... First edition'. Printed in the USA. A Dutton Prize Book. Pp.288. 196 x 130mm. Blue patterned cloth, goldstamped on the front and spine. Dust jacket white, printed in two shades of blue. 1027 copies 'apparently' (see GWC p.308).

The dedication is now 'To the Mother, To the Father'. Compared to the text of 1929a there are differences on at least 30 pages, mostly in the form of words or lines that are altered, inserted or omitted, but including some passages of the 1929a text where the lines follow the original 1921 text, which suggests either that Williamson decided to reinsert lines that he had previously taken out, or that the UK and American revisions were done independently, or that the American revisions were done first.

Listed in the bib note of 1929c are:
'First printing August, 1929'
'Second printing August, 1929'
'Third printing August, 1929'

1929c. E.P. Dutton & Co., Inc. New York. *Reprint of 1929b; the third text.*
'Fourth printing September, 1929'. Green linson, blackstamped.

1930. Faber & Faber Limited. *Reprint of 1929a; the second text.*
'Second impression January Mcmxxx'. Faber and Faber's 3/6 Fiction.
Grey cloth, redstamped on the spine. Dust jacket white, with a colour
illustration of a boy on a fence by Hookway Cowles.

1932. Faber & Faber Limited. *Reprint of 1929a, the second text; in The
Faber Library*
'Reprinted for this new edition Mcmxxxii'. The Faber Library No.3.
Green cloth, goldstamped. Dust jacket pink, printed in green and black.
Price 3/6.

1935. Faber & Faber Limited. *Reprint of 1929a; the second text; in The
Faber Library.*
'Reprinted ... November Mcmxxxv'. The Faber Library No.3. Green
cloth, goldstamped. Dust jacket light green, printed in red and blue,
with 'Second impression in this edition' on the front flap.

1936. In *The Flax of Dream* (A24, pp.11–245). *Reprint of 1929a, with further revisions; the fourth text.*
Printed from the 1929a type-setting but with new signatures and the
dedication and date and Note at the end of the text omitted. In the text
p.20 ends with a new sentence 'It's my father's, but he doesn't know
I've got it,' and p.64 ends with 'green shadows of the woodland spring,'
replacing the last two lines of the previous versions.

1942a. Faber & Faber Limited. *Reprint of 1936; the fourth text; in The
Faber Library.*
'Reprinted ... April Mcmxlii'. The Faber Library No.3. Pp.232. Green
cloth, silverstamped.
    Printed to War Economy Standard on thinner paper and fewer
pages by eliminating flytitles and other blank areas, with the pagination
and signatures adjusted accordingly. The dedication and date and Note

at the end of the text are restored, with the textual changes of 1936 now on pp.11, 55.

1942b. Faber and Faber Limited. *New edition of the second text.*
'Reprinted ... May Mcmxlii'. Printed by Purnell and Sons. Faber 'Q' Books. Pp.240. 180 x 124mm. Paperback. Covers printed in pink and black. Price 2/-.
Not a reprint as stated, but a new type-setting of 1929a.

1943. Faber and Faber. *Reprint of 1942b; the second text.*
'Reprinted ... December Mcmxliii'. Yellow cloth, goldstamped.

1944. Faber and Faber. *Reprint of 1942b; the second text.*
'Reprinted ... November Mcmxliv'. Yellow cloth. Dust jacket white, printed in red and black. Price 5/-.

1948. Faber and Faber. *Reprint of 1942b; the second text.*
'Reprinted ... June Mcmxlviii'. Yellow cloth, bluestamped. Dust jacket white, printed in red, blue-grey and black. Price 7/6.

1949. Penguin Books. *New edition of the fourth text.*
'Published in Penguin Books 1949'. Printed by Whitefriars Press. Penguin No.696. Pp.256. 178 x 112mm. Paperback. Covers printed in orange and black. Price 1/6.
Includes a publisher's note 'About This Book', unsigned, with the textual changes of 1936 now on pp.12, 61.

1952. Faber.
Listed by Homan (HWSJ 20); not seen.

1957. Faber.
Listed by Homan (HWSJ 20), paperback; not seen.

1967. Faber & Faber Limited. *Reprint of 1929a; the second text.*
'First published in this edition Mcmlxvii'. Faber paper covered Editions. Paperback. Price 7/6.

1969. Faber.
Listed by Homan (HWSJ 20), cloth and paperback; not seen.

1983. Zenith. *Reprint of 1929a; the second text.*
'Hamlyn paperbacks edition 1983'. The Hamlyn Publishing Group.
ISBN 0 600 20684 X. Paperback. Cover illustration from a painting 'A
Summer Noon' by John Atkinson Grimshaw. Price £2.50.
   A photo-reprint with print size enlarged.

Foreign-language edition:
1938. *Die Schönen Jahre.* Roman von Henry Williamson. S. Fischer
Verlag. Berlin. German-language edition of *The Beautiful Years* and
Dandelion Days in one volume.

A2 THE LONE SWALLOWS

In between each book of the *The Flax of Dream* Williamson published a
volume of miscellaneous writings collected from newspapers, magazines, or unpublished work. In the first of these, *The Lone Swallows*, most
of the pieces are short and about birds or the seasons, but 'Ernie' is a
cameo of a small boy, and two are fantasies, including 'Swallow Brow',
an anthropomorphic piece in the style of Richard Jefferies' *Wood Magic*.
   In the 'Compiler's Note' he gives no rationale for his selection other
than saying that 'Winter's Eve' was included as it was his 'first attempt
to describe the sights and sounds of the English countryside,' and
'London Children and Wild Flowers' because it was written 'in a
visionary fervour'.
   In a letter to Wilfred Meynell dated 26 November 1926 he wrote:
'Reviewers have generally said the stories of mine are "faked", but I
know they are (with one exception) "true but imaginary"'. In another
letter on 30 November he said that the book 'was written only 12
months after I had begun to write and therefore is full of faults, strain,
florescence, and perhaps self-consciousness. I am trying to make myself
to write carefully.'
   The first edition was never reprinted in its entirety and 'The Outlaw'
(the 'fake' story) was not reprinted in any issue, perhaps in response to
the critics. Redesigned for school use the book was put in Collins' New
World Series in 1924, then split into two as 'The Incoming of Summer'
and 'Midsummer Night' in the same year, and then put together again
with two new pieces and the original title in the Kings' Way Classics in
1928. In 1933 it was published by Putnam with additional material,

revised, reshaped, and illustrated by Tunnicliffe (to match *Tarka* 1932 and *The Old Stag* 1933).

1922. W. Collins Sons & Co. Ltd. *First edition; 31 titles.*
'Copyright, 1922'. Printed by Collins Sons and Co. Pp.x + 254. 213 x 138mm. Pale yellow paper boards, backed in black cloth with a white label printed in black; top edge trimmed, others untrimmed. No jacket. Price [8/6]. Published ?July 1922 (inscribed copies). 500 copies; some remaindered at 6d each (Girvan, D 1931).

Contents:
- quotation from Richard Jefferies on title-page;
- 'Compiler's Note' (3 pp.) with acknowledgement of sources and notes on some of the titles, dated 'Skirr Cottage, 11th November, 1921';
- text (pp.1–245) with 31 titles, ending with owl device:

	Notes:
The Lone Swallows	from *Saturday Review*; in LS 1933
Lady Day in Devon	from *Saturday Review*; in LS 1926 as 'March Day', and LS 1933 as 'Spring in Devon'
The Incoming of Summer	in LS 1933
Haunt of the Evejar (i, ii)	(i) from *Daily Express* (DE) 7.6.21; in LS 1933 as 'The Coming of Summer'; (ii) not in LS 1933
A Deserted Quarry in February	not in LS 1933
Vignettes of Nature (i)	from DE 23.4.21; in LS 1933 as 'May Day'
Vignettes of Nature (ii)	from DE 30.3.21; not in LS 1933
Hawk Notes	in LS 1933
Prophet Birds	from DE 6.9.21; in LS 1933
A Bird Mystic	from DE 19.7.21; in LS 1933
Samaritans	from DE 20.8.21; in LS 1933
Sportsmen of the Rubbish-Heaps	from DE 3.5.21; in LS 1933
Runaways	in LS 1933
London Children and Wild Flowers	from *English Review* 1921; in LS 1933 as 'The Passing of the Blossom' (the original title)
Meadow Grasses	in LS 1933
Tiger's Teeth	from *Wide World Magazine* 1922;

	in LS 1933
The Outlaw	see A57, 12 9.20; omitted from all later printings
Peregrines in Love	from *Field* 1921; in LS 1933
Midsummer Night	? from *English Review* 1920; in LS 1933
A Feathered Waster	in LS 1933 as 'A Very Bad Bird'
Invocation	from DE 1.7.21; in LS 1933 as 'The Drought (1921)'
Cockney Bird Trippers	in LS 1933
'Fullness After Dearth'	not in LS 1933
Cuckoo Notes	in LS 1933
Days of Autumn	in LS 1933
Swallow Brow: A Fantasy	not in LS 1933
Winter's Eve	in LS 1933
Ernie	in LS 1933
A Seed in Waste Places	in LS 1933
The Change: A Fantasy	not in LS 1924a; in LS 1926; in LS 1933 as 'The Change: A Fantasy of Whitefoot Lane'
Proserpine's Message	? from DE 15.9.21; in LS 1933
Strix Flammea	not in LS 1926; in LS 1928; in LS 1933

[1924a]. Collins' Clear-Type Press. *Reprint of 29 titles from the first edition; in The New World Series.*
No date. 'Manufactured in Great Britain'. The New World Series. Pp.vi + 214. Frontispiece and 3 plates, not reckoned. 190 x 125mm. Blue cloth, blackstamped on the covers and spine. Price [2/6]. Published [September] 1924.

Here the Compiler's Note is omitted together with two stories, 'The Outlaw' and 'The Change', and the titles rearranged, with new pagination and signatures, and four full-page photographs of birds, unattributed.

[1924b]. Collins' Clear-Type Press. *Reprint of 13 titles from 1924a.*
Titled THE INCOMING OF SUMMER.
No date. 'Manufactured in Great Britain'. The New World Series. Pp.vi + 110. Frontispiece and 1 plate, not reckoned. 190 x 125mm. Blue cloth boards, blackstamped on the front and spine. Price [1/9]. Also in

blue linen-covered card, blackstamped on the front only; perfect-bound. Price [1/6].
Contents consist of the first 13 titles listed in 1924a and two of the illustrations.

[1924c]. Collins' Clear-Type Press. *Reprint of 16 titles from 1924a.*
Titled A MIDSUMMER NIGHT on the cover, MIDSUMMER NIGHT on the title-page.
No date. 'Manufactured in Great Britain'. The New World Series. Pp.vi + 106. Frontispiece and 1 plate, not reckoned. 190 x 125mm. Blue cloth boards, blackstamped on the front and spine. Price [1/9]. Also in blue linen-covered card, blackstamped on the front only; perfect-bound. Price [1/6].
Contents consist of the 16 titles and two illustrations in 1924a that were not used in 1924b.

1926. E.P. Dutton & Company. New York. *American edition; 29 titles (not as 1924a).*
Subtitled 'And Other Essays of the Country Green'.
'Copyright, 1926'. Printed in the USA. Pp.xiv + 230. 195 x 129mm. Patterned paper boards in gold and black, backed in dark purple-grey cloth, with labels printed in red on the front and spine; pictorial endpapers in green by Charles E. Cartwright. Dust jacket white, printed in grey and red, repeating the endpaper design.
A new type-setting with 'Dedicated to Richard Jefferies' added and the 'Compiler's Note' rewritten as a 'Preface' for American readers, undated. Of the original titles 'The Outlaw' and 'Strix Flammea' are omitted (ie different from 1924a) and 'Lady Day in Devon' is retitled 'March Day'.

[1928]. W. Collins Sons & Co Ltd. *Reprint of 30 titles from the first edition, with 2 new titles; in The Kings' Way Classics.*
No date. 'Copyright'. Collins' Kings' Way Classics [No.38]. Pp.x + 246. 175 x 107mm. Fawn cloth with a green label, goldstamped, on the spine; top edge gilt. Dust jacket a) light brown, printed in black, with 'Henry T. [sic] Williamson' on the front panel; b) orangebrown, printed in mauve, with the same error on the front panel; series list to no.38 on the back panel. Price 3/6.
Compared to the first edition the quotation from Richard Jefferies is omitted, together with 'The Outlaw', and the titles rearranged, with

new pagination. New titles are 'The Crowstarver' (? from *Manchester Guardian* 1927) and 'Birds in London' which are added at the end accompanied by a brief 'Author's Note'.

[1929]. W. Collins Sons & Co Ltd. *Reissue of 1928; in Collins' Pocket Novels.*
No date. 'Copyright'. Collins' Pocket Novels series. Blue cloth, gold-stamped, with facsimile HW signature on the front. Dust jacket pale beige, printed in blue, with the series title and list on the back panel. Price 2/6.
The half-title and title-page are cancels.

1933. G.P. Putnam's Sons. *New edition; 43 titles; illustrated by Tunnicliffe.*
Subtitled 'And Other Essays of Boyhood and Youth'.

i) 'New enlarged and illustrated edition, 1933'. Printed by The Shenval Press. Pp.xvi + 244. Frontispiece and illustrations, reckoned. 190 x 122mm. Green cloth, goldstamped on the front (owl device) and spine. Dust jacket grey-green, printed in green and black, with the illustration from p.241 (swallows and spire) reproduced on the front panel; ads for TA and OS 'Uniform with this Volume' on the back panel. Price 5/-. Published [November] 1933.

ii) Cheaper issue: as i) but dust jacket white, printed in black, with the tailpiece from p.243 (two swallows on a wire) added on the spine panel, and a note 'This new cheap edition of *The Lone Swallows* together with the uniform editions of *Tarka*, *The Old Stag* and *The Peregrine's Saga* completes Henry Williamson's nature writings to date ...', with quotes from reviews, on the front flap; blurb from HW on the back flap; ads for TA, OS and PS 'Uniform with this Volume' on the back panel. Price 3/6. Published presumably in 1934, after PS.

Contents (compared to 1922):
    - new subtitle;
    - quotation from Jefferies omitted, 'Dedicated to Richard Jefferies' added (as 1926);
    - 'Compiler's Note' replaced by a 'Note to the New Edition' dated 1933 but causing some confusion as 'The Return' is referred to as 'The Nesting Boxes' and the dates given for some of the essays do not correspond with the ages at which Williamson says they were written;

- illustrations: frontispiece, 23 full-page wood-engravings and 35 line drawings as head or tailpieces or in the text, by C.F. Tunnicliffe;
- text (pp.1–242) made up of 27 titles from the first edition (all revised and some retitled) and 16 items from other sources (as below), followed by 'Here ends The Lone Swallows ...written mainly before 1921, slightly revised in 1933; and their fortune is with that which brought them to being':

	Notes:
Four Elegies:	
Fox	'Reynard' from 'Elegies Three' in PS 1923
Pig	'Corp' from 'Elegies Three' in PS 1923
Mouse	'Nor' from 'Elegies Three' in PS 1923
Boy	'The Crowstarver' from LS 1928
A Boy's Nature Diary	from ms. 1913; his earliest work
The Return	from ms.
Birds in London	from LS 1928
A London Owl	from PS 1923
The Old Pond	from OS 1926
The Country of the Rain:	from *New London Magazine* 1930–31
November	
December	
January	
February	
March	
April	
Migration	from *Daily Express* 5.4.33

1937. G.P. Putnam's Sons. *Reprint of 1933; illustrated.*
'Reprinted November, 1937'. Green cloth, goldstamped. Dust jacket white, with illustrations as 1933ii. Price 3/6.

1945. Putnam & Company Ltd. *Reprint of 1933; illustrated; limited issue.*
'Limited illustrated edition 1945'. 207 x 135mm. Green cloth, gold-stamped, with 'HW' monogram on the front, as one of The Henry Williamson Nature Books (see A33). 500 copies.

Not a new edition but a reprint with the title as running head and some marginal headings repositioned to match the HWNB format.

1946. Putnam & Company Ltd. *Reprint of 1945; illustrated.*
'Reprinted November 1946'. Green cloth, goldstamped. Dust jacket white, with an illustration of a swallow feeding young (not in the book) by Tunnicliffe on the front panel. Price 8/6.

1948. Putnam & Company Ltd. *Reprint of 1945; illustrated.*
'Reprinted March 1948'. Green cloth, goldstamped. Dust jacket as 1946. Price 8/6.

?1949. Putnam.
Announced in the 'School edition' of Tarka (TA 1949aii, p.281): 'For School Recreational Libraries, Nature Books by Henry Williamson, each 8/6. The Old Stag, The Lone Swallows, The Peregrine's Saga'; not seen.

1984a. Zenith.
Paperback, with illustrations by Tunnicliffe; not seen.

1984b. Alan Sutton. *Reprint of 1933, illustrated.*
'This edition published 1984'. ISBN 0 86299 193 5. Pp.x + 246. Paperback. Cover illustration from a painting 'Barn Owl at Dawn, Eccup' by Raymond Booth. Price £4.95.
    A photo-reprint with the illustrations well reproduced.

A3 DANDELION DAYS

The second book in *The Flax of Dream* is the story of Willie Maddison's schooldays. In a lengthy 'Epistle Apological' to his literary agent, printed only in the first edition, Williamson recalls the genesis of *The Flax* and explains that *Dandelion Days* has a hidden agenda, which is clearly based on his own years at Colfe's Grammar School in Lewisham from 1907–13:
    'Willie Maddison, I imagine, is nearly eighteen years of age when he stands at the eastern edge of the spinney and bids farewell to the fields and the trees which he has known for so long ... How valuable have been the lessons at Colham Grammar School, situate in the West Country, you must estimate for yourself; you must contrast the value of what is learned in the muggy atmosphere of the class-room with the sweet and lovely things seen in the countryside. It is to show this

contrast ... that I have written this book.

'... it is this instructional system that I would like to see considerably altered. Do not misunderstand me. I have no nihilistic tendencies towards schools. I do not intend, in my third volume to make Willie Maddison lead a punitive expedition against Colham Grammar School ... Rather I would have these school-master characters regarded with compassion. For years ... they have had to bear with numberless naughty boys, insolent boys, deceitful boys ... and boys like Willie Maddison ...

'You have read "The Beautiful Years," and here is Book II., and with it the boyhood of Willie Maddison definitely terminates. He is leaving for London; the month is July, and the year is nineteen-fourteen ...'.

Once again sales of the first edition were poor and it was not reprinted. In 1930 the whole book was rewritten ('toned-down' as Williamson put it), with additional changes in 1930c, 1932 and 1936.

1922. W. Collins Sons & Co. Ltd. *First edition.*
'Copyright 1922'. Printed by Collins Sons and Co. Pp.xiv + 306. 190 x 123mm. Blue cloth, orangestamped on the front and spine. Dust jacket white, printed in black and red, with a colour illustration of Maddison and eight named characters from the book, signed [C J Morse], on the front panel. Price 7/6. Published [October] 1922. 600 copies; some remaindered at 1Id each (Girvan, D 1931).

Contents:
- quotations from Richard Jefferies on title-page and pp.2, 62, 184, Walter de la Mare p.262;
- 'Inscribed to Andrew H. Dakers' (Williamson's literary agent);
- 'Epistle Apological to Mr. Dakers' (6 pp, not printed in later editions) explaining the ethos of the work, dated 27 January 1922;
- 'Addenda' with the subtitles of *The Flax of Dream* and notes, dated 7 March 1922;
- text (pp.3–299) in 4 sections, headed, with subheadings in the text, ending 'December, 1920 - September, 1921, Brockley - Georgeham', with owl device:

The Gardeners' Methods	3 subheadings
The Opening of the Flower	11 subheadings
Shadow and Sunlight	12 subbeadings
The Passing of the Blossom	4 subheadings

1930a. Faber & Faber Limited. *New edition, rewritten; the second text.*
i) 'First published in Mcmxxx'. Printed by Trend and Company. Pp.316.
198 x 127mm. Blue cloth, goldstamped on the spine. Dust jacket white,
printed in red and black, with a scroll device on the spine panel. Price
7/6. Published February 1930. [2500] copies.

ii) Signed, large-paper issue: as i) except: 'This edition printed on English
hand-made paper is limited to two hundred copies. This is number ...'
followed by the number and author's signature in ink, on recto of the first
leaf. 235 x 150mm. Yellow buckram, goldstamped on the front and spine;
top edge gilt, others untrimmed (uniform in style with the signed issues
of BY, DFW, PW). No jacket. Price 2 guineas. 200 copies.

In this edition a quotation from Robert Bridges is added to the title-
page and a new one from Richard Jefferies replaces the one from Walter
de la Mare. The original inscription, 'Epistle' and 'Addenda' are
omitted and replaced by a one-page letter 'To Andrew Dakers' in which
Williamson says 'Now I have rewritten the book, during the past
month, and only seventeen sentences remain of the original published
version. I think that I was unfair to our mutual friend Maddison in
those days ...', dated 'Shallowford, 6 November 1929'. At the end of the
text 'Brockley - Georgeham' is omitted and the 'Note' added as in BY
1929a.
    In the text the sections have new headings and are divided into 32
chapters, unheaded: 'One Petal Out' (chaps. 1–8), 'Opening of the
Flower' (chaps. 9–20), 'The Seed Loosening' (chaps. 21–27), 'Over the
Hills and Far Away' (chaps. 28–32), followed by an 'Epigraph' in the
form of a letter to 'Private W.B. Maddison' from his old schoolmaster.

1930b. E.P. Dutton & Co., Inc. New York. *American edition of the second
text.*
'Copyright, 1930 ... First edition'. Printed in the USA. Pp.320. 196 x
130mm. Green cloth, yellowstamped on the front and spine; top edge
yellow, foredge untrimmed. Dust jacket white, printed in green and
yellow, with a geometric pattern. Price $2.50.
    A new type-setting of 1930a including the letter to Andrew Dakers;
no revisions noted.

1930c. Faber & Faber Limited. *Reprint of 1930a, with further revisions; the
third text.*

i) 'Second impression April Mcmxxx'. Blue cloth, goldstamped on the spine.

ii) as i) but in yellow cloth, bluestamped on the spine. Dust jacket white, with a colour illustration of a boy and girl on a hillside by Hookway Cowles. Price 3/6.

This has the same pagination as 1930a but with the following alterations to the text: p.153 line 31: 'cormorants' instead of 'stags' (? originally meant to be 'shags') with the subsequent lines reset; p.173: four lines rewritten; p.211: fifteen lines rewritten; p.302: last paragraph of chapter 31 rewritten, ending 'the slight form shaking among the grasses withered at the roadside'.

1932. Faber & Faber Limited. *Reprint of 1930c, with a further revision; the fourth text; in The Faber Library.*
'New and cheaper edition Mcmxxxii'. The Faber Library No.9. Green cloth, goldstamped. Dust jacket pink, printed in green and black. Price 3/6.
'You can kiss my arse' is removed from p.269 lines 28–9 which are rewritten.

1936. In *The Flax of Dream* (A24, pp.247–550). *Reprint of 1932, with further revisions; the fifth text.*
This has new pagination and signatures and changes to the last few lines of chapter 32 which ends 'ripe for harvest[:] it was July, 1914'. The letter to Andrew Dakers and the previous date and Note at the end of the text are omitted and the Epigraph retitled 'The Alien Corn' (a subheading in BY 1921), with a quotation from Wifred Owen added on p.548.

1940. Faber & Faber Limited. *Reprint of 1936; the fifth text; in The Faber Library.*
'Reprinted June Mcmxl'. The Faber Library No.9. Pp.316. Green cloth, silverstamped.
The letter to Andrew Dakers, date and Note at the end of the text and the title 'Epigraph' are now restored, but the quotation from Owen is omitted.

1942. Faber & Faber Limited. *Reprint of 1940; the fifth text; in The Faber Library.*

'Reprinted ... April Mcmxlii'. The Faber Library No.9. Pp.300. Green cloth, silverstamped. Dust jacket yellow, printed in green. Price 3/6.

Printed to War Economy Standard on thinner paper and fewer pages with the quotations at the head of each section not on fly-titles.

1945. Faber and Faber Limited. *Reprint of 1942: the fifth text.*
'Reprinted ... Mcmxlv'. Green cloth, goldstamped. Dust jacket yellow, printed in brown. Price 5/-.

1947. Faber and Faber Limited. *Reprint of 1942; the fifth text.*
'Reprinted ... Mcmxlvii'. Green cloth.

1950. Penguin Books. *New edition of the fifth text.*
'Published in Penguin Books 1950'. Printed by C. Nicholls and Company. Penguin No.768. Pp.304. 180 x 112mm. Paperback. Covers printed in orange and black. Price 1/6.

Includes a publisher's note 'About this Book', unsigned, and a new dedication 'To Andrew Dakers' but the letter to him and the date at the end of the text are omitted.

1956. Faber and Faber Limited. *Reprint of 1942; the fifth text.*
'Reprinted ...Mcmlvi'. Green cloth. Dust jacket white, printed in red, yellow and black. Price 12/6.

1966. Faber & Faber Limited. *Reprint of 1932; the fourth text.*
i) 'This edition reprinted Mcmlxvi'. Orange cloth. Dust jacket white, printed in red, yellow and black. Price 15/-.

ii) 'First published in Faber paper-covered editions Mcmlxvi'. Paperback. Price 8/6.

After five reprints of the fifth text Faber now revert to the fourth text, but with the dedication 'To Andrew Dakers' and the letter to him and the Note at the end of the text omitted, as in the 1950 Penguin.

1969. Faber & Faber Limited. *Reprint of 1966; the fourth text.*
'Reprinted 1969'. Faber paper covered Editions. SBN 571 06755 7. Paperback. Price 9/- or 45p.

1983. Zenith. *Reprint of 1966; the fourth text.*

'Hamlyn Paperbacks edition 1983'. The Hamlyn Publishing Group. ISBN 0 600 20683 1. Paperback. Cover illustration from a painting by E.K. Brice. Price £2.50.
  A photo-reprint with print size enlarged.

Foreign-language edition: see BY (A1).

A4 THE PEREGRINE'S SAGA And Other Stories of the Country Green

Williamson's second volume of collected work, *The Peregrine's Saga*, consists of 16 stories 'written during the early days in Devon' that had either been published in magazines or were still in manuscript. Fewer but more substantial than the items in *The Lone Swallows* they are mainly about birds or animals, except for 'The Chronicle of Halbert and Znarr', the story of a cockney boy and a crow, 'Unknown', a tale of the paranormal, and 'A Weed's Tale', which epitomises his growing ability to make a good story out of something as insignificant as a dock-seed. It was this ability that would later generate full-length books about an otter, a fish and a pigeon.
  It was the first of his books to be illustrated but was never reprinted in its original form. In 1934 it was published by Putnam with new contents, revised, and illustrated by Tunnicliffe (to match *Tarka* 1932, *The Lone Swallows* 1933 and *The Old Stag* 1933). From this edition five pieces were collected again in *The Henry Williamson Animal Saga* (A46) and ten in *Collected Nature Stories* (A58).

1923. W. Collins Sons & Co. Ltd. *First edition; 16 titles; illustrated by Reynolds.*
'Copyright, 1923'. Printed by Collins Sons and Co. Pp.viii + 312. Frontispiece and 4 plates, not reckoned. 195 x 130mm. Green cloth, blindstamped on the front, goldstamped on the spine; top edge trimmed, others untrimmed. Dust jacket white, printed in red and black, with the frontispiece reproduced on the front panel. Price 7/6. Published [November] 1923. 600 copies; some remaindered at 10d each (Girvan, D 1931).

Contents:
- quotation 'Ad astra per aspera' on title-page;

- dedication: 'Inscribed to Esther Francis Stokes for many deeds in amity' (the mother of 'Annabelle' in SIS);
- illustrations: frontispiece and 4 plates of line drawings by Warwick Reynolds who had illustrated 'Raskil' in *Pan Fiction*;
- text (pp.3–301) with 16 titles, some with subheadings in the text, ending 'Georgeham 1922', with owl device:

	Notes:
The Saga of Chakchek the One-Eyed	from *Hutchinson's* 1923; in PS 1934 retitled
Bloody Bill Brock	? from *Pearson's Magazine*; in OS 1933 retitled; not in PS 1934
Li'l Jearge	from *Royal Magazine*; in PS 1934 retitled
The Bottle Birds	in PS 1934 retitled
Zoe	in OS 1933; not in PS 1934
Raskil the Wood Rogue	from *Pan Fiction* 1922; in PS 1934 retitled
Redeye	in OS 1933; not in PS 1934
A Weed's Tale	in PS 1934
Elegies Three	in LS 1933 as part of 'Four Elegies'; not in PS 1934
Aliens	in PS 1934
The Chronicle of Halbert and Znarr	in PS 1934 retitled
Bluemantle	in PS 1934
Unknown	in PS 1934
The Meal	in PS 1934
A London Owl	in LS 1933; not in PS 1934
The Saga of Mousing Keekee	in PS 1934 retitled

1925. E.P. Dutton & Company. New York. *American edition; 16 titles, revised; not illustrated.*
Titled SUN BROTHERS.
'Copyright, 1925'. Printed in the USA. Pp.x + 302. 196 x 129mm. Grey-green mottled paper boards, backed in grey-green cloth, with labels printed in green on the front and spine; pictorial endpapers in green. Dust jacket white, printed in green and red, repeating the endpaper design.
    Compared to the first edition the subtitle, illustrations, and date at

the end of the text are omitted, but an ornamented initial letter (unattributed) is added at the start of each item. The order of essays is rearranged and all show textual alterations, mostly limited to single words but occasionally whole lines.

[1927]. W. Collins Sons & Co. Ltd. *Reprint of 1923, with new revisions; not illustrated; in The Kings' Way Classics.*
No date. 'Copyright'. Collins' Kings' Way Classics [No.35]. Pp.viii + 304. 175 x 107mm. Fawn cloth with a green label, goldstamped, on the spine; top edge gilt. Dust jacket a) light orange, printed in black, with 'Henry T. [sic] Williamson' on the front panel; b) orangebrown, printed in purple, corrected to 'Henry Williamson', with the series list to No.38 on the back panel; c) printed in colour with a 'Greek pillar' design and 'Henry Williamson' on the front panel and a list of the first ten volumes in the series on the back panel. Price 3/6.

Here the order of essays is the same as in the first edition but 11 show textual alterations which are mostly independent of those in the American edition (1925) indicating that the two texts were treated separately. The only items that are unchanged are 'Bloody Bill Brock', 'Aliens', 'The Chronicle of Halbert and Znarr', 'The Meal' and 'A London Owl'. Collins had not wanted to make any changes but Williamson had insisted (D 1995).

[1929]. W. Collins Sons & Co. Ltd. *Reprint of 1927; in Collins' Pocket Novels.*
No date. 'Copyright'. Collins' Pocket Novels series. Blue cloth, goldstamped, with facsimile HW signature on the front. Dust jacket beige, printed in blue. Price 2/6.

1934. Putnam & Company. *New edition; 15 titles, with further revisions; illustrated by Tunnicliffe.*
Subtitled 'And Other Wild Tales'.

i) 'First illustrated edition published February 1934'. Printed by The Shenval Press. Pp.xii + 268. Frontispiece and illustrations, reckoned. 190 x 120mm. Green cloth, goldstamped on the front (owl device) and spine. Dust jacket blue-green, printed in black, with the illustration from p.189 (falcon in hand) reproduced on the front panel; ads for TA, OS, LS 'Uniform with this Volume' on the back panel. Price 5/-.

ii) Cheaper issue: as i) but dust jacket white, printed in black, with the illustration from p.232 (falcon at nest) on the front panel and vignette (falcon) from p.191 on the spine panel. Price 3/6.

Contents (compared to 1923):
   - illustrations are now a frontispiece, 23 full-page wood-engravings and 12 line drawings as tailpieces, by C.F. Tunnicliffe;
   - text (pp.1–265) made up of 1I titles from the first edition (all with new revisions and some retitled), and four from other sources, followed by 'Here ends The Peregrine's Saga, and other wild tales, written in Devon and London during 1921 and 1922':

	Notes:
The Mouse	'Li'l Jearge' from first ed.; collected in CNS
A Weed's Tale	from first ed.; collected in CNS
The Air Gipsies	'The Bottle Birds' from first ed.; collected in CNS
The Wood Rogue	'Raskil the Wood Rogue' from first ed.; collected in CNS
Aliens	from first ed.; collected in CNS
Chronicle of Halbert and Znarr	from first ed.; collected in CNS
Mewliboy	from OS 1926; collected in CNS
Bluemantle	from first ed.; collected in CNS
The Meal	from first ed.; collected in CNS
Unknown	from first ed.; collected in CNS
The Peregrine's Saga (5 parts):	collected in HWAS as 'Chakchek the Peregrine'
The Backbreaker's Bride	from *Harper's* 1932 or *Windsor Magazine* 1933
No Eel for Nog	from OS 1926
The Raid on London	'Chakchek's Raid on London' from OS 1926
Love and Death of The One-Eyed	'The Saga of Chakchek ' from first ed.
The Vigil of Mousing Keekee	'The Saga of Mousing Keekee' from first ed.

1937. Putnam & Company. *Reprint of 1934; illustrated.*
'Reprinted November, 1937'. Green cloth.

1945. Putnam & Company Ltd. *Reprint of 1934; illustrated; limited issue.*
'Limited illustrated edition 1945'. 207 x 135mm. Green cloth, gold-stamped, with 'HW' monogram on the front, as one of *The Henry Williamson Nature Books* (see A33). 500 copies.

Not a new edition but a reprint, with the title as running head and some marginal headings repositioned to match the HWNB format.

1946. Putnam & Company Ltd. *Reprint of 1945; illustrated.*
'Reprinted November 1946'. Green cloth. Dust jacket white, printed in black, with the illustration from p.184 (falcon making a kill) on the front panel and owl device on the spine panel. Price 8/6.

1948. Putnam & Company Ltd. *Reprint of 1945; illustrated.*
'Reprinted March 1948'. Green cloth. Dust jacket as 1946. Price 8/6.

?1949. Putnam.
Announced in the 'School edition' of *Tarka* (TA 1949aii, p.281): 'For School Recreational Libraries. Nature Books by Henry Williamson, each 8/6. The Old Stag, The Lone Swallows, The Peregrine's Saga'; not seen.

1960. In *The Henry Williamson Animal Saga* (A46, pp.419–477). *New edition of 5 titles from 1934, revised; not illustrated.*
The five stories that form 'The Peregrine's Saga' in the 1934 edition, now titled 'Chakchek the Peregrine' and numbered 1–5, with occasional alterations to words or lines and an introduction (2 pp.) giving background to the pieces, but no illustrations.

1970. In *Collected Nature Stories* (A58: pp.13–145). *New edition of 10 titles from 1934, revised; 14 illustrations by Tunnicliffe.*
This contains the 10 titles from 1934 that were not collected in HWAS (plus 'A Winter's Tale' from TME) with their associated full-page illustrations, a few revisions to words or lines and a one-page 'Preface' concerning the sale and publishing of HW's early books.

1982. Futura / Macdonald & Co. *New edition of 1970; not illustrated.*
'First Futura edition 1982'. Printed by Collins. The Heritage series. ISBN 0 7088 2201 0. Pp.viii + 152. 178 x 108mm. Paperback. All-round cover illustration from a painting of a seaside scene, unattributed. Price £1.50.

The text of 1970 including the Preface and 'A Winter's Tale' but no illustrations.

A5 THE DREAM OF FAIR WOMEN A Tale of Youth After the Great War

Readers of *Dandelion Days* might have expected the third book in *The Flax of Dream* to be about the War, but Williamson was saving that for *The Chronicle*. Instead it is 1919 and Willie Maddison is suffering the turbulence of desire for a woman who is 'free' in one sense, but not in another. In 1933 Williamson inscribed a reprint of the book 'To Gertrude Johnson who inspired me to write the erotic passages of this romance ...' By today's standards the eroticism is mild, but Gertrude may have been the Miss Johnson that Anne Williamson describes as 'a redoubtable lady vegetarian and nudist, who also took in paying guests,' and who lived in Georgeham (D 1995).

A brief note in the first edition states 'The characters in this book with one exception are imagined. The exception is the character called Peter White. The original of the portrait, an adolescent who wrote "The Document of Hysteria" reproduced here ... ceased to be a few hours after it was composed.' Elsewhere, however, he says that Maddison 'like all the other characters of this novel, was based on a real person' (FOD p. 987).

The Dream of Fair Women was the first of Williamson's books to be published in America but the last of his new works that Collins would agree to publish. One reason was the lack of commercial success. Referring to these works Williamson wrote: 'These "titles" failed to sell. Indeed not one earned its advance royalty payment of £25. When a year or two later, I asked the publishers if they would advance £25 on the option of my next book, which was to conclude *The Flax of Dream*, they wrote to advise me it was not their intention to exercise the option; that they were returning to me the copyrights of the five published books. This gave me the freedom to turn elsewhere ...' (CNS p.15). Another reason was the disagreement over revisions to *The Peregrine's Saga* (PS 1927).

1924a. W. Collins Sons & Co. Ltd. *First edition.*
'Copyright, 1924.' Printed by Collins Sons and Co. Pp.x + 422. 190 x 125mm. Blue cloth, orangestamped on the front and spine. Dust jacket white, printed in black, blue and red, with a colour illustration of figures at a costume ball (from a scene in the book), signed C Morse, on the front panel. Price 7/6. Published June 1924. 750 copies (Girvan, D 1931).

Contents:
- quotation from 'Philosophy of Martha' on title-page, anon p.2, 'Ode to the West Wind' p.134, Swinburne p.330;
- dedication: 'To my friend, J.D. Beresford, Book III. of The Flax of Dream' (Collins' reader who had recommended The Flax);
- note re characters in the book, ending 'Skirr Cottage, 27th Nov., 1923' (not included in later editions);
- text (pp.3–409) in 3 Parts, 34 chapters with headings, and a 'Valediction' which is here part of the narrative, ending 'London - Devon, November, 1919 - November, 1923', with owl device:

Part	I	The Weaver and the Flax	chaps.	1–13
	II	The Scarlet Thread		1–12
	III	The Broken Web		1–9
Valediction				

1924b. E.P. Dutton & Company. New York. *American edition of the first edition, with variant text.*
'Copyright, 1924'. Printed in the USA. Pp.xii + 468. 197 x 128mm. Light fawn, gilt-shot, patterned paper boards, backed in blue cloth, with labels printed in black on the front and spine; lower edge untrimmed. Dust jacket white, printed in blue, with a colour design of a thatched cottage and trees on the front panel. Published [October] 1924.

Changes in text compared to the first edition are: a footnote on p.12, changes to individual words on pp.12, 50, 228, 'while Billjohn whined and licked his hand' omitted from p.382 line 24, and 'avoiding the other's eyes' inserted on p.424 line 32. In his own copy Williamson wrote that these changes were unauthorised and they are not found in any other edition

1931a. Faber & Faber Limited. *New edition, revised; the second text.*
i) 'First published in June Mcmxxxi'. Printed by Trend and Company. Pp.448. 198 x 125mm. Brown cloth, goldstamped on the spine. Dust jacket white, printed in red and black, with a scroll device on the spine panel. Price 7/6. Published [June] 1931. 3500 copies (Girvan).

ii) Signed, large-paper issue: as i) except: 'This edition printed on English hand-made paper is limited to two hundred copies. This is number ...' followed by the number and author's signature in ink, on recto of the first leaf. 235 x 150mm. Red-brown buckram, goldstamped on the front and spine; top edge gilt, others untrimmed (uniform in style with the signed issues of BY, DD, PW). No jacket. Price 2 guineas. 200 copies, but unsigned, unnumbered, and 'Out of Series' copies are also known.

The subtitle, note concerning the characters, and date at the end of the text are omitted and only one of the previous quotations is used (from Swinburne, now on the title-page), with a revised dedication 'To J.D. Beresford, who helped the young writer much; coupled with the name of Walter de la Mare - friends seldom seen, but well beloved'.

The main text is now divided into three unnumbered sections with headings and 41 chapters without headings: 'The Policy of Reconstruction, or, True Reconstruction' (this was an early overall title for *The Flax of Dream*) (chaps. 1–13), 'The Scarlet Thread' (chaps. 14–28), 'The Broken Web' (chaps. 29–41), with the original Valediction rewritten and incorporated as chapter 41 which ends with 'her arm over her eyes,' followed by a new 'Valediction' (a flippant postscript on the fate of the characters) dated 'H.W. Manhattan Island. Fall, 1930'. The reworking of this text, which is heavy but less than in DD 1930a, was completed in three weeks in 1930 while the author was in New York.

1931b. E.P. Dutton & Co., Inc. New York. *American reprint of 1931a; the second text.*
'New and entirely rewritten edition. Copyright, 1931'. Printed in the USA. A Dutton Prize Book. Pp.448. 195 x 128mm. Blue cloth, gold-stamped on the front and spine. Also in red or beige linson, black-stamped. Dust jacket as 1924b. Price $2.50.

1933. Faber & Faber Limited. *Reprint of 1931a, with further revisions; the third text; in The Faber Library.*
'New and cheaper edition Mcmxxxiii'. The Faber Library No.14. Pp.440. 180 x 116mm. Green cloth, goldstamped. Dust jacket pink, printed in green and black. Price 3/6.

The Valediction of 1931a is now removed so the text ends with chapter 41 and 'her arm over her eyes'; other textual changes noted are: p.121–2: lines omitted or rewritten; p.128: the last line ends 'sacks' not 'weeping'; p.129: lines omitted or rewritten.

1936. In *The Flax of Dream* (A24, pp.551–987). *Reprint of 1933, with*

further revisions; the fourth text.
This has no dedication but a new quote from Wilfred Owen on p.554 and the first chapter headed 'June, 1916' (the errata slip indicates it should be 'June, 1919'). Textual changes are present in chapters 4, 8–11, 31, 33, 34 and 41, mostly limited to a few words or lines but sometimes involving lengthy passages or whole pages (eg chaps. 10, 11); chapter 41 now ends 'For ever, Quillie,' on p.981, followed by a piece headed 'Post-War' which is a reworked version of the Valediction of 1931a, undated.

1941. Faber & Faber Limited. *Reprint of 1936 without 'Post-War'; the fifth text; in The Faber Library.*
'Second impression December Mcmxli'. The Faber Library No.14. Pp.440. Green cloth, silver-stamped.
Reprinted from 1936 but with 'Chapter 1' (not 'June, 1916') on p.13, 'For ever, Quillie,' on p.439, and no 'Post-War' at the end; paginated as 1933.

1943. Faber & Faber Limited. *Reprint of 1941; the fifth text; in The Faber Library.*
'Third impression January Mcmxliii'. The Faber Library No.14. Green cloth, silverstamped. Dust jacket white, printed in blue. Price 3/6.

1945. Faber.
'Reprinted Mcmxlv' in the bib note of 1955; not seen.

1947. Faber and Faber Limited. *Reprint of 1941; the fifth text.*
'Reprinted ... Mcmxlvii'. Blue cloth, goldstamped. Dust jacket cream, printed in black and red-brown. Price 8/6.

1948. Faber.
Listed by Homan (HWSJ 20), paperback; not seen.

1950. Faber.
'Reprinted Mcmlv' in the bib note of 1955; not seen.

1955. Faber and Faber Limited. *Reprint of 1941; the fifth text.*
'Reprinted ... Mcmlv'. Blue cloth, goldstamped. Dust jacket white, printed in red and yellow. Price 15s.

1957. Faber.
Listed by Homan (HWSJ 20); not seen

1958. Faber.
Listed by Homan (HWSJ 20), paperback; not seen.

1968. Faber and Faber. *Reprint of 1936; the fourth text.*
i) 'First published in this edition Mcmlxviii'. Pp.448. Red cloth, gold-stamped. Dust jacket white, printed in blue, yellow and black. Price 30/-.

ii) 'First published in this edition Mcmlxviii'. Faber paper covered Editions. Paperback. Price 10/6.

Repaginated, with 'June, 1916' (uncorrected) on p.9, and 'Post-War' at the end.

1983. Zenith. *New edition of 1941; the fifth text.*
'Hamlyn Paperbacks edition 1983'. The Hamlyn Publishing Group. Printed by Hazell Watson and Viney. ISBN 0 600 20681 5. Pp.320. 197 x 129mm. Paperback. Cover illustration from a painting 'Sunflowers' by Helen Allingham. Price £2.50.
    Has 'Chapter 1' and no 'Post-War' as in 1941.

A6 THE OLD STAG Stories

The last of Williamson's early collections, *The Old Stag*, features accounts of staghunting, foxhunting and hare-coursing, tales of less common birds, including the heron, cormorant and red kite, and the now customary oddities in the form of 'The Yellow Boots', a tale of a convict escaped from Princeton jail on Dartmoor, and 'T'chackamma', an invented story, based solely on a crude sketch he had seen of an African baboon.
    Published by Putnam's, the book was reprinted in 1928 (the first time for one of Williamson's books) and then reshaped with different material and illustrated by Tunnicliffe, in 1933 (to match *Tarka* 1932). From this edition one piece was collected again in *The Henry Williamson Animal Saga* (A46) and eight in *Collected Nature Stories* (A58).
    In the two years between *The Dream of Fair Women* and *The Old Stag* Williamson met Loetitia 'Gipsy' Hibbert, daughter of a member of the Cheriton Otter Hounds. He was also working on his 'otter book' and

contributing to American magazines. These paid well and in HWAS
(p.422) he says: 'On this success I got married'.

1926. G.P. Putnam's Sons, Ltd. *First edition; 12 titles.*
'First published October 1926'. Printed by the Kemp Hall Press. Pp.viii
+ 300. 195 x 122mm. Red cloth, goldstamped on the front and spine; top
edge stained red. Dust jacket brown, printed in black, with a design of
a stag's head by Lionel Edwards on the front panel and owl device on
the front flap. Price 7/6. Published October 1926. 1500 copies (Girvan,
D 1931).

Contents:
- owl device on title-page (for the first time);
- dedication: 'To Windles' Mother' (Loetitia);
 - text (pp.1–298) with 12 titles, followed by a publisher's device:

	Notes:
Stumberleap	from *Saturday Evening Post, Collier's* 1925, or *Pearson's* 1925; in OS 1933
No Eel for Nog	from *Hutchinson's* 1925, or *Collier's* 1925; not in OS 1933; in PS 1934
Bill Brock's Good Turn	from *Saturday Evening Post,* or *Pearson's* 1925; in OS 1933 as part II of 'The Epic of Brock the Badger'
Mewliboy	from *Twenty-Story Magazine* 1925; not in OS 1933; in PS 1934
The Trapper's Mates	in OS 1933
The Flight of the Pale Pink Pyjamas	from *Collier's* 1925; in OS 1933
T'chackamma	in OS 1933
Chakchek's Raid on London	not in OS 1933; in PS 1934 retitled; (see 'The Outlaw' in LS 1922)
The Yellow Boots	not in OS 1933; in DH

	1935 retitled; collected in TME
A Day with the Jelly-Dogs	in OS 1933 retitled
The Five Lives of the Isle-of-Wight Parson	in OS 1933
The Old Pond	? from *Bermondsey Book* 1926; not in OS 1933; in LS 1933; (facsimile ms HWSJ 29)

1927. E.P. Dutton & Company. New York. *American edition; 12 titles*
'Copyright, 1927'. Printed in the USA. Pp.x + 348. 196 x 128mm. Pink paper boards, printed in purple, with a new design (stag and birds), unattributed, on the front and back, backed in purple cloth; foredge untrimmed. Dust jacket pink, printed in purple, repeating the cover design.

The only textual change noted is in 'Bill Brock's Good Turn' where the penultimate paragraph ends 'and lay down', replacing two lines of the original edition.

1928. G.P. Putnam's Sons, Ltd. *Reprint of the first edition.*
'Reprinted July 1928'. Red cloth, goldstamped on the front and spine. Dust jacket as 1926 but with 'Author of "Tarka the Otter" awarded Hawthornden Prize, 1928' on the front panel and 'Second Edition' on the spine panel. Price 7/6.

The gatherings are unsigned confirming that this is a new printing and not a reissue.

1933. G.P. Putnam's Sons. *New edition; 9 titles, revised; 33 illustrations by Tunnicliffe.*
Subtitled 'And Other Hunting Stories'.

i) 'First illustrated edition published February 1933'. Printed by The Shenval Press. Pp.xii + 288. Frontispiece and illustrations, reckoned. 190 x 122mm. Green cloth, goldstamped on the front (owl device) and spine. Dust jacket pale salmon-pink, printed in red and black, with the illustration from p.196 (Mr Tinker at the bar) on the front panel and ad for TA 'Uniform with this Volume' on the back panel. Price 5/-.

ii) Cheaper issue: as i) but in lighter green cloth, stamped in dull gold; dust jacket white, printed in black, with the illustration from p.283 (stag in river) on the front panel, tailpiece from p.286 (stag lying) on the spine panel and ads for TA, LS, PS 'Uniform with this Volume' on the back panel. Price 3/6.

Contents (compared to 1926):
   - illustrations are now a frontispiece, 24 full-page wood-engravings and 9 line drawings as tailpieces, by C.F. Tunnicliffe;
   - text (pp.1–286) made up of 8 individual titles previously published in books (all with some degree of revision) and 4 items brought together for the first time under one title as 'The Epic of Brock the Badger', followed by 'Here ends The Old Stag, and other hunting stories, written in Devon between the years 1921–1924':

	Notes:
The Trapper's Mates	from first ed.; collected in CNS
Zoe	from PS 1923, collected in CNS
The Five Lives of the Isle of Wight Parson	from first ed., collected in CNS
Redeye	from PS 1923; collected in CNS
T'chackamma	from first ed.; collected in CNS
The Flight of the Pale Pink Pyjamas	from first ed.; collected in CNS retitled
My Day with the Beagles	'A Day with the Jelly-Dogs' from first ed.; collected in CNS
The Epic of Brock the Badger:	collected in HWAS
The Epic of Brock the Badger	'Bill Brock's Farewell' part I, from *Outsiders* 1929
I	'Bloody Bill Brock' from PS 1923
II	'Bill Brock's Good Turn' from first ed.
III	'Bill Brock's Farewell' part II, from *Outsiders* 1929

Stumberleap   from first ed.; collected
                                                     in CNS

1942a. G.P. Putnam's Sons. *Reprint of 1933; 24 illustrations.*
'Reprinted June 1942'. Green cloth, goldstamped. Dust jacket white, printed in black, with ilustrations as 1933ii. Price 7/6.

Printed from 1933 on thinner paper with the type reset on pp.246–253 to eliminate the ugly line at the foot of p.247, no tailpieces, and an error on p.195 line 25 which now has 'Sor' instead of 'Sow'.

1942b. Penguin Books. *New edition of 1942a; 24 illustrations.*
'Published in Penguin Books 1942'. Printed by W.S. Cowell. Penguin No.395. Pp.192. Frontispiece, not reckoned. 180 x 110mm. Paperback. Covers printed in orange and black.

A note on recto of the half-title has 'For the Forces. Leave this book at a Post Office when you have read it, so that men and women in the services may enjoy it too.'

1946a. Putnam & Co. Ltd. *Reprint of 1942a with 33 illustrations; limited issue.*
'Limited illustrated edition 1946'. 207 x 135mm. Green cloth, goldstamped, with 'HW' monogram on the front, as one of *The Henry Williamson Nature Books* (see A33). 500 copies.

Printed from 1942a (with the error on p.195) but with the title as running head and the tailpieces from 1933 restored, to match the HWNB format.

1946b. Putnam & Co. Ltd. *Reprint of 1946a; 33 illustrations.*
'Reprinted November 1946'. Green cloth, goldstamped. Dust jacket white, printed in black, with the illustration from p.283 (stag in river) on the front panel and owl device on the spine panel. Price 8/6.

1948. Putnam & Company Ltd. *Reprint of 1946a; 33 illustrations.*
'Reprinted March 1948'. Green cloth. Dust jacket white, printed in black, with the illustration from p.283 on the front panel and a publisher's device (stork with 'P') on the spine panel. Price 8/6.

?1949. Putnam.
Announced in the 'School edition' of *Tarka* (TA 1949aii, p.281): 'For School Recreational Libraries. Nature Books by Henry Williamson, each 8/6. The Old Stag, The Lone Swallows, The Peregrine's Saga'; not seen.

1960. In *The Henry Williamson Animal Saga*. (A46: pp.377–417). *New edition of one title from 1933, revised; not illustrated.*
A new printing of the four parts that form 'The Epic of Brock the Badger' in the 1933 edition, renumbered, with an introduction (2 pp.), new page-headings, a few words altered, and no illustrations.

1970. In *Collected Nature Stories* (A58, pp.147–301). *New edition of 8 titles from 1933, revised; 23 illustrations.*
This contains the eight items in the 1933 edition that were not collected in HWAS with a new 'Preface' (5 pp.) giving background to the stories. 'Stumberleap' is restored as the lead item, as in the first edition, and all titles show textual changes, usually confined to words or lines, but quite extensive in 'The Flight of the Pale Pink Pyjamas' which is also retitled. The frontispiece and full-page illustrations that relate to the stories are included, with two of the tailpieces, but with poor reproduction.

A7 STUMBERLEAP A Story taken from The Old Stag

An ephemeral item issued shortly after *The Old Stag* was published, presumably to promote sales. One copy is rubber-stamped '18 Dec. 1926' and in *T.P's* and *Cassell's Weekly* of 29 January 1927 it was advertised as a 'booklet', available free from the publishers.

[1926]. G.P. Putnam's Sons. *First edition.*
'With Greetings from G.P. Putnam's Sons' printed on title-page. No date, edition statement, or printer's imprint. Pp.40. 192 x 177mm. Brown paper wrappers, printed in black, with the design by Lionel Edwards from the dust jacket of OS reproduced on the front; stapled. Issued probably December 1926.

Contents: text (pp.3–33) followed by ads (6 pp.) for Putnam's titles.
Printed from OS 1926, repaginated and with new running heads, it has 'turnip' instead of 'tur/nip' in the last line of p.8, and 'by the teeth of deer' added after 'half-cut' on p.18 line 11 with the following lines adjusted accordingly.

A8 TARKA THE OTTER His Joyful Water-Life & Death in the Country of the Two Rivers

By 1923 Williamson had learnt the ways of the otter hunt, had written about otters and had developed his narrative skills to the point where he was ready to undertake a whole book about one animal. The result was to become both influential and a classic of English natural history. In *Tarka* Williamson does not preach, or rant, or promote a cause, he simply tells a story and leaves the reader to form his own response - though he had his own ideas as to what that response would be. In a notebook for 1925 (1978b p.37) he wrote:

'The Otterhunters will say, we have no use for this man; he is one of those people who are are half inclined to be our enemies ...

'The Anti-Hunting Humanitarians will say, we have no use for this man; he is half inclined to side with the otter-hunting beasts ...

'The Otters will say, Nothing, for they will not know anything of it; and perhaps at the End of this Planet they will say, He understands us. Perhaps not ...'

It was perhaps because of this innate 'understanding' that the book had a greater impact than Williamson ever expected or intended. He had not set out to influence ecological thinking, but the book did, and there can be little doubt that it contributed at least indirectly to the eventual return of the otter to its native territory in the West Country and elsewhere.

The writing took more than three years, part of them spent looking after a sick wife and a baby (William) who was failing to thrive, and many drafts, but when it was finished his papers show that he sensed he had produced something special and was determined to get the best possible deal from a publisher. His statement in the Preface to *Collected Nature Stories* that 'In due course, *Tarka the Otter* went to Messrs. Putnam,' covers what was a lengthy, delicate and occasionally tetchy process.

Another response that was unexpected came in April 1928 when he was informed by the Committee for the Hawthornden Prize (a private foundation) that he was to receive the award for what they considered to be 'the best imaginative work of the year.' The immediate benefit was £100, but what really counted was the recognition. As he put it in a note to Grandmother Hibbert, 'In fact, one arrives.' (D 1995 p.114).

Since the original version of the book in 1927 there have been many foreign translations, a film by David Cobham, made in 1977, and more than 80 English or American printings, with various alterations and additions of which the most important are:

1928b   Putnam's, the second text
1928e   Dutton, the third text
1928f   Putnam's, the fourth text
1932   Putnam's, illustrated by Tunnicliffe
1949b   Penguin, new illustrations by Tunnicliffe
1960a   in HWAS, the fifth text; plus 'The Gentleman's River' and 'Apologia'
1961b   Longmans, illustrated by Barber
1962   Penguin, the sixth text
1963a   Penguin, map by Tunnicliffe
1964a   Nonesuch, new map and illustrations by Driscoll
1978b   Bodley Head, 'The Original Ending'; Introduction by R Williamson; photographs from the film
1982b   Puffin, glossary (from 'Apologia')
1985a   Webb and Bower, map redrawn; new Introduction by R Williamson; photographs by McBride
1995a   Puffin, illustrated by Large

1927a. Privately printed. *First edition; signed, numbered issue; 100 copies.* 'Privately printed for subscribers only Mcmxxvii' on the title-page; 'Printed in Great Britain' on verso. 'Of this edition printed at the Chiswick Press, Tooks Court, London, on English handmade paper, one hundred numbered copies, signed by the author are for sale to private subscribers only. This is no. ...' followed by the number, author's signature and owl device in ink on verso of the third leaf. Colophon: 'Here ends Tarka the Otter by Henry Williamson, begun in June 1923 and finished in February 1927 in the village of Ham in Devon, and printed at the Chiswick Press of Tooks Court in London', with publisher's device, on p.256. Pp.xvi + 256. Printed in brown and black antique Caslon type on large-paper, with owl device on the title-page and a small decoration at the start of each paragraph in the text. 250 x 160mm. Full vellum with brown leather label goldstamped on the spine; top edge gilt, others untrimmed. No jacket. Price 3 guineas. Published [August] 1927. 100 copies.

Printed separately to advertise the work was a 4–page 'Prospectus' which includes a brief description of the book, a short history of its numerous drafts, quotations from Sir John Fortescue's Introduction, and an order form, to be sent to 'Mr. Williamson, At the Sign of the Owl,

Georgeham, North Devon.' In 1987 this was reprinted by the Henry Williamson Society, to commemorate the diamond jubilee of the book's publication.

Contents:
- dedication 'To William Henry Rogers';
- 'Introduction' by Sir John Fortescue (4 pp.);
- decorations: small deer-slot design (in the Introduction) and leaf design (in the text) at the start of each paragraph, in brown (? by Lionel Edwards);
- text (3–255) with the first word 'Dimmity', in 2 sections and 20 Chapters with page headings in margins, followed by the colophon (as above):

| The First Year | chaps. | 1–10 |
| The Last Year | chaps. | 11–19 and Last Chapter |

1927b. G.P. Putnam's Sons. *First edition; large-paper issue; 1000 copies.*
As above except: publisher's imprint on the title-page. 'This edition is limited to eleven hundred copies printed in England, at the Chiswick Press, Tooks Court, London, of which one thousand copies only are for sale' on verso of the third leaf. 246 x 162mm. Brown cloth, backed in cream buckram (susceptible to browning) with leather label gold-stamped on the spine; top edge gilt, others untrimmed. No jacket. Price £1.1.0. Published October 1927. 1000 copies.

The reference to 1100 copies in the edition statement suggests that at this stage in the numbering of their editions of *Tarka* Putman's regarded the 100 signed copies (above) together with this item as constituting the 'first edition'.

1927c. G.P. Putnam's Sons. *First edition; cheaper issue.*
No edition statement. Colophon as 1927a. Pp.viii + 256. 194 x 124mm. Brown cloth, goldstamped on the spine. Dust jacket green, printed in black, with a lino-cut of an otter on a riverbank by Hester Sainsbury on the front panel. Price 7/6. A printed insert in one copy has 'Advance copy to be published Oct. 12th'.

A minor printing error in some copies (where the paragraph deco-ration is removed at the top of p.4) and other typographical evidence indicates that this was definitely printed from the original type-setting, but only in black and with modifications to the general format: no initial blank leaves; dedication moved to verso of the title-page; the Introduction repaginated, with the lines repositioned to give 34 lines to each page; page headings at the top of each page; and the decorations at the start of each paragraph omitted. Pagination and signatures in the main text are unchanged.

It is likely that this represents the item listed as 'Second edition, October 1927' in 1928a which is otherwise unknown, but it is certainly not a new edition and must therefore be classified either as a separate issue of the first edition, or as a reprint. As it carries no reprint statement and was put out at the same time as 1927b, the former is preferred. Girvan (D 1931) states that the type was 're-imposed' which could refer to the modifications but is not correct for the main text.

1928a. G.P. Putnam's Sons. *Reprint of 1927c; the first edition.*
'Third edition, January 1928'. Brown cloth, goldstamped on the spine. Dust jacket as 1927c. Price 7/6.

1928b. G.P. Putnam's Sons. *Reprint of 1927c, revised, the second text.*
'Fourth edition, slightly revised, following suggestions of "T.E.L.," June 1928'. Brown cloth, goldstamped on the spine. Dust jacket blue-green, as 1927c, but with 'Awarded Hawthornden Prize 1928' on the front panel and 'Fourth edition' on the spine panel, both printed in black. Price 7/6.

Changes noted from the original text are: p.3: text starts with 'Twilight' instead of 'Dimmity' (see 1990 below); p.45: the last 3 lines and the first on p.46 are rewritten with the sentence ending 'into the drab hues of decay'; p.161: in the last paragraph a sentence of 3 lines is omitted before 'Every ten yards' which is followed by 'small bright beads' instead of 'tiny silver beads', and 'dipping streak' instead of 'silver streak'.

1928c. G.P. Putnam's Sons. *Reprint of 1928b, the second text.*
'Fifth edition, July 1928'. Brown cloth, goldstamped on the spine.

1928d. G.P. Putnam's Sons. *Reprint of 1928b; the second text.*
'Sixth impression, September 1928'. Brown cloth, goldstamped on the spine. Dust jacket as 1927c but with 'Hawthornden Prize 1928' on the front panel and 'Sixth impression' on the spine panel, both in red (very liable to fade). Price 7/6.

1928e. E.P. Dutton & Company. New York. *American edition of the first text, with new revisions, the third text.*
'Copyright, 1928'. Printed in the USA. Pp.xiv + 262. Decorated initial letter to each chapter, unattributed. 195 x 127mm. Green wavy-patterned cloth, goldstamped on the front and spine. Dust jacket green, printed in darker green, with a design of an otter on a rock, unattributed, on the front panel.

A variant in green buckram is reported by Homan (HWSJ 16).

This text has none of the changes noted in 1928b but new text on p.4 where lines 9–15 are partly rewritten from 'At the tail of the pool ...' to 'Alder and sallow grew on its banks.' With the change of publisher the colophon is reduced to 'Here ends Tarka the Otter by Henry Williamson, begun in June 1923 and finished in February 1927 in the village of Ham in Devon', with no device.

1928f. G.P.Putnam's Sons. *Reprint of the second text, with the revisions of 1928e; the fourth text.*
'Sixth edition, November 1928'. Brown cloth, goldstamped on the spine.

Printed from 1928b but incorporating the changes made in 1928e (with 'grew on its banks' now on p.4 line 11) to form a 'combined revised' text which is then unchanged until HWAS (1960a).

1928g. G.P. Putnam's Sons. *Reprint of 1928f, the fourth text.*
'Seventh impression, December 1928'. Brown cloth, goldstamped on the spine.

1929a. G.P. Putnam's Sons. *Reprint of 1928f; the fourth text.*
i) 'Eighth impression, May 1929'. Brown cloth, goldstamped on the spine. Dust jacket as 1928d but with 'Eighth impression' on the spine panel. Price 7/6.

ii) as i) but in green cloth, blackstamped on the spine; dust jacket white, printed in black, with a design of an otter in moonlight signed 'K' (Kermode, HWSJ 16) on the front panel and 'Popular edition' on the spine panel. Price 3/6.

1929b. G.P. Putnam's Sons. *Reprint of 1928f; the fourth text.*
i) No copy in brown cloth dated 1929 has been seen, but a dust jacket similar to 1928d with 'Ninth impression' on the spine panel is known, price 7/6, which suggests that this printing may also have been issued

in two formats as 1929a.

ii) 'Ninth impression, September 1929'. Green cloth, blackstamped. Dust jacket as 1929aii 'Popular edition'. Price 3/6.

1929c. E.P. Dutton & Company. New York. *Reprint of 1928e; the third text.*
'Second printing. September 1929'. Green cloth, goldstamped. Dust jacket green, printed in darker green, as 1928e.

1929d. G.P. Putnam's Sons. *Reprint of 1928f; the fourth text.*
'Tenth impression, November 1929'. Green cloth, blackstamped. Dust jacket as 1929aii 'Popular edition'. Price 3/6.

1929e. Putnam.
'Eleventh impression, November 1929' in the bib note of 1931; not seen.

1930a. G.P. Putnam's Sons. *Reprint of 1928f; the fourth text.*
'Twelfth impression, November 1930'. Green cloth, blackstamped. Dust jacket as 1929aii 'Popular edition'. Price 3/6.

1930b. Bernhard Tauchnitz. Leipzig. *German edition of the second text (in English).*
i) 'Tauchnitz Edition. Collection of British and American Authors. Vol. 4927' on the front cover and half-title. Pp.288. 162 x 115mm. White paper covers, printed in black; no endpapers; perfect-bound.

ii) as i) but in red cloth, goldstamped on spine, with endpapers.

1931. G.P. Putnam's Sons. *Reprint of 1928f; the fourth text.*
'Thirteenth impression, October 1931'. Green cloth, blackstamped. Dust jacket as 1929aii 'Popular edition'. Price 3/6.

1932. G.P.Putnam's Sons. *New edition of the fourth text; 40 illustrations by Tunnicliffe.*
i) 'First illustrated edition published 1932'. Printed by The Shenval Press. Pp.xiv + 282. Frontispiece and illustrations, reckoned. 190 x 122mm. Green cloth, goldstamped on the front (owl device) and spine. Dust jacket white, printed in black, with the illustration from p.193 (hounds at the holt) on the front panel, no illustration on the spine

panel, ad for OS on back panel. Price 5/-.
A variant with the owl device blindstamped has been noted.

ii) Cheaper issue: as i) but dust jacket has the frontispiece (otter underwater) reproduced on the front panel, tailpiece from p.216 (otter-prints
in reeds) on the spine panel and ads for PS, LS, OS 'Uniform with this
Volume' on the back panel. Price 3/6.

The text and Introduction of 1928f with a frontispiece, 23 full-page
woodcuts, captioned, and 16 line drawings as tailpieces by C.F.
Tunnicliffe, who is acknowledged in the end-note on p.280 which now
reads 'Here ends Tarka the Otter by Henry Williamson ... illustrated by
C.F. Tunniclffe by the Taw and Torridge Rivers in 1932'. Tunnicliffe had
offered his services after reading the book and though he had not previously done book illustration was soon commissioned to illustrate
matching editions of LS, OS and PS.

1935. G.P. Putnam's Sons. *Reprint of 1932; the fourth text; illustrated.*
'Reprinted September 1935'. Green cloth, goldstamped.

1936a. Putnam & Co. Ltd. *Reprint of 1932; the fourth text; illustrated.*
'Reprinted November 1936'. Green cloth, goldstamped. Dust jacket as
1932ii. Price 3/6.

1936b. E.P. Dutton & Company, Inc. New York. *Reprint of 1928e; the
third text.*
'Third printing. November 1936'. Greeny-blue cloth, blackstamped on
the front and spine. Dust jacket green, printed in brown, with the
design as 1928e and 'Awarded the Hawthornden Prize' on the front
panel; printed on the front flap is a note that the Prize was open only to
writers 'under the age of 41'.

1937a. Penguin Books. *New edition of the fourth text.*
'Published in Penguin Books 1937'. Printed by Hazell, Watson and
Viney. Penguin No.81. Pp.256. 180 x 110mm. Paperback. Covers printed
in orange and black. Price 6d.
    The text and Introduction of 1928f with the subtitle and owl device
omitted; end-note as 1928e (USA).

1937b. Penguin Books Limited. *Reprint of 1937a; the fourth text.*

'Reprinted June 1937'. No.81. Pp.256. Paperback.

Printed from 1937a with the subtitle restored, lines repositioned and spaces closed up to accommodate a publisher's catalogue (8 pp.) dated September 1937.

1937c. Penguin
'Reprinted October 1937' in the bib note of 1940; not seen.

1939a. Putnam & Co. Ltd. *Reprint of 1932; the fourth text; illustrated.*
'Reprinted January 1939'. Green cloth, goldstamped. Dust jacket as 1932ii. Price 3/6.

1939b. Penguin Books Limited. *Reprint of 1937b; the fourth text.*
'Reprinted October 1939'. No.81. Paperback.

1940a. Penguin Books. *New edition of the fourth text.*
'Reprinted May 1940'. Printed by Wyman and Sons. No.81. Pp.192. Paperback. Covers printed in orange and black.

A new type-setting on fewer pages with the full subtitle but no owl device; end-note as 1928e (USA).

1940b. Putnam
Listed by Homan (HWSJ 16), but not in the bib note of 1941.

1941. Putnam & Co Ltd. *Reprint of 1932; the fourth text; illustrated*
'Reprinted April 1941'. Green cloth, goldstamped. Dust jacket white, printed in black, with design as 1932i on the front panel, no illustration on the spine panel. Price 3/6.

1942a. Penguin Books. *New edition of the fourth text.*
'Reprinted December 1942'. Printed by R.R. Clarke. No.81. Pp.160. Paperback. Covers printed in orange and black.

Contents as 1940a but on even fewer pages with a note on recto of the half-title: 'For The Forces. Leave this book at a Post Office when you have read it, so that men and women in the Services may enjoy it too.'

1942b. Penguin Books. *Reprint of 1942a; the fourth text.*
'Published in the Forces Book Club, 1942'. No.5 (on spine). Paperback. Covers printed in pink and black. No price (£3 annual subscription).

1945. Putnam & Company Ltd. *Reprint of 1932; the fourth text; illustrated; limited issue.*
'Limited illustrated edition 1945'. 208 x 135mm. Green cloth, gold-stamped, with 'HW' monogram on the front, as one of The Henry Williamson Nature Books (see A33). 500 copies.

Printed from the 1932 type-setting but with the title as running head, chapter headings moved from the margins to above the text and lines adjusted accordingly.

1946. Putnam & Co. Ltd. *Reprint of 1945; the fourth text; illustrated.*
'Reprinted November 1946'. 190 x 122mm. Green cloth, goldstamped. Dust jacket white, printed in black, as 1932i on the front panel, owl device on the spine panel. Price 8/6.

1948. Putnam and Company Ltd. *Reprint of 1945; the fourth text; illustrated.*
'Reprinted March 1948'. Green cloth, goldstamped. Dust jacket white, printed in black, as 1932i on the front panel, publisher's device (stork with 'P') on the spine panel. Price 8/6.

As 1945 but with no owl device on the title-page.

1949a. Putnam & Company Ltd. *Reprint or reissue of 1948; the fourth text; illustrated.*
i) 'School edition first published 1949'. Green linson, goldstamped. Dust jacket white, printed in black, as 1932i on the front panel, no illustration on the spine panel. Price 12/-.

ii) as i) but in lighter green fabric, stamped in dull gold; dust jacket not seen. Price 8/6.

'For School Recreational Libraries. Nature Books by Henry Williamson, each 8/6. The Old Stag, The Lone Swallows, The Peregrine's Saga' on p.281.

1949b. Penguin Books. *New edition of the fourth text; 20 new illustrations by Tunnicliffe; in Puffin Story Books.*
'Published in Puffin Story Books 1949'. Printed by Hunt, Barnard and Co. No.60 (on spine); PS 81 (on half-title). Pp.240. 180 x 110mm. Paperback. Covers printed in blue, black and brown, with a pictorial design (otter on front, hounds on back) by Tunnicliffe. Price 1/6.

In this edition the subtitle is omitted and the Fortescue Introduction replaced by 'How the Book Came to be Written' (pp.7–11) by Eleanor Graham, the series Editor. The illustrations are 20 new headpieces (one to each chapter) by C.F. Tunnicliffe, but whether they were prepared for the 1932 edition and not used, or commissioned by Penguin for this edition, is not known; end-note as 1928e (USA) but with owl device (the first time in any printing of *Tarka*).

1951. Penguin Books. *Reprint of 1949b; the fourth text; illustrated.*
'Reprinted 1951'. A Puffin Story Book. No.60. Paperback. Covers as 1949b. Price 2/-.
The subtitle is restored but shortened to 'His Joyful Water-life and Death in the Two Rivers'.

1955. Penguin Books. *Reprint of 1951; the fourth text; illustrated.*
'Reprinted 1955'. A Puffin Story Book. No.60. Paperback. Covers as 1949b. Price 2/6.

1959. Penguin Books.
'Reprinted 1959' in bib note of 1962; not seen.

1960a. In *The Henry Williamson Animal Saga* (A46: pp.11–199).
New edition of the fourth text, with further revision and new material; the fifth text.
Compared to previous editions:
 - subtitle in full;
 - now 'Dedicated to the memory of William Henry Rogers, Esquire late Tutor in college at Eton and sometime Master of the Cheriton Hunt';
 - Introduction by Fortescue omitted and replaced by 'The Gentleman's River' (pp.13–22), an account of the genesis and writing of the book (the same title is in *Modern Man* 1951 with a few passages of common text, and *Country Life* 1952 with different text);
 - illustrations, end-note and owl device omitted;
 - text (pp.23–194) with alterations to words or phrases on pp.28, 45, 67, 69 and 91 where chapter 8 ends 'he passed the animals, and went more easily towards the light'.
 - 'Apologia Pro Verba Mea' (pp.196–99) which is a response to comment about dialect words and hunting terms used in the book, signed 'Henry Williamson. North Devon 12 December, 1927' (see 'Provincialisms' in *London Mercury* 1928 and LL).

1960b. Looking Glass Library. New York. *American edition of the fifth text; 40 illustrations by Tunnicliffe.*
'Distributed by Random House' on the title-page. 'Copyright 1960 ... This book is published by Epstein and Carroll Associates, Inc ...' on verso of the title-page. Printed by The Colonial Press, Clinton, Mass. Looking Glass Library No.19. Pp.320. Frontispiece and illustrations, reckoned. 190 x 123mm. Blue-green paper boards, printed in black with the illustration from p.221 (hounds at the holt) reproduced on the front and from p.131 (otter and gulls) on the back, with otter vignette (detail from p.241, reduced) on the spine. Dust jacket white, printed in blue-green and black, repeating the cover design. Price $1.95. Published September 1960 (review slip).

A compact 'no-nonsense' edition that combines the contents and latest text of 1960a with all the illustrations from the 1932 edition in their original order.

1961a. Penguin Books. *Reprint of 1951; the fourth text; illustrated.*
'Reprinted ... 1961'. A Puffin Story Book No.60. Paperback. Covers as 1949b. Price 2/6.

1961b. Longmans. *New edition of the fourth text; illustrated by Barber.*
'First published in The Heritage of Literature Series ... 1961'. Printed by the Northumberland Press. Series number 'A 83' on the back cover. Pp.viii + 240. Frontispiece and illustrations, reckoned. 170 x 110mm. Red linson, goldstamped on the spine; brown-patterned endpapers.

This has the full subtitle but no dedication, Introduction, end-note, or owl device. Illustrations comprise a frontispiece and 5 full-page drawings, captioned, by John Barber.

1961c. Longmans. *Reprint of 1961b; the fourth text; illustrated (Barber).*
'Second impression 1961'. The Heritage of Literature Series. No.83. Red linson.

1962. Penguin Books. *Reprint of 1951, with further revisions; the sixth text; illustrated.*
'Reprinted with revisions by the author 1962'. No.60. Pp.240. Paperback. Covers as 1949b. Price 2/6.

Contents and illustrations are as 1951 but with words changed on pp.36, 71, 74 and a line omitted on p.102 where chapter 8 ends 'The man played on, moving away from the seal'.

1963a. Penguin Books. *Reprint of 1962; the sixth text; illustrated; with a map by Tunnicliffe.*
'Reprinted with map 1963'. No.60. Paperback. Covers as 1949b. Price 3/-.
The end-note and owl device are now on p.237 with a map titled 'The Country of the Two Rivers' captioned 'Map of Tarka's journey, drawn especially for this Puffin edition by C.F. Tunnicliffe' on pp.238–9.

1963b. Longmans. *Reprint of 1961b; the fourth text, illustrated (Barber).*
'Third impression 1963'. The Heritage of Literature Series. No.83. Red linson.

1964a. The Nonesuch Press. *New edition of the fifth text; illustrated by Driscoll.*
'This Nonesuch Cygnet, designed by Sir Frances Meynell, first published 1964'. Printed by William Clowes and Sons. Pp.iv + 268. Illustrations, reckoned. 240 x 150mm. Green cloth, orange panel on the front, goldstamped on the front and spine; endpapers printed in blue with a map of 'North Devon, the country of Tarka's life and death'. Dust jacket white, printed in green and black, with a publisher's device on the front panel and 'T5013' on the front flap. Price 30/-.
This has the dedication and text of 1960a followed by an 'Appendix' containing the original Introduction by Fortescue, 'The Gentleman's River' and 'Apologia Pro Verba Mea'. The illustrations are 19 full-page line drawings (with the one from p.83 reduced and repeated on title-page) and the endpaper map, by Barry Driscoll. Owl device on p.241 with an end-note which now reads '... begun in June 1923 and finished in the village of Ham in North Devon in 1926,' though why the book should now have been finished earlier than was stated in the first edition is unclear.

1964b. Franklin Watts, Inc. New York. *American issue of 1964a; the fifth text; illustrated.*
'First American publication 1964'. Printed by Williams Clowes and Sons. (UK). A Nonesuch Cygnet. Book as in 1964a. Dust jacket as in 1964a except for 'Watts' at the foot of the spine panel and 'Printed in Great Britain' on the front flap with no number. Price $7.95.

1965a. Penguin Books. *Reprint of 1963a; the sixth text; illustrated.*
'Reprinted 1965'. No.60. Paperback. Covers as 1949b. Price 3/6.

1965b. Longmans.
A fourth impression of 1961b; The Heritage of Literature Series; not seen.

1965c. The Bodley Head. *New edition of the fifth text; 36 illustrations by Tunnicliffe.*
'This edition first published by ... 1965'. Printed by William Clowes and Sons. Pp.236. Illustrations, reckoned. 204 x 128mm. Blue-green linson, goldstamped on the spine. Dust jacket white, printed in black, with the illustration from p.46 (otter and cubs) on the front panel and a photograph of the author by Oswald Jones on the back panel. Price 18/-.
Items in this edition are the original Introduction by Fortescue, the text of 1960a, and the illustrations by Tunnicliffe from 1932 (omitting the tailpieces to chapters 6, 11, 13 and 16, which could not be accommodated in the new type-setting); end-note as 1932, with no owl device.

?196–. No publisher. *Reprint of 1965c; the fifth text, illustrated.*
No date. 'This edition published by arrangement with The Bodley Head Ltd. Edito-Service S.A., Geneva, Publishers'. Title in red on the half-title and title-page. Frontispiece photograph of HW by Oswald Jones (from the dust jacket of 1965c). Purplish cloth-facsimile, ornately gold-stamped, with marker tab.
A photo-reprint of 1965c with print size reduced, cased in the style of Heron Books (the only one of Williamson's books known to have received the treatment) and repaginated, with the illustrations facing different pages. The date of issue is unknown but probably between 1965c and 1969a.

1966a. Longmams. *Reprint of 7961b; the fourth text; illustrated (Berber)*
'Fifth impression 1966'. The Heritage of Literature Series. No.83. Yellow paper-covered boards, printed in black.

1966b. Penguin Books.
'Reprinted ... 1966' in the bib note of 1973; not seen.

1967a. Penguin Books.
'Reprinted ... 1967' in the bib note of 1973; not seen.

1967b. An Avon Camelot Book. New York. *New American edition of the*

fifth text, 34 illustrations by Tunnicliffe.
'First Avon Camelot printing, January, 1967'. Printed in the USA. Avon ZS110. Pp.224. Illustrations and map, reckoned. 180 x 105mm. Paperback. Edges red. Cover illustration (otter) by Hugh Baker. Price 60 cents.

Contents as 1960a without the subtitle but with the illustrations by Tunnicliffe from 1932 (omitting six tailpieces) and his map from 1963a, placed on the inside of the covers and facing pages.

1969a. The Bodley Head. *Reprint of 1965c; the fifth text; illustrated.*
'Reprinted 1969'. SBN 370 00988 6. Blue-green linson, goldstamped on the spine. Dust jacket as 1965c but printed 'Second impression'. Price 18/- (£0.90).

As 1965c but with owl device on p.234 after the end-note.

1969b. Longmans.
'This edition first published by Longmans, Green and Co Ltd ... 1969' in the bib note of 1973a. Pleasure in Reading series; not seen.

1969c. Penguin Books.
'Reprinted ... 1969' in the bib note of 1973b; not seen.

1971. Penguin Books. *Reprint of 1963a; the sixth text; illustrated.*
'Reprinted ... 1971 (twice)'. A Puffin Book. ISBN 0 14 030060 0. Paperback. Covers as 1949b. Price 25p.

1972. Penguin or Puffin.
'Reprinted ... 1972' in the bib note of 1973b; either the last issue with the Penguin imprint or the first with the Puffin imprint; not seen.

1973a. Longmans. *Reprint of 1969b; the fifth text; illustrated.*
'Second impression 1973'. Pleasure in Reading series. ISBN 0 582 18658 7. Pp.236. Grey paper-covered boards, printed in black and white, with an illustration (otter in snow) by David Cook.

As 1965c with the Tunnicliffe illustrations but no subtitle or owl device.

1973b. Puffin Books. *Reprint of 1963a; the sixth text; illustrated.*
'Reprinted ... 1973'. ISBN 0 14 030060 0. Paperback. All-round cover illustration (otter with fish) by David Carl Forbes. Price 30p.

1974. Puffin
'Reprinted ... 1974' in the bib note of 1975; not seen

1975a. Puffin Books. *Reprint of 1963a; the sixth text; illustrated.*
'Reprinted ... 1975'. ISBN 0 14 030060 0. Paperback. Covers as 1973b.
Price 50p.

1975b. The Bodley Head. *Reprint of 1969a, with additions; the fifth text; 35 illustrations by Tunnicliffe.*
'This edition first published 1975'. ISBN 0 370 10964 3. Pp.244. Blue-green linson, goldstamped on the spine. Dust jacket as 1965c.

The tailpiece on p.233 is removed and replaced by the end-note and owl device, with the map and 'Apologia' from 1964a now included on pp.234–40.

1976. Puffin Books. *Reprint of 1963a; the sixth text; illustrated.*
'Reprinted ... 1976 (twice)'. ISBN 0 14 030060 0. Paperback. Covers as 1973b. Price 50p.

1977. Puffin
'Reprinted ... 1977' in the bib note of 1978; not seen.

1978a. Puffin Books. *Reprint of 1963a; the sixth text; illustrated.*
'Reprinted ... 1978'. ISBN 0 14 030060 0. Paperback. Cover design (otter and heron on front, owl and hunt on back) by David Carl Forbes. Price 70p.

1978b. The Bodley Head. *Reprint of 1964a; the fifth text; with new material and colour illustrations.*
'This edition first published 1978'. ISBN 0 370 30146 3. Pp.256. 8 colour plates, not reckoned. Dark green linson, goldstamped on the spine. Dust jacket white, printed in yellow and white on a colour photograph of otter cubs by Steve Downer. Price £4.50.

In this volume the main text is reprinted from 1964a with the subtitle, dedication, end-note and map from that edition, but without the Introduction by Fortescue, 'The Gentleman's River', 'Apologia', or the Driscoll illustrations. In their place, however, are important new elements in the form of an Introduction (30 pp.) by Richard Williamson which provides much background information on the book and the film, 'The Original Ending' (2 pp.) signed 'H.W.', and 16 full-page colour photographs, mostly of wildlife, taken by Steve Downer on location in 1977.

1979a. Book Club Associates. *Reprint of 1978b; the fifth text; illustrated (colour).*
'This edition published 1989 ...' Book and jacket as 1978b.

1979b. Puffin Books. *Reprint of 1963a; the sixth text; illustrated.*
'Reprinted ... 1979'. ISBN 0 14 030060 0. Paperback. Covers as 1978a. Price 70p.
Another copy otherwise identical has 'Reprinted ... 1979 (three times)'.

1981a. Puffin.
'Reprinted ... 1981' in the bib note of 1984; not seen

1981b. Macmillan Education. *Reprint of 1975b; the fifth text; illustrated.*
'First published in M Books 1981'. ISBN 0 333 30602 3. White paper boards, printed in red and black, with a colour photograph of an otter on the front.

1981c. Ulverscroft. *New edition of the fifth text, in large print.*
'First large print edition published February 1981'. Published by F.A. Thorpe. Printed by T.J. Press. Ulverscroft Large Print Series. ISBN 0 7089 0545 5. Pp.x + 390. 220 x 135mm. White paper boards, printed in green and black.
Contents as 1978b but without the map, illustrations or owl device.

1982a. The Bodley Head. *Reprint of 1978b, with modifications; the fifth text; 33 illustrations by Tunnicliffe.*
'This edition first published 1982'. ISBN 0 370 30919 7. Pp.256. Frontispiece and illustrations, reckoned. Red linson, goldstamped on the spine. Dust jacket white, printed in green and red, with the illustration from p.21 (otter and owl) on the front panel and a photograph of the author on the back panel. Price £6.95.
Mostly printed from 1978b but with the Introduction by Fortescue in place of the one by Richard Williamson and the addition of 'Apologia' (both reprinted from 1964a), with illustrations by Tunnicliffe from 1932 (omitting seven tailpieces) instead of the colour plates, and no owl device.

1982b. Puffin Books. *Reprint of 1963a, with a glossary; the sixth text; illustrated.*
'Reprinted ... 1982'. ISBN 0 14 030060 0. Paperback. Cover design as 1978a. Price £1.25.
Includes a one-page 'Glossary' condensed from 'Apologia' (1960a) on p.240.

1984. Puffin Books. *Reprint of 1982b; the sixth text; illustrated.*
'Reprinted ... 1984'. ISBN 0 14 030060 0. Paperback. Covers as 1978a. Price £1.75.

1985a. Webb and Bower. *New edition of the sixth text, with new material; illustrated by McBride; 12 illustrations by Tunnicliffe.*
'This edition published ... 1985'. Printed by Mandarin Offset International, Hong Kong. ISBN 0 86350 074 9. Pp.208. Illustrations, reckoned. 256 x 190mm. Olive-green simulated cloth, stamped white and fawn on the front and spine; olive-green endpapers. Dust jacket white, printed in white and black on an all-round colour photograph by Simon McBride. Price £12.95.

Contents: new Introduction by Richard Williamson (pp.7–13) with two photographs and three facsimiles, map of 'The Country of the Two Rivers' (pp.14–15) redrawn from previous versions, text (pp.16–207) as 1962, and 'Glossary' as 1982b; end-note as 1928e, with owl device. Elements that are not included are the Introduction by Fortescue, 'The Gentleman's River ' and 'The Original Ending'.
    Additional illustrations comprise 60 photographs in black and white and 55 in colour, some double spread, by Simon McBride, plus 12 of the 20 headpieces by Tunnicliffe from 1949a now used as tailpieces.

1985b. Penguin Books. *Reprint of 1982b; the sixth text; illustrated.*
'Reprinted in this edition 1985'. Penguin Country Library. ISBN 0 14 059011 0. Paperback. Cover design by Paul Robinson. Price £2.95.
    A photo-reprint with print size enlarged.

1986a. Webb and Bower. *Reprint of 1985a; the sixth text; illustrated.*
'Second impression 1986'. Book and jacket as 1985a. Price £12.95.

1986b. Puffin Books. *Reprint of 1982b; the sixth text; illustrated.*
'Reprinted ... 1986'. ISBN 0 14 030060 0. Paperback. Cover design by

Terry Riley. Price £1.95.

1987. Bodley Head.
Reported but not seen.

1990. Beacon Press. Boston. *American reprint of 1945; the fourth text, illustrated.*
i) 'First Beacon paperback edition published in 1990'. Printed in the USA. Serial numbers 96–90 and 1–8. The Concord Library. ISBN 0 8070 8507 3. Pp.xxxvi + 284. Paperback. Cover design by Christine Raquepaw including a repeat of the frontispiece (otter underwater).
A photo-reprint of 1945 (limited issue) with map by courtesy of Webb and Bower 1985 and an Introduction (pp.ix-xxxii) by Robert Finch, Brewster, Massachusets, undated, in which Finch refers to the book starting with the word 'Dimmity' (as in the first UK and American texts). Unfortunately in this printing it starts with 'Twilight' (as in the second text of 1928b) so Finch and the publishers were clearly not working from the same text - an example of the need to know about Williamson's revisions for which this author is much obliged.

ii) as i) but with 'Introduction copyright [symbol] 1990 by Beacon Press' added to the edition statement and the serial numbers now 99–95 and 2–8, on verso of the title-page.
Text altered to start with 'Dimmity' instead of 'Twilight'.

1995a. Puffin Books. *New edition of the sixth text; illustrated by Large.*
'This edition published in Puffin Books 1995'. Printed by Clays Ltd. Puffin Modern Classics. ISBN 0 14 036621 0. Pp.vi + 282. 198 x 129mm. Paperback. Cover illustration of an otter by John Butler. Price £5.99.
Contents as 1982b but with no subtitle or owl device, 'How the Book Came to be Written' placed after the text, headed 'Afterword', and 21 line drawings by Annabel Large, one on the title-page and 20 as headpieces to each chapter.

1995b. The Folio Society. *New edition of the fifth text; 38 illustrations by Tunnicliffe.*
'This edition is reprinted by kind permission of The Bodley Head'. Printed at the Bath Press. Pp.xvi + 224. Frontispiece and illustrations, reckoned. Hamilton Wove paper; endpapers green, with a new map.

227 x 155mm. Green cloth, goldstamped on the front and spine, with the frontispiece (otter underwater) reproduced on a paper label on the front, in green card patterned slip-case. Price £19.95.

The contents of 1982a without 'The Original Ending' but with a new map, 'North Devon, the Country of Tarka's life and death' by Denys Baker, and 38 illustrations by Tunnicliffe from 1932 (omitting two tail-pieces).

Foreign-language editions (seen* or from HWSJ 16):

1929. *Tarka Der Otter.* Reimer - Vohsen. Berlin.*

1930. *Tarka La Loutre.* Delmain Et Boutelleau. Paris.

1930. *Tarka La Lontre.* Fratelli Treves Editori. Milano.

1932. *Tarka Jugendzeit, eine Ottergeschichte.* Reimer - Vohsen. Berlin. Abridged.*

c1932. *Uttern Tarka.* Knut Lindberg. Sweden. Paperback.

1938. *Tarka vodni poutnik.* Drūzstevni práce v Praze. Illustrations by Tunnicliffe.*

1947. *Tarka Der Otter.* Werner - Degener - Verlag. Hannover.

1960. *Tarka, Uttern.* Wahlstroms Bokforlag. Stockholm.*

1963. *Tarka Der Otter.* Scherz. Bern Und Stuttgart.

1964. *Odderen Tarka.* Forlaget Fremad. Denmark. Illustrations by Driscoll.*

1967. *Tarka La Loutre.* Editions Stock. Paris. Paperback.*

1969. *Tarka La Lontra.* Bompiani. Milano. Paperback. Illustrations by Tunnicliffe.*

1969. *Vodn Poutnik Tarka.* Klub Mladych Ctenaru. Praha. Prague.

?1971. *Tarka De Otter.* Van Holkena & Warendorf - Bussum, Unibok. Belgium.

1979. Moscow. Illustrations by Tunnicliffe.

A9 THE PATHWAY

In the final volume of *The Flax of Dream* Willie Maddison is living at 'Scur Cottage' in Devon and writing a book called 'The Star-Born'. It is 'a sort of fantasy' that he hopes will deliver mankind from the culture of war but his personal 'pathway' leads only to turmoil and despair and the 'dream' dies.

In a Preface (printed only in 1931b) Williamson states: 'The scenes and characters were not planned beforehand; they arose before me as I wrote'. Part-way through the writing he felt he was 'an alchemist, transmuting energy into dream,' but when he had finished he was 'vaguely disappointed that it was not as I intended ... I had wasted my power during the indolent years'.

In concept *The Flax of Dream* was always intended to be a 'tetralogy' but what had actually emerged at this stage was a trilogy of books that had been planned and written in sequence, and published in a uniform and attractive style by one publisher, followed four years later (and after *Tarka*) by one that was unplanned and issued in an uninspiring format by a third-choice publisher (Collins had refused it, and he had been unable to agree terms with Putnam's). This, however, was the one that attracted serious critical attention, both in the UK and America, prompting Williamson to undertake a major revision of the first three volumes which were then published by Faber from 1929–31. With *The Pathway* there was no need for a major overhaul and revisions were limited to a series of lesser changes made in 1929a, 1929b, 1936 and 1944.

1928a. Jonathan Cape. *First edition.*
'First published Mcmxxviii'. Printed by Butler & Tanner. Pp.416. 198 x 128mm. Green cloth, goldstamped on the spine. Dust jacket white, printed in red and black, with a fourpointed device on the spine panel and a misprint 'Last Generation' instead of 'Lost Generation' in the blurb on the front flap. Price 7/6. Published October 1928. 2000 copies

(Girvan, D 1931); 11000 copies including reprints (letter from Cape 1969).

Contents:
- quotation 'I am the Way ...' on title-page;
- text (pp.9–416) in 4 sections, headed, and 18 Chapters, unheaded, ending 'November 1924 - September 1928. London - Devon', with owl device:

Winter	chaps.	1–4
Spring		5–8
Summer		9–14
Autumn		15–17 and 'Last Chapter'

1928b. Jonathan Cape. *Reprint of the first edition.*
'Second impression Mcmxxviii'. Green cloth, goldstamped. Price 7/6.

1928c. Jonathan Cape. *Reprint of the first edition.*
'Third impression Mcmxxviii'. Pp.418 (added blank). Green cloth, gold-stamped.

1929a. Jonathan Cape. *Reprint of the first edition, revised; the second text.*
'Fourth impression Mxmxxix'. Pp.424 (new fly-titles). Green cloth, goldstamped. Dust jacket design as previously but with 'Fourth impression' on the spine panel and the misprint corrected. Price 7/6. One copy seen has 'Overseas Edition' stamped in purple on recto of the front free endpaper.

After p.405 line 28 there are 18 lines of new text ending 'It was pure beauty,' which are accommodated by reducing the quotation on p.414 to two lines, the first quotation on p.416 to three lines and omitting the owl device.

1929b. E.P. Dutton & Co., Inc. New York. *American edition of the second text, with a further revision; the third text.*
'Copyright 1929' and 'First edition'. Printed in the USA. Pp.400. 196 x 129mm. Green cloth, goldstamped on the front and spine; top edge pink, fore-edge untrimmed. Dust jacket white, printed in red and blue-green, with a design of birds flying over waves, signed 'HR' on the front panel. Price $ 2.50.

A new type-setting with 'waiting' instead of 'sitting' in the first line of the previously added text (now p.386 line 17), and the two shortened quotations (now on pp.394 and 396) restored to their original length. Later bib notes indicate that within four months there were at least 10 printings of this edition, which suggests either massive demand or small print runs. All were issued in the same format and for ease of reference are listed here rather than as individual entries (seen*):

'First printing	February, 1929'
'Second printing	February, 1929'
'Third printing	February, 1929' *
'Fourth printing	February, 1929'
'Fifth printing	February, 1929'
'Sixth printing	February, 1929' *
'Seventh printing	June, 1929'
'Eighth printing	June, 1929'
'Ninth printing	June, 1929'
'Tenth printing	June, 1929' *

1929c. Jonathan Cape. *Reprint of 1929a by a different printer; the second text.*
'Sixth impression Mcmxxix'. Printed by John Wright and Sons, Bristol. Green cloth, goldstamped.

This appears to have been numbered incorrectly and is probably the 'Fifth impression Mcmxxix' which is listed in the bib note of 1931a but otherwise unknown.

1931a. Jonathan Cape. *Reprint of 1929a by another printer; the second text.*
i) 'Sixth impression Mxmxxxi'. Printed by The Alden Press. Green cloth, goldstamped. Dust jacket design as previously but with 'Sixth impression' on the spine panel and front flap. Price 7/6.

ii) Cheaper issue: 'Sixth impression Mcmxxxi'. Printed by The Alden Press. Cape's Half-Crown Fiction No.21. Orange cloth, blackstamped. Dust jacket tan, printed in black and purple. Price 2/6.

1931b. Jonathan Cape. *Reprint of 1929a; the second text; signed issue on large-paper.*
'Limited and signed edition in Mcmxxxi'. This edition printed on English hand-made paper is limited to two hundred. This is number ...' followed by the number and author's signature in ink, on recto of the

second leaf. Printed by The Alden Press. Pp.x + 426 (new fly-titles and a blank). 235 x 150mm. Green buckram, goldstamped on the front and spine; top edge gilt, others untrimmed (uniform in style with the signed issues of BY, DD, DFW). No jacket. Price 2 guineas. 200 copies.

Includes a 'Preface' by HW (pp.1–7) concerning the writing of the book that is not present in any other printing (collected by John Gregory in A67).

1933. Faber & Faber Limited. *Reprint of 1929a; the second text, in The Faber Library.*
'First reprinted in this new edition June Mcmxxxiii'. The Faber Library No.16. Green cloth, goldstamped. Dust jacket pink, printed in green and black. Price 3/6.

1936. In *The Flax of Dream* (A24, pp.988–1416). *New edition of the second text, with further revisions; the fourth text.*
Textual changes are present on at least 50 pages with alterations to words or lines, omissions, and the insertion of new passages and paragraphs; they are more common in the last two sections and particularly in the last chapter, where the last paragraph now consists of 6 lines commencing 'He did not need to change'. After the text, the date and place are omitted and replaced by the owl device with 'Here ends The Flax of Dream, arisen from the battlefield of Christmas, 1914'.

1940. Faber & Faber Limited. *Reprint of 1936; the fourth text; in The Faber Library.*
'First reprinted ... and in February Mcmxl'. The Faber Library No.16. Pp.432. Green cloth, goldstamped. Dust Jacket yellow, printed in red. Price 3/6.

Printed from the 1936 type, repaginated, with the original date and place restored at the end but no owl device.

1942. Faber & Faber Limited. *Reprint of 1940; the fourth text; in The Faber Library.*
'Reprinted October Mcmxlii'. The Faber Library No.16. Green cloth, silverstamped. Dust jacket cream, printed in red. Price 3/6.

1944. Faber and Faber Ltd. *Reprint of 1929a, with parts of 1936, and further revisions; the fifth text.*
'Reprinted in December Mcmxliv'. Pp.420. Red or brown cloth, gold-

stamped.

Many of the changes made in the 1936 version are included here (with the type re-set) but others are dropped; additional changes to words or lines are noted on pp.45–47, 51 and 413 line 15 where 'They walked on, hand in hand' is added; ends with the date and owl device.

1947. Faber and Faber Ltd. *Reprint of 1944; the fifth text.*
i) 'Reprinted in June Mcmxlvii'. Fawn cloth. Dust jacket white, printed in red and black. Price 8/6.

ii) as i) but dust jacket yellow, printed in green, price 6/-.

1969. Faber and Faber Ltd. *Reprint of 1944; the fifth text.*
i) 'First published in this edition 1969'. SBN 571 09022 2. Khaki cloth. Dust jacket cream, printed in black, green and red-brown. Price 30/-, £1.50.

ii) edition statement as i). Faber Paper Covered Editions. SBN 571 09021 4. Paperback. Price 10/-, £0.50.

[1983]. Zenith. *New edition of the fifth text.*
No date. 'Zenith books (Hamlyn Paperbacks) are published by The Hamlyn Publishing Group Ltd...' Printed by Hazell Watson and Viney. ISBN 0 600 20682 3. Pp.384. 198 x 179mm. Paperback. Cover illustration from a painting 'Madonna Lillies' by Ernest Chadwick. Price £2.95.

No date, place or owl device at the end.

A10 THE ACKYMALS

The Ackymals (local dialect for the blue-tit or great-tit) is a short story first printed in *The London Mercury* of January 1927 then revised and published as a fine-press limited edition in the USA in 1929.

That year marked the end of what can be regarded as the first phase of Williamson's career. Until then he had been occupied largely with *The Flax of Dream* and *Tarka*, but over the next twenty he would expand his range beyond nature writing and novels to include fantasy, satire, autobiography, war, travel, village life, and a tale for children. In the final phase, from 1949, he would narrow the focus again to just one major work, *A Chronicle of Ancient Sunlight*.

It was also the year in which he built a 'writing hut' that he was to use throughout the rest of his life, in a field at Ox's Cross (as he called it) on the hill above Georgeham. In the autumn, with a second son (John) and a third child on the way, the family left Georgeham and moved to Shallowford Cottage at Filleigh, near South Molton.

1929. The Windsor Press. [San Francisco]. *First edition.*
'Printed at The Windsor Press. 1929' on the title-page; signed by the author in red ink on verso. Colophon: 'This first edition of The Ackymals is limited to 225 copies, each signed by the author. Printed by James and Cecil Johnson at The Windsor Press, with decorations by Julian Links', followed by a Press device and 'Copy No...' with the number written in red or green ink by the author, on p.24. Pp.vi + 24. Publisher's device printed in green on the titlepage and a headpiece vignette in green and black on p.2. 234 x 160mm. Floral-patterned paper boards with grey cloth spine, goldstamped; top edge trimmed, in blue card slip-case. The price and month of publication are not known but Girvan (D 1931) and Anne Williamson (D 1995) both place it before the other books published in this year. 225 copies stated, but unnumbered copies have also been noted.

Contents: 'The Ackymals' (pp.2–23); no date or owl device.

1930. In *The Village Book* (A14, pp.273–292). *New edition; revised.*
The first three pages of the American text are omitted and words or phrases changed on pp.273–5, 280, with 'Hole Farm' instead of 'Foot Farm', 'The Lower House' instead of 'The Stag and Tufters', etc.

1945. In *Tales of a Devon Village* (A31, pp.93–104). *New edition, with further revlsions.*
Changes from the 1930 text include 'tomtits' instead of 'ackymals' twice on p.95, a new sentence on p.98 lines 6–7 and 'planting' instead of 'tilling' on the same page.

A11 THE WET FLANDERS PLAIN

Williamson's personal experience of war on the Western Front amounted to about six months in total (D 1998) but its effects were to last for the rest of his life. In 'Apologia' at the start of *The Wet Flanders*

Plain he tells how being in the belfry of the church at Georgeham when the bells were rung evoked memories of the bombardment: 'the powerful wraith of those four year of the War enters into me ... I see men arising and walking forward; and I go forward with them, in a glassy delirium ... up and down, across ground like a huge ruined honeycomb ...' That he would write about the Great War was inevitable. He was already planning to do it in semi-fictional form in *A Chronicle of Ancient Sunlight* where it occupies five books, but they were many years in the future; what he could do in the meantime was approach it though reminiscence.

He had gone back to the battlefields in 1925 on honeymoon and again with his brother-in-law, William Busby, formerly of the Tank Corps, in 1927, and *The Wet Flanders Plain* is a fusion of these visits arranged in a loose diary form with a chapter devoted to each 'Day', merging his recollections with the contemporary scene. In a copy inscribed to C.R.W. Nevinson he says that most of it was actually written in 1925.

The first edition was limited to 400 copies and was not reprinted (Beaumont would not do a cheap edition) but later in the year it was published by Faber in revised form and in 1987 it was republished with photographs taken in 1925 and articles commissioned by *The Evening Standard* in 1964 for the fiftieth anniversary of the War.

1929a. The Beaumont Press. *First edition.*
i) Numbered issue: no imprint on the title-page; 'Printed and made in England' on verso; 'The Certificate. This is the twenty-fourth book issued by the Beaumont Press. 80 copies (five of which are not for sale) have been printed on hand-made parchment vellum signed by author artist and publisher and numbered 1 to 80 and 320 copies (fifteen of which are not for sale) on hand-made paper numbered 81 to 400. This is No....' with the number written in ink, on verso of the first leaf. Colophon: '... The Cover and Title-page designed by Randolph Schwabe The Typography and Binding arranged and the book produced by Cyril William Beaumont and printed at his Press Completed on the eighth day of May Mdccccxxix' with publisher's device, on p.98. Pp.vi + 98. 230 x 140mm. Paper boards patterned in black and brown, backed in fawn cloth, goldstamped; fore-edge untrimmed. No jacket. Price 25/-. Published June 1929. 320 copies.

ii) Signed, numbered issue: as i) but printed on parchment vellum and with the signatures of Williamson, Schwabe and Beaumont in ink below the Certificate on p.ii, backed in vellum. Price 50/-. 80 copies.

Contents:
- title-page vignette in black and orange, by Schwabe;
- 'Apologia pro vita mea' (pp.1–6);
- text (pp.9–96) headed 'The Diary', and divided into nine chapters, headed: First Day, Second Day, Third Day, Fourth Day, Fifth Day, Sixth Day, Seventh Day, Eighth Day, Last Day, with subheadings in the text, ending with owl device.

1929b. Faber & Faber Limited. *New edition, revised; the second text.*
'The revised edition ... was first published in Mcmxxix'. Printed by Butler and Tanner. Pp.148. 192 x 123mm. Black cloth, goldstamped on the spine; top edge brown. Dust jacket brown, printed in red and black, with a quote from Humbert Wolfe - 'easily the best antiwar book written in English ...' on the front panel, all corners clipped; some with a wraparound advertisement band printed in yellow and black quoting Arnold Bennett and Humbert Wolfe. Price 5/-. Published October 1929. 2990 copies (Girvan, D 1931)).

A variant has been noted that is slightly taller (194mm) with the foredge rough-trimmed and the jacket unclipped.

Changes from the first edition are: quotation '... lost forever in ancient Sunlight, which arises again as Truth' on the title-page, unattributed; dedication 'To C R.W. Nevinson'; in 'Apologia' the two penultimate paragraphs are partly rewritten with 'This year ... I was called a traitor by my father' removed. In the text: p.33: last sentence changed to 'I can sleep all night!'; p.56: three lines omitted at the bottom of the page; p.79: lines 5 and 6 have new text; p.148: ends 'Ypres, Roclincourt, Ham, 1927', with owl device.

1929c. E.P. Dutton & Co., Inc. *American edition of the second text.*
'Copyright, 1929' and 'First edition'. Printed in the USA. Pp.128. 203 x 128mm. Black and yellow cloth with geometric design and a label printed in black on the spine. Dust jacket yellow and black with a geometric design of fixed bayonets, unattributed, on the front panel.

No changes in text noted.

1987. Gliddon Books. *Reprint of 1929a; the second text, illustrated, with new material and an Introduction.*

i) 'Reissued by Gliddon Books 1987 with new material'. ISBN 0 947893 04 0. Great War Classics series. Pp.xx + 172 (pagination is incorrect). 4 photographic plates, not reckoned. 223 x 135mm. Black cloth, gold-stamped on the spine. Dust jacket white, printed in red and black, with a photograph of HW in 1915 on the front panel, and in 1964 on the back panel.

ii) as i) except: ISBN 0 947893 22 9. Paperback. Cover photograph of HW in a war cemetery on the front and in March 1915 on the back.

New elements are an eight-page Introduction by Richard Williamson giving background to the work, reproductions of 14 photographs taken in 1925, and 'Return to Hell' - the five articles that Williamson wrote when he returned to the battlefields in 1964.

A 12 THE LINHAY ON THE DOWNS

The first book with this title (see also A20) contains two short stories, both of which appeared later in other books, issued in a fine-press edition, numbered and initialled by the author. Why he should give the same title to two different books has not been explained, but *As the Sun Shines* is also used twice (in LL 1933 and A28).

1929. Elkin Mathews & Marrot. *First edition.*
'Five hundred and thirty numbered copies of this story have been set in Monotype English Poliphilus, and printed by Robert MacLehose & Co. Ltd., at the University Press, Glasgow; Nos.1–500 only are for sale and Nos.501–530 for presentation. This is copy No...' with the number written and initialled by the author in ink, on verso of the title-page. The Woburn Books Number 12. Pp.28. 205 x 143mm. Grey sugar-paper boards and endpapers, printed in a green floral design signed 'J.G.P. '28'. Dust jacket grey sugar-paper, with the same design as the covers. 530 copies.

Contents:
- 'The Linhay on the Downs' (pp.3–19); published previously in the *Atlantic Monthly* and *Fortnightly Review* 1927; later in LOD (A20) revised, and TDV (A31) without further changes;
- 'The Firing Gatherer' (pp.21–26) followed by owl device; published in

Time and Tide 1927 (Girvan D 1931, not yet confirmed); later in VB (A14) with one word changed ('spring' to summer' in th last paragraph), and LDV (A32) with a few additional changes.

A13 THE PATRIOT'S PROGRESS Being the Vicissitudes of Pte. John Bullock

In his own copy of *The Wet Flanders Plain* Williamson wrote: 'Why have I a war-complex? Terrified by war, I now love to let my mind dwell on the immense destructive power and desolation of war. Is this a form of neurosis? I love to imagine guns flashing, and troops marching, and the vastness of our army's movements and operations. This is of course, in retrospect very different from the war that actually was.'

The war that actually was is in *The Patriot's Progress*, a book that came about largely by accident. In 1928 Williamson had been approached on behalf of William Kermode, a Tasmanian-born artist living in England who had served in the war, in the hope that he would provide some captions for a book of war illustrations that Kermode was preparing.

The response was not what Kermode expected. Williamson had just addressed his war through reminiscence in *The Wet Flanders Plain* but this was a chance to do it for real and he chose to deliver a whole book written around Kermode's lino-cuts, effectively relegating them to the role of supporting cast. Some diplomatic moves by Williamson's literary agent were required to reconcile the conflicting views of the project.

The result, however, was a most effective combination with Williamson's raw evocation of the soldier's lot perfectly complemented by the rough style and subtle humour of Kermode's images. Williamson later thought that the writing was 'mannered to the anti-Staff period of the infantryman's war of 1915–17,' but this is what gives it much of its force. John Bullock's mindset was an integral part of how it 'actually was'.

In 1968 he added a Preface and Epigraph, quoting opinions and correspondence about the book, and in 1999 it was reprinted with an historical Introduction and Biographical Note.

1930a. Geoffrey Bles. *First edition; illustrated by Kermode; signed, numbered issue.*

i) Verso of the title-page blank. 'This edition on large paper is limited to three hundred and fifty signed copies, this is number ....' numbered and signed by Williamson and signed by Kermode in ink, on verso of the half-title. Colophon: 'Here ends The Patriot's Progress which was cut in lino by William Kermode at Kew Gardens in Surrey in Mcmxxix, written by Henry Williamson in the village of Ham in Devon in the same year, printed by the Euston Press ... London ... published by Geoffrey Bles ... Mcmxxx', with owl device, on p.196. Pp.xii + 196. Illustrations, reckoned. 249 x 155mm. Maroon cloth, backed in white parchment-vellum, goldstamped; top edge gilt, others untrimmed. No jacket. Price 2 guineas. Published April 1930 (see below). 350 copies.

ii) edition statement as i), numbered '197', in ink, but not signed by author or artist; a public library copy in light khaki cloth with red leather label on the spine, edges untrimmed.

iii) verso of the half-title blank with no edition statement or number and unsigned; bound as i). [50] copies (see below).

iv) verso of the half-title blank, as in iii), but in blue, diagonal-ribbed cloth, goldstamped on the spine, top edge unstained. [100] copies (see below).

Note: in this issue the illustration on p.93 is of poplar trees alongside a road, that on p.141 is of a soldier outside a street-corner brothel, and the illustration of two women in a brothel is on p.144 (the arrangement in the American printing, 1930d).

In *John O'London's Weekly* on 15 March 1930 Bles announced that 'In March I am publishing [The Patriot's Progress] (10s 6d net) ... The Limited Edition of 350 copies at £2.2s is already over-subscribed'. In response to enquiries in 1966, however, Jocelyn Gibb (then managing director of Bles) wrote that the records showed that the month of publication was April, that 500 copies of the limited edition were printed, but only 400 were bound, and only 350 signed and numbered. It is likely therefore that item iii) represents the 50 that were bound but unsigned, and that item iv) represents the 100 copies that were originally unbound.

Contents:
- 'Dedication': a lino-cut of a grave, no text;

- illustrations: 124 linocuts by William Kermode in the text, plus one on the dust jacket and the sign on p.81;
- text (pp.1–194) in 5 sections, headed, followed by 'Epilogue' (a lino-cut) p.195, colophon and owl device:

First Phase
Second Phase
Third Phase
Fourth Phase
Fifth Phase

1930b. Geoffrey Bles. *First edition; cheaper issue.*
i) 'First published, April, 1930'. Verso of the half-title blank. Colophon, pagination and illustrations as 1930a. 230 x 140mm. Red buckram, gold-stamped on the spine; top edge red. Dust jacket white, printed in red and black, with an additional lino-cut by Kermode on the front panel, repeated on the back. Price 10/6. Published April 1930. 5000 copies (letter from Gibb 1966).

ii) as i) but cut to 220 x 138mm; red cloth, blackstamped on the spine, top edge plain; dust jacket as i), cut to size.

Note: in this issue the illustration on p.93 is of men marching on a long straight road, that on p.141 is of a 'crown and anchor' board, and the illustration of two women in a brothel is on p.143 (the arrangement in all later UK printings).

1930c. Geoffrey Bles. *Reprint of the first edition.*
i) 'Reprinted, April, 1930'. As 1930bi. Dust jacket printed with 'Second impression'. Price 10/6. 2000 copies (letter from Gibb 1966).
ii) as 1930bii; red cloth, blackstamped.

1930d. Geoffrey Bles. *Reprint of the first edition.*
i) 'Reprinted, May, 1930'. As 1930bi but top edge unstained. Dust jacket printed with 'Third impression'. Price 10/6. 1000 copies (letter from Gibb 1966).

ii) as 1930bii; red cloth, blackstamped.

1930e. E.P. Dutton & Co., Inc. New York. *American reprint of the first*

edition.
'Copyright, 1930'. Printed in the USA. Pp.x + 196. 210 x 137mm. Blue, wavy-patterned cloth, goldstamped on the front and spine; top edge pink, foredge untrimmed. Dust jacket pink/red, printed in black, with the illustration from p.28 reproduced on the front panel. Price $2.50.
Illustrations as in 1930a; colophon shortened to 8 lines omitting the UK printer and publisher.

1968. Macdonald. *Reprint of the first edition, with additional material.*
'This edition first published 1968'. SBN 356 02455 5. Pp.xxii + 198. 203 x 128mm. Dark olive linson, goldstamped. Dust jacket blue-green, printed in red and black, with the linocut as 1930b on the front and back panels. Price 21/-. 2500 copies (letter from Macdonald 1970).
Printed from 1930b but with additional material by Williamson comprising a 'Preface' (pp.xi-xx) with the text of a review of the original book by Arnold Bennett, a letter from T.E. Lawrence (writing as T.E. Shaw), and an 'Epigraph' (pp.196–7) signed 'H.W. 1 July, 1968' including the obituary of Kermode from *The Times* of 6.2.59.

1976. Macdonald and Jane's. *Reprint of 1968.*
'Second impressison 1976'. ISBN 0 356 02455 5. Blue linson, silver-stamped. Dust jacket white, printed in blue and red, with lino-cut as 1968. Price £3.50.

1978. Sphere Books Limited. *Reprint of 1968.*
i) 'First Sphere Books edition 1978'. ISBN 0 7221 9181 2. 177 x 109mm. Paperback. Cover illustration of soldiers advancing, unattributed. Price 85p.
A photo-reprint with print size reduced.

ii) as i) except: ISBN 0 7221 3183 9. Cut to 173 x 106mm. Paperback. Cover design of a cross, poppy and barbed wire, unattributed. Price £1.10.

1991. Cardinal. *Reprint of 1968.*
'Published in Cardinal by Sphere Books Ltd 1991'. ISBN 0 7474 0805 X. Paperback. Cover design from a photograph of a soldier in silhouette (Imperial War Museum). Price £4.99.

1999. Sutton Publishing. *Reprint of 1968, with an Introduction and Note.*

'First published in this edition in 1999 ...' ISBN 0 7509 2234 6. Pp.xxviii + 196. Paperback. Cover design from *The Illustrated London News* and 'The Soldiers of the Gloucestershire Museum'. Price £6.99.

Includes the Preface from 1968 but not the Epigraph, with an 'Introduction' (4 pp.) by K.W. Mitchinson (historian) and a 'Biographical Note' (3 pp.) by Anne Williamson.

A14 THE VILLAGE BOOK

Soon after Williamson moved to Georgeham ('Ham') he began to write about its life and inhabitants and soon after he left he published the collection of tales and sketches that make up *The Village Book*. In the Note to the first edition of *The Labouring Life* (A16) he says: 'While writing the antecedent Village Book it seemed that property was the root of all evil; but since the writer has left the village of Ham, where most are small property-owners, there has been time for reflexion, whereafter it would appear that the problem is one of narrowness of mind.'

In the note of dedication there is the ritual disclaimer that this 'is an imaginative work which should not be read as the history of any particular village, and certainly not of any man or woman,' but in the Preface to the signed issue of *The Labouring Life* (1932ii) he acknowledges that the characters are based on real people.

In 1945 most of the contents of this and *The Labouring Life* were rearranged and revised to form *Tales of a Devon Village* (A31) and *Life in a Devon Village* (A32).

1930a. Jonathan Cape. *First edition.*
i) 'First published 1930'. Printed by The Alden Press. Pp.344. Frontispiece, not reckoned. 209 x 136mm. Brown cloth, goldstamped on the front (owl device) and spine. Dust jacket cream, printed in red and black. Price 7/6. Published July 1930. 5000 copies (letter from Cape 1969).

Page 276 line 24 has the comma incorrectly printed in bold.

ii) Signed, numbered issue: as i) except: 'Five hundred and four copies of this special signed edition of The Village Book have been printed for sale. This is copy number ...' followed by the number and author's signature in ink, on verso of the first leaf. 209 x 136mm. Green cloth, vellum backed; top edge gilt, others untrimmed. Dust jacket glassine with paper flaps, some printed with 'Limited edition 504 copies signed. £2.2.0.' Published July 1930.

On p.276 line 24 the previous comma in bold is now a quotation mark in bold.

Contents:
- quotation from Old Ploughman of Ham on title-page;
- dual dedication to Mrs. Hibbert (great-grandmother of his children) and Petre Mais 'our old striding friend of the Sussex Downs';
- illustrations: frontispiece photograph of the author with dogs at Skirr Cottage, captioned; facsimiles of two sketches by the author pp.168, 293;
- text (pp.11–342) with 55 pieces grouped in the Contents pages under two main headings - The Spirit of the Village, Winter and Spring / Air and Light of the Fields and the Sea, Winter and Spring - but in a different order in the text (as below), ending with owl device:

	Notes:
The Donkey	in LDV in 'On Scandal'
The Badger Dig	from *T.P.'s and Cassell's* 1926; in TDV
Night in the Estuary	
Scandal and Gossip	in LDV in 'On Scandal'
The Poor Fowl	
A Mason's Week	in LDV in 'On Scandal'
A Winter Fresh	
Washing Day	in LDV in 'A Farmer's Life'
The Linnets	
The Village Inns (1) The Lower House	from *Monthly Criterion* 1928; in LDV
'Muggy,' The Rabbit Agent	from *Manchester Guardian* 1929; in LDV
The Vacant Fields	in LDV
The Village Inns (2) The Higher House	from *Monthly Criterion* 1928; in LDV
The Buzzards	
Old Woolacott	in LDV

The Sawyers	from *London Mercury* 1928, in LDV
The First Day of Spring (1)	in LDV
In the Village	
The Lane to the Sea	
Wind, Grass and Sun	
The Brook	
The Cattle Path	
The Engboo	
The Problem of Peace	
The First Day of Spring (2)	in L.DV, excluding 'Interlude'
The Origin of Ghosts	
Vention Lane	
The Blackbird of the Blasted Tree	
The Foreigners	
The Blackthorn Brake	
The Ravens of Bloodhill	
Authentic Cases of Salvation	
Interlude	
The First Day of Spring (3)	in LDV
The Peregrine Falcon	
Man to Animal	
The Wall above South Side	
Middlehill Lane	
The Way Home	
Ham Saint George	
The Old Cob Cottage	from *Sunday Dispatch* 1928; in TDV
A Boy on the Headland	from *Daily Telegraph* 1928
Billy Goldsworthy's Barn	in TDV
The Gaping Raven of Morte	
Scriddicks	in LDV in 'On Scandal'
Flight of the Falcon	
The Ackymals	see A10; in TDV
The Water Ousels	
A Farmer's Life (1–4)	in LDV
Swallows in Cliffs	from *Daily News* 1925
A Romance of Old-World Courting	in TDV as 'An Old-World Courting'

My Owls (1–2) — in LDV as 'Birds of Skirr Cottage, 1–2'

The Zeale Brothers — from *London Mercury* 1929, in TDV

The Firing Gatherer — see A12; in LDV

1930b. E.P. Dutton & Co., Inc. New York. *American reprint of the first edition*
'Copyright, 1930 ... First edition'. Printed in the USA. Pp.344. Frontispiece, reckoned (no first blank). 210 x 137mm. Brown cloth, gold-stamped on the front and spine; fore-edge untrimmed. Dust jacket cream, printed in red and black, as 1930a; some with a wraparound advertisement band printed in blue and black, quoting a cable from Frank Swinnerton.
Page 276 line 24 has the comma in bold as 1930ai.

1930c. Jonathan Cape. *Reprint of the first edition.*
'Reprinted September 1930'. Brown cloth, goldstamped on the front and spine. Dust jacket design as 1930a but with 'Second impression' printed on the spine and front flap. Price 7/6.
Page 276 line 24 now has the comma corrected and p.307 has the last five lines reset and punctuated to separate the Jefferies quotation from Williamson's text.

1933. Jonathan Cape. *Reissue of 1930c, in The Life and Letters Series.*
'Re-issued in The Life and Letters Series 1933'. No.53. 206 x 134mm. Green cloth, goldstamped on the front and spine. Dust jacket white, printed in green. Price 4/6.
Printed as 1930c but with the half-title and title-page as an integral cancel on slightly stiffer paper. Item 1930c is relatively uncommon which suggests that the bulk of that printing may have been issued in this format.

1937. Jonathan Cape. *Reprint of 1930c, with a revision; in The Travellers'Libary.*
'First issued in the Travellers' Library 1937'. No.217. Pp.344. Khaki cloth, bluestamped on the spine; also in blue cloth, goldstamped. Dust jacket yellow, printed in green and black. Price 3/6.
Print size reduced, including the facsimile sketches, with no frontispiece or quotation on the title-page. On p.307 the penultimate line of

'Swallows in Cliffs' has 'forsake the old sheds and shadowed barns' instead of 'desert the old sheds and barns'.

A15 THE WILD RED DEER OF EXMOOR A Digression on the Logic and Ethics and Economics of Stag-Hunting in England To-day

Published in the interval between his two books on Georgeham, *The Wild Red Deer of Exmoor* is a short collection of Williamson's thoughts on stag-hunting after a day spent as a guest of the local meet. Part I is a revised version of 'Hunting to Kill' which was published in *Brittania* on 2 November 1928, but the rest is new material, including a report of an antihunt protest meeting, a section on Lenin, and an account of his experiences with the hunt.

As in *Tarka*, his position is one of rational ambivalence: 'The sportsman wants to continue his sport, the humanitarian wants to stop it. Having both sets of feelings within myself, I believe that I understand both types. Also I have my personal reactions to both of them ... transfer the set of ideas of the one to the other, and their intolerant attitudes are identical.'

1931a. Privately Printed. *First edition.*
No publisher or printer's imprint. 'London. 1931' on the title-page. 'Seventy-five copies only have been printed of this Edition. This copy is No ...' followed by the number in ink, on verso of the title-page. Pp.64. Hand-made paper. 192 x 130mm. Orange-red cloth, goldstamped on the spine; top edge gilt, others untrimmed, in green card slip-case. Not offered for sale (Girvan, D 1931). 75 copies.
'Printed for the author July 1931' in 1931b.

Contents:
- dedication 'To the Gentle Reader';
- text (pp.7–64): parts I-IV, unheaded, with no date or owl device.

1931b. Faber and Faber Limited. *Reprint of the first edition.*
'Reprinted July 1931'. Printed by R. Maclehose and Company. Pp.64. 193 x 124mm. Orange paper-covered boards, greenstamped on the spine; top edge green. Dust jacket white, printed in green and red. Price

2/6. Published August 1931 (letter from Faber 1966).
Also with the dust jacket price-clipped and printed 1/- on the front flap.

A16 THE LABOURING LIFE

In the Note to the first edition Williamson says 'The Labouring Life is not intended as a guide to farm-work; it is a collection of short stories and sketches which have bases in reality, or what seemed to have happened in one village and its neighbourhood ... Like its fellow, The Village Book, it is an imaginative work, created for two reasons: first, for the reader's entertainment; second that the spirit and letter of village life in the decade following the Great War be contained for future students of English country life ...

'The characters are not meant to represent any living persons; rather they are essences of personalities ... All personal prejudices of the author in extracting the various essences of personality have been excluded, in so far as his intelligence permits ...'

In the Preface to the signed issue (1932ii) referring to the Rector, he adds: 'I call him an imaginary character, because I have manipulated him, for the purposes of fiction ... Therefore the character is Williamson-rector ... At the same time, it would be contemptible and dishonest to deny that the character is based upon the incumbent of the village where I lived for several years ... and the other characters are based upon living people, too.'

Printed on the endpapers is a sketch-map of Georgeham and its environs, drawn and captioned by the author. In 1945 the contents of this and The Village Book were rearranged and revised to form Tales of a Devon Village (A31) and Life in a Devon Village (A32).

1932. Jonathan Cape. *First edition.*
i) 'First published 1932'. Printed by The Alden Press. Pp.496. Frontispiece, not reckoned. 210 x 135mm. Green cloth, goldstamped on the front (owl device) and spine; bottom edge untrimmed; endpapers white, with a hand-drawn map of the village and its environs printed in green and brown signed 'H.W. fecit 1932'. Dust jacket fawn, printed in blue and red, with a floral design signed 'C.J' on the front panel. Price 7/6. Published May 1932. 4000 copies (letter from Cape 1969).

A copy has been noted with the half-title and title-page uncancelled and frontispiece present, cased in the format of 'The Life and Letters Series' of 1934 (as below).

Text preceded by a 'Note' (2 pp.) on the background to the book dated 'Shallowford, Christmas, 1931'.

ii) Signed, numbered issue: as i) except: 'This signed edition is limited to one hundred and twenty-two copies, of which one hundred and eighteen are for sale. This is number ...' followed by the number and author's signature in ink, on recto of the first leaf. Pp.viii + 492. Brown cloth, vellum backed; top edge gilt, foredge untrimmed. Dust jacket glassine, with marbled paper flaps. 122 copies (matched to the number of subscribers).

Additional to the 'Note' is a 'Preface, or What You Will' (7 pp.) in two numbered parts, dated 25 February 1932, in which Williamson addresses the issue of 'truth' in the book with reference to an incident he had deleted from 'Surview and Farewell'. Part 1 of this piece was revised and used as the 'Note' to the American printing of 1933 and later in A28, but part 2 was not reprinted until both parts were collected by John Gregory in A67.

Contents:
- quotation from the Bible on title-page;
- frontispiece photograph of the author fishing, captioned;
- 'Note' in i); 'Note' and 'Preface' in ii);
- dedication 'To all my friends in Ham, including Arty, who asked for it, this book (excluding morel [sic] characters) is dedicated', followed by a supposed 'letter' from Arty which includes 'morel';
- text (pp.13–491) with 30 pieces grouped in the Contents pages under two main headings - The Spirit of the Village, Summer and Autumn / Air and Light of the Fields and the Sea, Summer and Autumn - but in a different order in the text (as below), ending with owl device:

	Notes:
Chapter 1	'samples' of the contents of LL and VB
The Life of the Stream	in LDV as 'The Stream'
Old Men	in LDV in 'On Scandal'
Summer Afternoon by the Sea	in LDV as 'Summer Afternoon'

The Well	in TDV
Star-Flights of Swifts	in LDV as 'Birds of Skirr Cottage 3'
The Labourer and 'A Labourer's Life'	in LDV as 'My Neighbour 'Revvy''
The White Witch and the Blackbird	
The Darkening of the Doorway	in TDV
Above the Needles, June 1928	from *Daily News* 1927, or *Outsiders* 1929
Village Children	in LDV
A Summer Day on Dunkery	in LDV as 'A Day on Dunkery'
Cemetery, or Burial Ground?	in TDV
Otters in the West Country	
The Fox in the Moonlight	in TDV
The Long-Toms	
The Mystery of Dark Cottage	in TDV
'Devonshire Cider'	in LDV
The Fair, Morning	in LDV
What the Doctor Said	in LDV
The Fair, Afternoon	in LDV
A Bird-Blasted Wood	from *Sunday Express* 1928
A Village David and Goliath	in TDV
P.C. Bullcornworthy	in TDV
Billy Goldsworthy's Cow	from *John O'London's* 1932; in TDV
Consecration of the New Burial Ground	in LDV same title and part in 'On Scandal'
A Devon Hillside, October 1928	in LDV
'Provincialisms'	from *London Mercury* 1928
Surview and Farewell	in LDV
Windwhistle Cross	from *Sunday Express* 1928

1933. E.P. Dutton & Co., Inc. New York. *American reprint of the first edition.* Retitled AS THE SUN SHINES (also used for A 28).

'Copyright, 1933 First edition'. Printed in the USA. Pp.494 (no initial blank). 212 x 138mm. Blue cloth, goldstamped on the front and spine; fore-edge untrimmed. Dust jacket white, printed in green and red.

No endpaper maps, frontispiece or dedication. The 'Note' is a slightly revised version of part 1 of the 'Preface ' from 1932ii, undated and unsigned, and it is this version which is reprinted with the last sentence omitted as the prelude to 'Devonshire Cider' in A28 (pp.99–101). Chapter 1 is retitled 'Village Sayings' in the text, running heads, and Contents.

1934. Jonathan Cape. *Reissue of the first edition, in The Life and Letters Series.*
'Re-issued in The Life and Letters Series 1934'. No.60. 206 x 135mm. Green cloth, goldstamped on the front and spine. Dust jacket white, printed in green. Price 4/6.

Apart from the copy noted in 1932i the half-title and title-page are cancels, but with variations in the make-up of individual copies:

a) no frontispiece, endpaper maps or publisher's catalogue; dust jacket with a list of the series titles to no.54 on the back panel;

b) no frontispiece but endpaper maps present; publisher's catalogue (20 pp., undated) added at the end, listing the series titles up to no.83; dust jacket not seen.

A17 THE GOLD FALCON or The Haggard of Love, being the adventures of Manfred, airman and poet of the World War, and later, husband and father, in search of freedom and personal sunrise, in the city of New York, and of the consummation of his life.

A year after its publication Williamson stated that 'The Gold Falcon was written with its Old Testament theme of the search for God in a modern setting, an entirely objective and deliberated work ... the falcon was honour, or the soul, or God, awaiting and finally claiming the pilgrim whose life was search, however vain and awkward, for integrity and truth,' continuing with unconvincing logic, 'Because of its theme, the book must be anonymous ...' (LOD p.182).

'Deliberated' it may have been, but it was hardly 'objective'. Much of it is a fictionalised account of the winter he spent in New York from 1930–31 when he had a brief but intense affair with Barbara Sincere (a member of Dutton's staff depicted as 'Barbara Faithfull' in the book), laced with unflattering sketches of some well-known figures in the literary world under false names.

The reviewers, naturally, were intrigued. Eda Walton, an American critic, found it 'A terrifying and fascinating, annoying and amusing anonymous novel,' but J.B. Priestley, recognising himself (and the author) posed the question: 'What is one to say about a writer who will not put his name to a novel and yet introduces into it, under the thinnest of disguises, a number of fellow-writers?'

Not surprisingly, publishers in the UK and USA had been reluctant to take it on. When it did appear there was a brief period of speculation before Williamson was confirmed as the author (Robert Graves was suspected, and felt insulted) but it was not until 1947 that the identity of the author and various characters were openly acknowledged in the book.

1933a. Faber & Faber Limited. *First edition, published anonymously.*
i) 'First published in February Mcmxxxiii'. Printed by Latimer Trend and Co. Pp.416. 193 x 123mm. Blue cloth, blindstamped with a falcon design on the front, with a second falcon design, goldstamped, on the spine. Dust jacket cream, printed in gold, red and black, with the subtitle in full on the front panel and the falcon designs repeated on the front and spine panels. Price 7/6. Published February 1933 (letter from Faber 1966).

Initial leaves are: blank, half-title, title-page.

ii) Special issue, without dedication: edition statement and printer as i). Pp.416 (including stub). 200 x 130mm. White vellum, goldstamped on the front and spine; top edge gilt, others untrimmed.

Initital leaves are: half-title, title-page and a stub (the dedication leaf of 1933b excised). An unidentified cutting suggests there were 10 copies of this issue.

Contents:
- quotations (p.7) from Donne, Webster's Dictionary (definition of 'Haggard') and Wilfred Owen;
- text (pp.13–415) in 4 parts, headed, and 66 sections, unheaded, with no date, name or owl device:

Migration	sections 1–15
Greenwich Village Eyrie	sections 16–24
The Vision in Eldorado	sections 25–56
Homecoming	sections 57–66

1933b. Printed for the Author. *First edition; special issue, with dedication.*
Copy a): as 1933aii except: no edition statement on verso of the title-page; pp.5–6 present as a full leaf with a printed dedication 'To "T.E. Lawrence" by whose taken thought the author added a cubit to his stature' on recto, verso blank.

Initial leaves are: half-title, title-page, dedication. An unpublished letter to HW from Lawrence, writing as 'T.E. Shaw' and dated 13.2.33, indicates that this copy at least was sent out by Faber at the same time as the book was published (and that Lawrence had soon worked out who was responsible).

Copy b): as copy a) but with a printed dedication 'To John Heygate who gave unconsciously to the making of this book whatever virtue of restraint there be in the character of Manfred' on recto, verso blank. Facing this (on verso of the title-page) is a handwritten statement by Williamson: 'This is one of 15 Special Copies printed with various acknowledgements for private distribution. No.4, for John Heygate Esquire. S.S. 42'.

It seems unlikely that Faber would have agreed to 15 copies with different printed dedications, so the figure Williamson gives may include 10 copies of the undedicated issue (1933aii) and five with dedications; if this is the case then three copies with printed dedications remain unaccounted for.

1933c. Faber & Faber Limited. *Reprint of the first edition.*
'Second impression February Mcmxxxiii'. Blue cloth, stamped as 1933a. Dust jacket white, with a colour illustration of a blonde female head against a background of sea and sky by Hookway Cowles. Price 3/6.

1933d. Faber & Faber Limited. *Reprint of the first edition.*
'Third impression February Mcmxxxiii'. Blue cloth, yellowstamped on spine. Dust jacket as 1933c. Price 3/6.

1933e. Harrison Smith and Robert Haas. New York. *American reprint of the first edition, with revision; the second text.*
'Copyright, 1933'. Printed in the USA. Pp.416. 197 x 129mm. Green cloth, stamped as 1933ai; fore-edge untrimmed. Dust jacket cream, printed in red and gold, with the falcon designs, but no subtitle on the front panel. Price $2.50. Published [August] 1933.

On p.18 lines 19–21 are replaced by four lines ending 'awaiting something which could not be formulated.'

1947a. Faber and Faber Ltd. *New edition, with the author's name; revised; the third text.*
'By Henry Williamson' on the title-page; 'Second edition Mcmxlvii' on verso. Printed by Purnell and Sons. Pp.viii + 392. 190 x 121mm. Blue cloth, goldstamped on the spine. Dust jacket white, printed in blue, yellow and brown. Price 8/6.

This has a quotation from Francis Thompson in place of the subtitle and quotations from Psalm 134 and Ronsard on p.357. 'The Vision in Eldorado' now contains sections 25–62 and 'Homecoming' sections 63–66, with no date, name or owl device at the end. In the text the change noted in 1933e is not present, but more than half the pages show alterations, with words, lines and paragraphs added, omitted or rewritten, and some real names instead of fictional ones:

First edition:	This edition:
Channerson	Nevinson
G.B. Everest	T.E. Lawrence
Torrence	D.H. Lawrence
Sherston Savage	Siegfried Sassoon
Adolf Stucley	Aldous Huxley
Enoch Potter	Arnold Bennett
Horace Whipple	Hugh Walpole
P.B. Bradford	J.B. Priestley
Edward Waggoner	Edmund Blunden; etc.

In an unpublished note Williamson said ' I have rewritten the Revised Edition; it is the best so far, with new scenes to replace much of the "old acid" of Manfred (and his appalling rudeness to his wife in the early Chapters).'

1947b. Faber and Faber Ltd. *Reprint of 1947a; the third text.*
'Reprinted February Mcmxlvii'. Blue cloth, goldstamped.

Foreign-language edition:
1933. *Il Falco d'Oro.* Valentino Bompiani. Milano. An Italian pirated edition.

A18 THE STAR-BORN

In the light-hearted 'Valediction' to *The Flax of Dream* (DFW 1931a, p.446) Williamson says that apart from 'The Policy of Reconstruction' Maddison wrote one other book, '"The Star-born", of which certain people have enquired by letter to Jonathan Cape, Ltd., Publishers, of London. Will it be published? The answer is yes. "The Star-born" also was composed, and lost, very much in the manner described in *The Pathway*. The extraordinary memory of a friend who heard it read one September night, in a Devon cottage ... has been largely responsible for the recovery of many of its authentic scenes and sayings; but otherwise it is inevitably lessened by an inferior hand and mind, namely that of Maddison's biographer . '

In the event, however, Williamson preferred to use the more plausible device of a discovered 'second version' of Maddison's manuscript to construct a book that is an artistic and logical sequel to *The Flax of Dream* but not structurally part of it. In advertisements and lists of works he described it as a 'pendent' volume.

It is his most sustained piece of imaginative writing, telling the story of a young boy, taken from his mother, nurtured by spirits and then returned to the world and his family but in altered form. At times poignant and compelling it is a blend of Nature and the Other World, flavoured throughout with his own preoccupations, dreams and disillusionments.

The first edition was illustrated by Charles Tunnicliffe, who is said to have been 'completely baffled' when he tried to interpret the text, and the second by Mildred Eldridge.

1933. Faber & Faber Limited. *First edition; illustrated by Tunnicliffe.*
i) 'First published in May Mcmxxxiii'. Printed by Latimer Trend and Co. Pp.240. Illustrations, reckoned. Vellum paper and endpapers. 228 x 145mm. Green cloth, goldstamped on the spine; top edge gilt, others untrimmed. Dust jacket cream, printed in red and black, with a design of a barn owl and skull by Tunnicliffe (additional to those in the book) on the front panel. Price 15/-. Published May 1933 (letter from Faber 1966). 2000 copies (advert).

ii) Cheaper issue: as i) except: endpapers not vellum paper; tighter weave green cloth; top edge plain; dust jacket blue-green. Price 7/6.

iii) Signed issue: as i) except: 'This edition printed on English hand-made paper is limited to seventy signed and numbered copies. This is number ...' followed by the number and author's signature in black ink, on recto of the first leaf. Endpapers not vellum paper. Green parch-ment-vellum. No jacket. Price 2 guineas. 70 copies, but unnumbered and unsigned copies stamped 'Out of Series' are also extant.

Some unused copies of the first gathering (16 pp.) which have recently emerged, signed by HW in red ink but unnumbered, indicate that this issue was originally going to be limited to 50 copies.

Contents:
- dedication 'To my Mother';
- 'Introduction' (pp.9–10) dated 'Devon, 1932. Henry Williamson' and establishing the fiction that this is the second version of the book that Maddison was writing before he met his death;
- illustrations: 15 full-page wood-engravings, 18 tailpieces and 2 vignettes by C.F. Tunnicliffe, plus the dust jacket design
- text (pp.15–235) in 4 parts, headed, and 26 sections, with no date or owl device:

Beyond	The House in the Forest, and sections 1–6
Translation	sections 7–10
Wayward	sections 11–17
Homecoming	sections 18–25

1948. Faber and Faber Ltd. *New edition, revised; illustrated by Eldridge.*
'This edition first published in Mcmxlviii'. Printed by Latimer Trend and Co. Pp.204. 8 plates, not reckoned. 208 x 130mm. Light purple cloth, silverstamped on the spine. Dust jacket light blue-green, printed in red and black, with the design from p.71 repeated on the front panel. Price 12/6.

Also with the dust jacket price-clipped and printed 7/6 on the front flap.

Here the 'Introduction' is shortened to two paragraphs, stating that the present version is based on 'some old notebooks, containing alter-native passages' which have recently come to light, ending '1948. H.W.' In the main text there are additions, alterations or omissions on at least 80 per cent of pages and 'The House in the Forest' is almost completely rewritten, eliminating all dialogue, to create a more convincing dream-state. Illustrations are 8 full-page lithographs and 35 line drawings by

Mildred Eldridge.

1973. Cedric Chivers Ltd. *Reprint of the first edition.*
'This edition published ... at the request of the London & Home Counties Branch of the Library Association 1973'. SBN 85594 871 X. Pp.236 (fewer blanks). 218 x 135mm. Green linson, goldstamped on the spine; fore and lower edges speckled pink. Dust jacket white, printed in green and black, with a new design of an owl and waterfall by Tunnicliffe on the front panel. Price £2.

A19 ON FOOT IN DEVON or Guidance and Gossip being a Monologue in Two Reels

In an unpublished note referring to this work Williamson wrote: 'it was written in 48 hours, and filled up with nonsense - Beachcomber stuff - to satisfy a young publisher I met at a party and promised to do a book in his series - On Foot In ... etc. Later I said the book I started turned into something else - for Cape - "Devon Holiday" - and he'd have to wait. He threatened me. So I did the On Foot thing at once and turned it in.'

In fact the writing took nearly two months (D 1995) and delivered a book that is a light and readable narrative of excursions to the north and south Devon coasts (hence the 'Two Reels' in the subtitle), including a return to Georgeham with its past associations and connections to his own books, in a style closer to present-day travel-writing than the conventional guidebooks of the period. As T.E. Lawrence observed he 'could make even Bradshaw interesting'.

With a dust jacket by Tunnicliffe and endpaper maps it went through various issues but was not apparently reprinted.

1933. Alexander Maclehose & Co. *First edition; illustrated.*
Date on the title page. No edition statement. Printed by Robert Maclehose and Co. Pp.xii + 196. Frontispiece and 7 plates, not reckoned. 190 x 123mm. Brown cloth of varying shades, blackstamped on the front and spine; map of North Devon on the front endpaper and South Devon on the rear fixed endpaper, signed 'A'. Dust jackets printed in blue with an illustration of farm buildings and a pond by Tunnicliffe on the front panel, but with differing blurb, adverts and prices indicating a series of issues over time:

i) White or cream (darkens to brown), price 5/- on spine panel, no price on front flap; blurb ends 'meditation' without quotes from reviews; 'Books of the Open Air' with 4 titles on back panel; list of 7 titles 'Uniform with this Volume', some 'in preparation', on back flap. Published June 1933.

ii) Blue-green (? faded), price 5/- on spine panel; further details not known.

iii) Green (fades to blue-green), no price on spine panel, 3/6 sticker on front flap; blurb ends with quote from J.C. Squire; back panel and flap blank.

iv) Green (fades to blue-green), no price on spine panel, 2/6 on front flap crossed out and 3/6 written in pencil; blurb ends with quote from J.C. Squire; back panel and flap blank.

v) Green (fades to blue-green), 3/6 sticker on spine panel and front flap; blurb ends with quote from J.C. Squire; 'Books of the Open Air' with 15 titles on back panel; back flap blank.

vi) Green (fades to blue-green), price 2/6 on spine panel and front flap; blurb ends with quote from J.C. Squire; 'Books of the Open Air' with 15 titles on back panel; back flap blank.

Contents:
- dedication ' To Miss A.T. who did all the work' (Ann Thomas);
- illustrations: 8 photographic plates of Devon views (6 by Judges' Ltd.; 2 from *The Times*);
- text (pp.1–196) with descriptive subheadings, no owl device, comprising:

Reel I   chapters I-XIII
Reel II   .chapters XIV-XXII
Final Chapter

A20 THE LINHAY ON THE DOWNS And Other Adventures in the Old and the New World

This version of *The Linhay on the Downs* (the other is A12) consists mainly of 50 items that Williamson contributed to a weekly paper, *The Sunday Referee* (SR), between May 1933 and May 1934, mostly under the heading 'The Notebook of a Nature-Lover' (NNL, numbered 1–45) or 'A Nature-Lover in the New World' (NLNW) but occasionally unheaded. Added to these are some miscellaneous pieces, the title story from A12, passages from 'The Sun in the Sands' that do not appear later in the book (A30), and five 'Essays on Books and Authors', the first of which is composed largely of correspondence about *Tarka*.

Under the terms of the contract for the book, he was supposed to have provided the publishers with a work of 'continuous prose' but in Cape's view (understandably) *The Linhay on the Downs* was not continuous prose; they also objected to the inclusion of the 'Essays', but Williamson was insistent. When the book was published sales were poor and the critics unimpressed.

1934. Jonathan Cape. *First edition; illustrated.*
'First published 1934'. Printed by The Alden Press. Pp.320. Frontispiece and 7 plates, not reckoned. 206 x 135mm. Blue-green buckram, gold-stamped on the spine; top edge green. Dust jacket cream, printed in red and black. Price 7/6. Published November 1934. 4000 copies (letter from Cape 1969; may include later issues).
Noted also in green cloth, not buckram.

Contents:
- dedication 'To Miss Louise of Le Manoir Fleuri (Mrs. Robert de l'Aigle Reese) in grateful memory of many happy days in the South ...' referring to his visit to the USA from March to April 1934;
- illustrations: 8 plates with 10 family photographs listed and captioned;
- text (pp.13–315) in 3 Parts, headed, with 48 items, titled, followed by owl device:

Notes:

Part 1: England
   The Linhay on the Downs   from LD (A12), revised
   A Fresh Start
   Salmon Fishers

The Sex-Life of Rooks	NNL no.43 'Are Rooks "Civilised"?', 11.3.34
A West Country Trout Farm	NNL no.16 'Trout', 3.9.33
Traps and Trapping	NNL no.8, 9.7.33
My Partridges	NNL no.4 'Partridges', 11.6.33
The Fishers	
Science, or, Sentiment	part 1 is NNL no.9 'Fact or Sentimentality?', 16.7.33
Rise of a Village	
'Some Marvels of Pond Life'	
The Gold Fish	NNL no.11 'The Goldfish', 30.7.33
The Old Trout	NNL nos.5, 6 'The Old Trout', 18.6, 25.6.33, and no.7 'The End of the Old Trout', 2.7.33
'The Dear One'	NNL no.2, 28.5.33
Dimmit Light	NNL no.10, 23.7.33
Stag Hunting	NNL no.12, with new paragraphs, 6.8.33
Heat Wave	NNL no.13, 13.8.33
Wasps	NNL no.14, 20.8.33, and no.15 'The Wasp's Nest', 27.8.33
August Evening	NNL no. 17 'September Evening', 10.9.33
Harold	NNL no. 19 'A Modern Boy', 24.9.33
Wane of Summer	NNL no. 18, 17.9.33
A London Sanctuary	NNL no. 20, 1.10.33
Moonlight	NNL no 21, 8 10 33
Potwallopers' Marsh	NNL no.22, 15.10.33
The Spate	NNL nos.23, 24, 22.10, 29.10.33
The Harmony of Nature	NNL no.41 'Through the Mist', 25.2.34, and no.42 'The Rats' Feast', 4.3.34
Hill of Winds	NNL no. 25 'Hill with a View', 5.11.33

A Night on Salisbury Plain	NNL no.28 'In the Fog', 26.11.33
Still the Drought	NNL no.30 'Spawning Salmon', 10.12.33
Morning Tide	NNL no.31, 17.12.33
The River Freezes	NNL no.32 'A River Freezes', 24.12.33
Flighting	NNL no.33 'Birds on the Wing', 31.12.33
The Yule Log	
Sea and the Wind: North Devon	NNL no.34, 7.1.34
The Glory of the Gale	NNL no.36, 21.1.34
Ravens	NNL no.44 'Cautious Ravens', 18.3.34
High Peak Canal	part 1 is NNL no.39 untitled, 11.2.34; part 2 is no.40 'Hill-Top Meditations', 18.2.34
Wood Fires	NNL nos.26, 27, with 2 pp. of new text, 12.11, 19.11.33
From 'The Sun in the Sands'	part 1 not traced (it is not in A30); part 2 includes NNL no.29 'The Last Swallow', 3.12.33

Part 2: Essays on Books and Authors
On Otters
Reading in Bed
Izaak Walton
A Brave Book

Reality in War Literature	from *London Mercury* 1929, revised

Part 3: America

S.S. Berengaria	NNL no.45 'North Atlantic', 25.3.34
Manhattan 1	[NLNW no.I] 'Here is New York', 1.4.34
2	NLNW no.II 'Now that April's Here', 8.4.34

Southern Sun	1	NLNW no.III 'Southern Sun', 15.4.34
	2	NLNW no.IV 'Always the Sun', 22.4.34
	3	
	4	NLNW no.V 'An American Cameo', 29.4.34
	5	'A Prison in Augusta', SR 3.6.34
	6	NLNW no.VI 'De Swanee Ribber', 6.5.34
	7	parts of "Bus Ride to Florida', SR 27.5.34
	8	parts of "Bus Ride to Florida', SR 27.5.34
	9	NLNW no.VII 'A Florida Wilderness', 13.5.34
	10	'By the Gulf of Mexico', SR 20.5.34
	11	
	12	
To England		

1938. Jonathan Cape. *Reissue of the first edition, in The Life and Letters Series.*
'Re-issued in the Life and Letters Series 1938'. No.42. Pp.316 (fewer blanks). Green cloth, silverstamped. Dust jacket white, printed in green. Price 4/6, or 6/- on sticker.
The half-title and title-page are cancels with the subtitle omitted.

1944. Faber and Faber Limited. *Reissue of the first edition, by Faber.*
'Reissued in Mcmxliv'. Pp.316. Green cloth, goldstamped on the spine. Dust jacket cream, printed in red and black. Price 8/6.
Faber and Faber acquired the title in 1944 and are said to have re-bound 838 copies, with new cancels for the half-title and title-page.

1984. Alan Sutton. *Reprint of the first edition.*
'This edition published 1984'. The Sovereign series. ISBN 0 86299 194 3. Paperback. Cover illustration from a painting 'Winter Sunset with Barn Owl' by Raymond Booth. Price £4.95.

A photo-reprint with print size reduced, the subtitle restored and the illustrations grouped between pp.64–65.

A21 DEVON HOLIDAY

Devon Holiday is not about any particular holiday but is just a patch-work of material (some old, some new) tacked together as a tour of the Devon Moors (mainly Exmoor) in the company of four fictionalised friends, who have little in the way of adventures but wander around reminiscing, swapping stories and discussing the merits or otherwise of their own literary works, including, of course, *Tarka*.

Williamson described it as 'a rather silly volume, a sort of bogus guide and walking-tour affair' (CNS p.306) but Cape's lawyers saw it as potentially libellous and demanded cuts. Then, just before publication, T.E. Lawrence ('G.B. Everest' in the book) died, which meant that a jocular reference to the great Celebrity had to be neutralised by a 'Postscript' (placed at the front of the book) that casts a shadow on the whole exercise.

Devon Holiday was an opportunity for Williamson to do for the moors what he had done for the coasts in *On Foot in Devon* but he was not committed to it. On this occasion he had provided Cape with 'continuous prose', as required by his contract, but discontinuous thought. Clearly they were not getting his best work and it was the last of his books that they would publish. The serious work he was doing was on *Salar* and that had already been sold to Faber.

1935. Jonathan Cape. *First edition.*
'First published 1935'. Printed by The Alden Press. Pp.320. 204 x 134mm. Green buckram, goldstamped on the spine; top edge green. Dust jacket cream, printed in black and green. Price 7/6. Published June 1935 (letter from Cape 1969). 2500 copies.

Binding variants:
a) as i) but with the two previous blank leaves used as endpapers (ie pp.316);
b) as i) but in green cloth, not buckram, top edge plain.

Contents:
- quotation 'And How' on title-page;

- 'Postscript' concerning the recent death of 'G.B. Everest' (ie T.E. Lawrence) with a transcript of his last telegram p.7;
- text (pp.11–317): Chapters 1–18 and 'Last Chapter' with narrative subtitles and incorporating five previously published items (collected again in TME 1953):

			Notes:
Chap.	VI	The Dog that Ate his Punishment	from *Windsor Magazine* 1933
	VIII	Swagdaggger Crosses a Field	'The White Stoat' from *Passing Show* 1934
	IX	The Heller	from *Atlantic Monthly* or *Cassell's*, 1928
	XVI	The Story of the Poisoned Hounds	'The Yellow Boots' from OS 1926 etc
Last Chapter		The Maiden Salmon	from *Nash's* 1934.

A22 SALAR THE SALMON

The challenge that Williamson set himself in writing *Salar* was to convert the life-cycle of a fish into a commercially-successful novel. He was not sure he could do it, but Faber clearly thought he could and bought the rights even before the book was started. In return Williamson surrendered the manuscript of 'The Sun in the Sands' as security in case he should fail to deliver on 'the salmon book' (D 1995). The outcome, however, was a work that demonstrates his ability to create a narrative out of natural phenomena even more impressively than in *Tarka*.

In a press report the month before publication Williamson stated 'I spent altogether 5,000 hours simply watching the pools and eddies, until I "knew" the stream just as an author should "know" the environment in which his characters live ... I had to learn exactly how they moved and reacted to every change of current ... the descriptive passages, for instance had to be true and yet have variety. They had to make the reader know the bed of the river and its changing moods.'

Writing had begun in earnest in January 1935 but Faber wanted to publish in October, so the schedule was tight; by August he was receiving proofs of the early chapters, while still writing the later ones and there was no time for revision. Tunnicliffe had completed the illustrations he had been asked to do, but perhaps because of the pressure for publication or as part of a strategy for a second edition, they were not used until the following year.

Prior to publication thirteen sets of proof sheets were individually bound as 'The Shallowford Edition' of which ten were advertised for sale, though only one sold. Of the many subsequent printings the most important are the 1936 editions illustrated by Tunnicliffe (first in America, and then with colour plates and more illustrations in the UK), and the new edition illustrated by Loates and with an Introduction by Richard Williamson by Webb and Bower in 1987.

1935a. No publisher, place or printer. *Proofs of the first edition, bound and issued as 'The Shallowford Edition'.*
Copy number 7: 'This edition consists of thirteen copies of the first printed version, handcorrected by the author at Shallowford during the summer of 1935' printed at the foot of the title-page. 'Of thirteen copies of the original draft ten are for sale, corrected by the author and signed. This is Number 7. Henry Williamson' written in brown ink on recto of the first leaf. 202 x 125mm. Half-bound in black Morocco with raised bands, goldstamped with the title, author and 'Shallowford Edition' on the spine; Cockerell marbled paper boards and endpapers.

Made-up from galley-proofs, printed by Faber, with 3 blank leaves, half-title, title, dedication, Contents, ditto, fly-title, leaves numbered 19–323 and 3 blank leaves, with an additional typewritten page. Printed and numbered on rectos only, with over 300 corrections by the author in brown ink. Printed at the end is: 'Finished 5 August 1935, in the field above Ham, hot sunshine and the author exhausted and flat now that it is all over,' followed by an inscription in the author's hand: 'The above bibliographical note was scribbled on the last page of Mss, & typed by the typist, on the copy which went straight to the printers ...', ie the printing of the note was a mistake and Williamson's addition was required to fulfil the promise of 'an original bibliographical note by the author' that was made when the work was advertised.

Other examples of this issue have not been seen but are likely to vary in their printing, collation, binding, corrections and author's notes. In a letter dated December 1950 Williamson wrote 'I advertised 13 copies, leather bound, for sale in the TLS autumn 1935, proceeds to the widow of V.M. Yeates. One only sold £15.15.0 (purchaser later asked for a refund). I took the remaining 12 to Norfolk, they lay in a box all the 8 years, both moth and worm in. Gave one to Fr. Bruno Scott-James of Stiffkey Old Hall ...'

1935 b. Faber and Faber Limited. *First edition.*
'First published in October Mcmxxxv'. Printed by R. MacLehose and Company. Pp.320. 195 x 120mm. Brown cloth, goldstamped on the spine; top edge red; endpapers green, printed in black with a hand-drawn map of North Devon, unsigned, but the quality and style suggest Tunnicliffe (see SNF 1941). Dust jacket white, printed in brown, with an all-round colour illustration of salmon leaping by C.F. Tunnicliffe; blurb on the front and back flaps, followed by a list of HW books up to *The Wild Red Deer of Exmoor.* Price 7/6. Published October 1935 (flyer).

Contents:
- dedication 'To T.E. Lawrence of Seven Pillars of Wisdom and V.M. Yeates of Winged Victory';
- decorations: fishtail vignette on title-page, salmon device with 'H.W.' p.320, by Tunnicliffe (attributed on the dust jacket of 1936a);
- text (pp.15–319) in 4 Books and 25 Chapters, with headings, followed by 'Here ends Salar the Salmon by Henry Williamson, begun in January 1935 at Shallowford and finished in August 1935 in the field below Windwhistle Spinney in Devon' (printed part-way down p.320), with the 'H.W.' salmon device:

Book One:	Tideways	chaps.	1–6
Two:	Spring Spate		7–14
Three:	Summer River		14–20
Four:	Winter Star-Stream		21–25

1935c. Faber and Faber Limited. *Reprint of 1935b; the first edition.*
'Second impression November Mcmxxxv'. Brown cloth, goldstamped; top edge red. Dust jacket white, printed in silver, blue and red, with the 'H.W.' salmon device enlarged on the front and back panels; 'Second impression' on the spine panel and front flap. Price 7/6.
    The end-note on p.320 is printed at the top of the page not part-way down.

1935d. Faber and Faber Limited. *Reprint of 1935c; the first edition.*

i) 'Third impression December Mcmxxxv'. Brown cloth, goldstamped. Dust jacket as 1935b. Price 7/6.
End-note printed as 1935c.

ii) as i) but in pink/red cloth of varying shades, silverstamped on the spine; top edge plain. Dust jacket as 1935b but with new blurb, quoting reviews, on the front flap; list of HW books on the back flap including his *Richard Jefferies* which was not published until July 1937 and 'Tales of My Children' which must refer to his series in *Family* (Section C). Price 3/6.
Also with the dust jacket price-clipped and printed 4/- on the front flap.

1936a. Little, Brown, and Company. Boston. *American edition; 32 illustrations by Tunnicliffe.*
'Published June, 1936'. Printed in the USA. An Atlantic Monthly Press Book. Pp.x + 302. Frontispiece and illustrations, reckoned. 213 x 138mm. Green cloth, goldstamped on the front and spine. Dust jacket cream, printed in black, green and red, with a composite design taken from the illustrations on the front panel and a note on C.F. Tunnicliffe on the back panel.
The first illustrated edition with illustrations by C.F. Tunnicliffe comprising: a) headpieces to each of the 25 chapters and the Contents page; b) four full-page black and white [scraperboards] as frontispiece and on pp.131, 201, 287, and c) the two decorations from the first edition, with the fishtail vignette now used as the endpiece (without the end-note) and the salmon device now on the title-page (without the 'H.W.'), both reduced in size. Why the first illustrated edition should have been published in America is not clear, but the quality of the illustrations is better than in any other edition, eg the headpiece to chapter 1 is clearly an image of an island at night, whereas in most UK printings it is little more than a dark moonscape.

1936b. Little, Brown, and Company. Boston. *Reprint of 1936a; illustrated.*
'Reprinted June, 1936'. Green cloth, goldstamped on the front and spine.

Listed in the bib note of 1938 are:
    'Reprinted October, 1936'
    'Reprinted December, 1936'

1936c. Faber and Faber Ltd. New UK edition; *66 illustrations by Tunnicliffe.*
'First published in this edition in October Mcmxxxvi'. Printed by R. Maclehose and Company. Pp.324. 16 plates and 15 stubs, not reckoned. 228 x 140mm. Purplish silver-patterned cloth, silverstamped on the spine; top edge silver, fore-edge untrimmed; endpapers green, printed in black, with numerous vignettes by Tunnicliffe. Dust jacket white, printed in blue and black, with an additional illustration by Tunnicliffe (men in a boat, pointing towards an estuary) on the front panel and vignette of a fish on the spine panel. Price 15/-
A new type-setting of the text including all the illustrations from 1936a except the four full-page illustrations which are reworked here as colour plates, and the endpiece, with the previous headpieces photo-enlarged and 39 new illustrations by Tunnicliffe, comprising: a) 16 colour plates, from watercolours, not printed in any other issue, b) tail-pieces to 20 chapters, and c) 3 vignettes - two on the title-page and one on verso of the Contents page.

1936d. Bernhard Tauchnitz. Leipzig. *German edition (in English); not illustrated.*
'Copyright 1936 by Bernhard Tauchnitz'. Pp.224. 180 x 110mm. White paper covers.

1938. Little, Brown, and Company. Boston. *Reprint of 1936a; illustrated.*
'Reprinted October, 1938'. Green cloth, goldstamped. Dust jacket as 1936a. Price $2.50.

1941. Faber and Faber Limited. *Reprint of 1935c; the first edition; in The Faber Library.*
'First published in this edition July Mcmxli'. The Faber Library No.52. Green cloth, silverstamped. Dust jacket yellow, printed in blue. Price 3/6.
The title-page decoration is omitted; end-note printed as 1935c.

1943. Faber and Faber Limited. *Reprint of 1941; the first edition; in The Faber Library.*
'Reprinted January Mcmxliii'. The Faber Library No.52. Green cloth, silverstamped.

1944. Faber and Faber Ltd. *New edition; not illustrated.*

'First published in this edition Mcmxliv'. Printed by Latimer Trend and Co. Pp.188. 187 x 118mm. Green cloth, goldstamped; fore-edge untrimmed. Dust jacket pale blue, printed in red and black. Price 5/-.

Printed to Wartime Economy Standard with fewer pages and smaller type.

1945. Faber and Faber Ltd. *Reprint of 1944; the first edition.*
'Second impression July Mcmxlv'. Green cloth, silverstamped. Dust jacket grey. Price 5/-.

1946. Putnam & Co. Ltd. Faber & Faber Ltd. *New edition; 48 illustrations by Tunnicliffe.*
'This limited edition published 1946'. Printed by Unwin Brothers. Pp.x + 278. Frontispiece and illustrations, reckoned. 207 x 135mm. Green cloth, goldstamped with 'HW' monogram on the front, as one of *The Henry Williamson Nature Books* (see A33). 500 copies.

As Putnam's had not previously published Salar this type had to be reset to match the format of the other HWNB, making it the only one of the five that is genuinely a new edition and not just a reprint. Compared to 1936c the 16 colour plates and 3 tailpieces (chaps. 9, 12, 17) are omitted, with other tailpieces rearranged and the headpieces reduced in size. The only added feature is a frontispiece of men in a boat with another on shore pointing to the estuary, which is clearly another version of the illustration on the dust jacket of 1936c and is not present in any other issue.

1948a. Faber and Faber Ltd. *Reprint of 1944; the first edition.*
'Reprinted ... April Mcmxlviii'. Green cloth, silverstamped. Dust jacket grey. Price 6/-.

1948b. Faber and Faber. *New edition; 48 illustrations by Tunnicliffe.*
'This new edition first published in Mcmxlviii'. Printed by Latimer Trend and Co. Pp.232. Illustrations, reckoned. 210 x 134mm. Green cloth, silverstamped; endpapers cream, printed in brown with illustrations as 1936c. Dust jacket blue-green, printed in red and black.

A new type-setting with no new illustrations but some changes in composition compared to 1946: frontispiece and 2 tailpieces replaced by 2 previous tailpieces and a vignette, with some rearrangement but giving the same total number of illustrations as 1946; headpieces restored to the same size as 1936c but with one reversed (chap. 11).

1949. Penguin Books. *New edition; not illustrated.*
'Published in Penguin Books 1949'. Printed by Hunt, Barnard and Co.
Penguin Books 712. Pp.224. 180 x 110mm. Paperback. Covers printed in
orange and black. Price 1/6.

1950. Little, Brown, and Company. Boston. *Reprint of 1936a; illustrated.*
'Reissued February 1950'. Cut to 210 x 135mm. Green cloth, goldstamped on front and spine.

1959. Faber and Faber. *Reprint of 1948b; illustrated.*
'First published in this new edition Mcmlix'. Faber paper covered
Editions. Paperback. Cover illustration from the vignette on p.67. Price
5/-.
   Not a new edition but a photo-reprint of 1948a with print size
reduced and no endpaper designs. An advert inside the front cover
offers 'Another and more durable edition ... at 10s 6d ... strongly bound
in cloth' (? this printing in boards or an unknown).

1960. In *The Henry Williamson Animal Saga* (A46, pp.201–375). *New
edition, revised; the second text; not illustrated.*
The main text (pp.206–370) has changes to words or lines noted on 11
pp., with 'Welsh mountains' instead of 'Snowdon mountain' in the
fourth paragraph of chapter 2, and 'bliddy 'errin 'ogs' in the fourth line
from the end of chapter 3. Preceding the text is 'The Sun in Taurus', a
brief note on salmon and river pollution, and at the end 'A Personal
Note' by HW concerning the writing and publication of the book.

1961. Faber and Faber. *New edition of the second text; 46 illustrations by
Tunnicliffe.*
'Published in this new edition Mcmlxi'. Printed by Western Printing
Services. Pp.210 (pagination is incorrect). Illustrations, reckoned. 205 x
130mm. Pink cloth, silverstamped on the front and spine; top edge
green. Dust jacket white, printed in pink and black, with the tailpiece
from p.64 repeated on the front panel. Price 15/-.
   A new type-setting with 46 illustrations from the 1948b edition omitting one tailpiece, the salmon device at the end and the endpaper
designs.

1962. Faber and Faber. *Reprint of 1959; the first text; illustrated.*
'Reprinted in Mcmlxii'. Faber paper covered Editions. Paperback. Price 6/6.

1965. A Signet Book. New York. *New American edition; the first text; 29 illustrations by Tunnicliffe.*
'First printing, October, 1965'. Printed in the USA. Signet P 2716. Pp.192. 180 x 105mm. Paperback. Edges red. Cover photograph of a seascape, unattributed. Price 60c.

Illustrations: 29 in total comprising 3 full-page illustrations, 25 head-pieces and one tailpiece. The statement 'Published by arrangement with Little, Brown (who supply a hardcover edition)' suggests there may be American printings between 1950 and 1965 that are not recorded here.

1967. Faber and Faber. *Reprint of 1959; the first text; illustrated.*
'Reprinted in ... Mcmlxvii'. Faber paper covered Editions. Paperback. Price 9/-, £0.45; on a sticker.

1969. Faber.
Reported but not seen.

1972. Faber and Faber. *Reprint of 1961; the second text.*
i) edition statement in ii) has 'ISBN 0 571 04152 3. (hard bound edition)'; not seen.

ii) 'Published in this edition 1972'. Faber paper covered Editions. ISBN 0 571 04811 0. Pp. 212 (correcting the pagination from 1961). Paperback. Cover design from wood engravings by Elizabeth Trimby. Price 95p.

1973. Faber.
Listed by Colin Stanley in A62; not seen.

1978. Faber and Faber. *Reprint of 1972ii; the second text; illustrated.*
'Reprinted 1978'. Faber Paperbacks. ISBN 0 571 04811 0. Paperback. Price £2.50.

1986. Faber and Faber. *Reprint of 1972ii; the second text; illustrated.*
'Reprinted ... 1986'. Faber Paperbacks. ISBN 0 571 14811 0. Paperback. Cover illustration from the tailpiece on p.58. Price £3.95.

The title-page vignette is omitted.

1987. Webb & Bower. *New edition of the second text, with a Foreword and Introduction; illustrated by Loates.*
'This edition published by Webb & Bower (Publishers) Limited 1987'.

Printed in Spain. ISBN 0 86350 152 4. Pp.208. Frontispiece and illustrations, reckoned. 254 x 190mm. Brown linson, whitestamped on the spine; endpapers green, patterned with a fish design. Dust jacket white, printed in green, with the illustration from pp.163 repeated on the front panel and from p.55 on the back panel. Price £14.95.

Contents:
- 'Foreword' (pp.7–9) signed Mick Loates, Kingsbridge, S. Devon;
- 'Introduction' (pp.11–17) signed Richard Williamson;
- Illustrations: 31 colour illustrations (16 full-page), and 18 b/w illustrations (four also repeated), by Michael Loates; frontispiece photograph of HW and 5 family photographs, unattributed;
- text (pp.20–207) followed by the end-note but no salmon device.

1990. David R. Godine. Boston. *American reprint of 1987; the second text; illustrated.*
'Published in 1990 by ... first printing'. Printed in Hong Kong. ISBN 0 87923 845 3. 245 x 190mm. Paperback. Cover illustration from p.163 on the front and from p.208 on the back.

Foreign-language editions:

1946. *Nesmrtelny Losos.* Vladimir Pour, Novy Bydzov. (Czech).

1953. *Salar Der Lachs.* Fischer Bucherei. Hamburg. Paperback, not illustrated.

1956. *Salar, historien om en laks.* Asmodts Forlag. Kobenhaven. (H WSJ 3).

1964. *Salar il Salmone.* Bompiani. Milan.

A23 CHRISTMAS

This is the full text of an article by Williamson that was published in *The Atlantic Monthly* of December 1934 (and elsewhere) appropriated and produced as a small pamphlet by an American couple in 1935 as a Christmas greeting to their friends, with the permission of the magazine but not the author.

1935. No publisher. *First edition.*
No title-page or pagination. 'Two hundred copies of this brochure printed for Mr. & Mrs. Frederic W. Main so that they may share with friends their pleasure in reading this charming essay on the joys of anticipation of the Christmas season. Nineteen Berkeley Street, Springfield, Mass. December, nineteen-thirty-five ... Edmund B. Thompson, printer, Hawthorn House, Windham, Connecticut' on p.8. Pp.8. 132 x 102mm. Cream paper wrappers made double by folding along the top edge, printed in red and black, with title and author on the front cover; sewn. Not for sale. Issued December 1935. 200 copies.

Contents:
- note on verso of front wrapper: 'Henry Williamson, a frequent contributor to *The Atlantic Monthly*, is the winner of the Hawthornden Prize with his novel *Tarka the Otter'*;
- text (pp.1–7) titled 'Christmas'.

A24 THE FLAX OF DREAM A Novel in Four Books

Fifteen years after the first book appeared and five years after the series was revised *The Flax of Dream* was finally published in one volume. Its title was taken from the phrase 'to whom the Weaver gives the flax of Dream' in a book written by one of Williamson's aunts (Mary Leopoldina). Williamson evidently saw himself as the 'Weaver' and the 'Dream' was the belief (later moderated) that he would write a book that would 'help to alter the thought of the entire world' after the First World War.

In a Preface to *The Pathway* (in 1931b) he wrote: 'In thinking of and planning *The Flax of Dream* the form of the writing was intended to symbolise the form of a young man's life - the first Book to have the simplicity and clarity of the child; the second Book to show the sapling spirit bent and stressed by the influence of certain little-minded ideas in action, in this case, education at a small public-school; the third Book to have the feverishness and incoherency of youth after an European War directly caused by the ideas of unchildlike men; the fourth Book to show the child-man free of and outside those unnatural ideas ...

'Although the four Books were planned to be self-contained, each with its own peculiarities typical of its period and with its own climax, *The Flax of Dream* was intended for eventual presentation as one novel ...'

In the Foreword to this edition he says: 'This long novel telling the story of one human unit of Europe immediately before and after the War, has for its theme the unhappiness of the child ... The tale is neither wholly fiction, nor is it autobiography. It may be autopsychical. I cannot tell ... Willie Maddison appears to me as a younger brother, whose life has been recreated from scenes we both knew and sometimes shared ... it is a novel of cause and effect.' The 'cause' here is the system of education he had described, and the 'effect' is the First World War.

In the Bibliographical Note he adds: 'In the various revisions, many untruths, exaggerations, incidents of false characterisation and false writing were either cut out or replaced by new pages ... however, it was always the author's determination that the spirit of each Book should remain as in the original version.'

At over 1400 pages the book had to be printed on India paper to get it into one volume and, not surprisingly, it has not been reprinted in this form. Bibliographically the book is a hybrid: the first three books are simply reprints of previous editions with further revisions, while the fourth is genuinely a new edition also revised.

1936. Faber and Faber Limited. *First edition.*
i) 'First published in one volume in March 1936 ...' Printed by Latimer Trend and Co. Pp.1416. Printed on India paper, with errata slip headed 'Correction' tipped-in on p.8 and listing one error on p. 9 line 26 which should have 'the' instead of 'this'. 195 x 125mm. Blue cloth, gold-stamped on the spine. Dust jacket blue, printed in red, with all-over silver stars, a list of Faber Library titles nos.1–30 on the back panel, blurb on the front flap and blurb with reviews of *Salar* on the back flap. Price 8/6. Published May 1936. 10,000 copies (GWC p.163; letter from Faber 1966) including all issues.

ii) as i) except: errata slip on p.8 headed 'Printer's Corrections', listing errors on pp.9 (a further change), 546, 555. Blue cloth of varying shades and weave. Dust jacket blue or blue-green, printed in red and black, with quotes from reviews in the blurb on the front flap and a list of books by HW on the back flap headed by *The Children of Shallowford* which was not published until 1939. Price 10/6. Probably the second issue.

iii) as ii) except: the back flap of the dust jacket has a list of books by HW including *The Story of a Norfolk Farm*, *Genius of Friendship* and *As the*

Sun Shines, all of which were not published until 1941. Price 10/6. Probably the third issue, but other variants may also exist.

Normally the cheaper issue of a book indicates a later issue, but here the situation appears to be reversed: the fact that copies in the dust jacket with stars have no review quotes, have only one error noted, and do not list any of Williamson's later works, suggest strongly that they were issued first. If the other issues were not put out until 1939 or later then wartime conditions might explain the rise in price. As yet no copy is known in which the printer's corrections have been made which suggests that all are derived from the original printing.

Contents:
- 'Bibliographical Note' by the author concerning revisions, on verso of title-page;
- 'Dedicated to All who fought for freedom in the World War, and who are still fighting';
- 'Foreword' (pp.7–10) explaining the origins of the work and ending 'H.W. Shallowford, Christmas Day, 1935';
- texts:

Book I	The Beautiful Years (pp.11–245); a reprint of 1929a, the second text, with further revisions, making the fourth and final text (see A1);
Book II	Dandelion Days (pp.247–550); a reprint of 1932, the fourth text, with further revisions, making the fifth and final text (see A3);
Book III	The Dream of Fair Women (pp.551–987); a reprint of 1933, the third text, with further revisions, making the fourth text (see A5).
Book IV	The Pathway (pp.989–1416); a new edition of the second text, with further revisions, making the fourth text (see A9); followed by owl device and 'Here ends The Flax of Dream, arisen from the battlefields of Christmas, 1914'.

The Main Characters:
Names are listed once only and generally in the order of their first

significant appearance in this edition (the previous ones sometimes differ). References in brackets indicate characters that also feature in *A Chronicle of Ancient Sunlight* (A36).

The Beautiful Years:
John Maddison, WM's father (DL)
Big Will'um, Mr Temperley's foreman, widower
Biddy (Mrs Crane), JM's cook
Mr Temperley, owner of Skirr Farm, and Mrs Temperley (DL)
William Maddison (L'ill Will'um or Willie), JM's son (YPM)
Jim Holloman, WM's friend
Jack Temperley, son, WM's friend (HDL)
Dolly, Temperley's maid
Doris and Margaret (Peggy), Jack's sisters
'Old Bob' Lewis, Tetley's head keeper
Colonel Tetley, landowner, widower
John Strong-i'-th'arm, blacksmith
George Davidson, mason
Bill Adams, the local atheist
Mr Norman, an artist, and Mrs Norman, at 'The Firs'
Elsie Norman, their daughter (HDL)
Mary Ogilvie, Elsie's friend (IWN)
Mr Rore, headmaster of Colham Grammar School
Slater, Chapman and Dennis, schoolboys
Rupert Bryers, a new boy
Mr 'Eyesicks' Isaacs, landowner, magistrate
Fred and Harry, under-keepers

Dandelion Days:
Clemow and 'Bony' Watson, schoolboys
Mr 'Rattlethrough' Rapson, French master
Mr 'Bunny' Kenneth, English master
'Soapy Sammy' Crinkle, school porter
Mr Eustace 'Useless' Worth, woodwork and drawing master
Mr 'Taffy' Croodbrane, Physics master
Effish, Beckelt, Macarthy and Farthing, schoolboys
Charlie Cerr-Nore, elder son of Rev and Mrs Odo Cerr-Nore
Bill Nye, a crowstarving boy, and great-grandmother Aholibah Nye
John Fry, preacher
Tom Sorell, quarryman

Mr Zimmerman, oral French master
Phillip Maddison, WM's cousin (DL)
Richard Maddison, WM's uncle (DL)
Sir Heland H Donkin, old Colhamean, composer of the school song

The Dream of Fair Women:
Mrs Evelyn (Eveline, Eve or Lina) D'Arcy Fairfax (TD)
Captain Patrick Colyer, friend of Evelyn
Albert Gammon, landlord of the Nightcrow Inn
Muggy Smith, the village wit
Billy 'Brownie' Brown, a labourer, Mrs Brown, and Megan, their daughter
Jack o' Rags, an ex-miner and hermit
Julian Warbeck (Jay Double-u), friend of Evelyn (TD)
Major Lionel Fairfax, Evelyn's husband
Jonquil (Quillie) Fairfax, their daughter
Lord 'Naps' Spreycombe, Viscount and M.F.H. (IM)
Mr Archibald Dodder, O.B.E.
Martha, the Fairfax's maid
Peter White, Sandhurst cadet
Miss Pamment, and Mrs Pamment, her mother, aunt of Mary Ogilvie
Grandfather (Rev Vernon) Fairfax
Mrs Margery Beayne, and Miss Millicent Fairfax, his daughters
Aubrey de la Hay, theatrical writer and performer
Sir Rudolph Cardew, actor and local celebrity

The Pathway:
Mrs Constance Ogilvie, widowed niece of Sufford Chychester, Mary's mother
Benjamin Chychester, son of Fiennes, 'adopted' by Sufford
Sufford Calmady Chychester Esq., Mary's great-uncle (IWN)
Miss Edith Chychester, Sufford's sister
Jean Ogilvie, Mary's sister
Ron and Pam Ogilvie, the younger children
Luke, fisherman and boatman
Howard de Wychehalse, friend of Mary Ogilvie, and sister Gwen
Diana Shelley and Mrs Shelley, her mother
Miss Virginia 'Old Jig' Goff, a 'pillar of the church'
Reverend Aubrey 'Glasseyes' Garside, Vicar of Speering Folliot
Mr John 'Jan' Mules, sexton, postman and verger, and Mrs Mules (IWN)

A25 GOODBYE WEST COUNTRY

By the spring of 1936 Williamson had decided to leave Devon and had bought over 200 acres of farmland at Stiffkey, near Cromer in Norfolk. One reason was that he had begun to feel stale; in the opening pages of *Goodbye West Country* he writes: 'My work in the West Country is finished ... No more humus left for me in this soil ... fertility gone,' but another was a concern that if war was to come then the nation's survival would depend on its agriculture, and that he ought to be a part of it.

Written in 1937 the book is arranged in the form of a diary or calendar of the months from January to December for an unspecified year, but it is a virtual diary, not a literal one. It has no serial record of events or consistent theme and is essentially a collection of literary loose ends from the Devon years that are placed under the various dates wherever they happen to fit.

Much of the text relates to 1936 but by not stating the year Williamson is able to shift the time-frame, so that January includes a conference on mechanisation that he attended in 1937, while December has his fortieth birthday which was in 1935. Overall the 'entries' are an entertaining mix of memories, impressions, reflections, correspondence, and previously unused sketches of West Country life, with a long account of his visit to Germany and a Hitler rally in 1935, and a detailed description of writing a script for the BBC. Generously illustrated with photographs, mostly taken by the author, the book has an emotional coherence that is notably lacking in *Devon Holiday*.

1937. Putnam. London. *First edition; illustrated.*
i) 'First published in September, 1937'. Printed by Unwin Brothers. Pp.viii + 400. 30 plates, not reckoned. 222 x 138mm. Reddish-brown cloth of varying shades, goldstamped on the spine. Dust jacket cream, printed in black and brown, with a portrait of the author signed 'K' on the front panel and ads for 3 books on the back panel. Price 10/6. Published September 1937.

A variant in almost maroon cloth has the last plate facing p.398 (instead of p.400) but the same dust jacket and price.

ii) Cheaper issue: as i) except: shade of cloth more reddish than brown; dust jacket of the same design but printed in blue and black, with ads for 2 books on the back panel and new blurb, price 5/-.

Contents:
- dedication 'To the migrants - Loetitia, Ann, Robin, Windles, John, Margaret, Robert, Rosemary, and Richard' (his wife, Ann Thomas, Loetitia's brother and all the children);
- illustrations: 30 plates with 31 photographs relating to the author and text, captioned but unattributed;
- text (pp.3–399): Chapters numbered 1–12, unheaded, followed by owl device.

1938. Little, Brown and Company. Boston. *American reprint of the first edition, shortened and with fewer illustrations.*
'Published March 1938'. Printed in the USA. Pp.x + 370. 8 plates, not reckoned. 226 x 145mm. Green cloth, goldstamped on the front and spine. Dust jacket cream, printed in yellow and green, with a colour illustration of an angler by Allen Pope Jr. on the front panel.

In this printing only 8 of the original illustrations are used and pp.277–306 and the first paragraph of p.307 of the first edition are omitted, with the subsequent pages repaginated. The text taken out relates to Williamson's script and broadcast for the BBC which would have been of little interest to American readers.

A26 THE CHILDREN OF SHALLOWFORD

Written at Stiffkey before the Second World War started and while he was trying to revive the farm, *The Children of Shallowford* is a fluent, affectionate and mostly literal account of the early years of Williamson's growing family, based partly on a series of articles called 'Tales of My Children' which he had contributed to *Family* in 1935.

Starting with the birth of William and John in Georgeham, the book covers the period from the move to Shallowford in 1929 to the departure for Norfolk at the end of 1937, during which time four more children arrived - three of them (Margaret, Charles Robert and Richard) born to Loetitia and one (Rosemary) to Ann Thomas ('A'Bess' in the book). Illustrated with unassuming family photographs it is a celebration of the excitements and tribulations of childhood and parenthood, recalled in a way that is evocative without being sentimental.

In the revised edition of 1959 there are a few passages of new text, but nine of the original chapters are taken out for reworking in *A Chronicle of Ancient Sunlight* (PD, PG), and there are no photographs though some new ones were included in the reprint of 1978.

1939. Faber and Faber Ltd. *First edition; illustrated.*
'First published in October Mcmxxxix'. Printed by Latimer, Trend and Co. Pp.292. Frontispiece and 16 plates, not reckoned. 210 x 130mm. Green cloth, goldstamped on the spine. Dust jacket cream, printed in green, pink and black. Price 8/6. Published September 1939 (letter from Faber 1966). 4000 copies.

Contents:
- dedication 'To Merriel [sic] North, Friend of all Children';
- illustrations: frontispiece and 16 plates of family photographs, captioned but unattributed;
- text (pp.13–292): 25 Chapters with headings, ending 'September, 1937', with owl device:

Chapter:		In 1959 edition:
1	17–18, February 1926	
2	Confusion of Feeling	
3	The Simple Life Becomes Complicated	
4	Son and Mother	Chap. 1
5	The Flax of Dream	
6	29 October, 1928	
7	We Move to Shallowford	
8	Enter Coneybeare	
9	15 April, 1930	
10	Exit Coneybeare	
11	On Dream, Irritability, and Death	Chap. 2
12	The Way of Life	First part chap. 3
13	Cold Pudding Becomes the Family Friend	Second part chap. 3
14	Galloping Annie's Terrier	First part chap. 4
15	Riddy, A'Bess, Robbie and Rosie	Second part chap. 4; first part chap. 5
16	Life is Sometimes Fun	Second part chap. 5; chap. 6
17	The Hut on the Hilltop	Second part chap. 7
18	The Beacon on Ox's Cross	First part chap. 7

19	Winds of Heaven	Chap. 8
20	River in Flood	Chaps. 9, 10
21	Companionship	Chap. 11
22	Innocent Winter Buttercup	Chap. 13
23	Ancient Sunlight	First part chap. 15
24	John's Book	Second part chap. 15
25	And So Goodbye	

1959. Faber and Faber. *New edition, with additions and omissions; not illustrated.*

'Reissued in this new and revised edition, with additional scenes, Mcmlix'. Printed by Latimer Trend and Co. Pp.218. 208 x 132mm. Green cloth, goldstamped on the spine. Dust jacket pink, printed in green and black. Price 15/-.

The dedication is now 'To Meriel North'. Text (pp.9–218) made up of 15 chapters from the first edition (revised, retitled and rearranged), extracts from Goodbye West Country (rewritten) and some passages of new text including an 'Epigraph', ending '1937– 1958, Norfolk-Devon', with owl device:

Chapter:		Source of text:
1	Mother and Son	1939, chap. 4
2	On Irritability, Dream and Death	1939, chap. 11
3	Cold Pudding is the Family Friend	1939, chaps. 12, 13
4	On Terriers, Ghosts, Trout and Sport	1939, chaps. 14, part of 15
5	Nature, and Some Natural History	1939, part of chaps. 15, 16
6	We Go Travelling	1939, part of chap. 16
7	The Beacon on Ox's Cross	1939, chaps. 18, 17
8	Winds of Heaven	1939, chap. 19
9	Freshet	1939, part of chap. 20
10	John Shows a Cool Head	1939, part of chap. 20
11	Threshing	1939, chap. 21
12	Wind, Sand and Sea	Part from GWC pp.76–85
13	Life Catches Up	1939, chap. 22
14	Seven Year Cycle	From GWC pp.390–395
15	St. Martin's Little Summer	1939, chaps. 23, 24
16	Soliloquoy on a Tea-chest	New text, and part of GWC pp.377–382

Epigraph   New

1978. Macdonald and Jane's. *Reprint of 1959, with new illustrations and an Afterword.*
'This edition, with illustrations, and an Afterword by Richard Williamson, published in 1978 by ...' ISBN 0 354 04313 7. Pp.224. 8 plates, not reckoned. 223 x 137mm. Fawn linson. Dust jacket white, printed in light brown, designed by Paul Chevannes, photographed by John Lawson. Price £5.50.
New elements are: 8 plates with 22 family photographs, captioned but unattributed, of which 17 are new and 5 from the first edition; and a four-page 'Afterword' by Richard Williamson dated May 1978 in which the lives of the children are brought up to date.

A27 THE STORY OF A NORFOLK FARM

Williamson's occupation of the land at Old Hall Farm, Stiffkey, lasted nearly eight years from December 1937 to September 1945 and in *The Story of a Norfolk Farm* he provides a moving and seemingly effortless account of the early years of the project, from its origins in 1935 to the summer of 1939, with an 'Epigraph' written in June 1940. A sequel was soon commenced but was turned into *Lucifer Before Sunrise* (A55) and for the rest of the farm story the reader has to turn to this or other books including *The Phasian Bird* (A34), *In the Woods* (A49) and *A Solitary War* (A54), or his contemporary contributions to *The Evening Standard* (collected in A63, 64 and 73) and *The Eastern Daily Press* (collected in A68, with recollections of the period by Bill Williamson).
Illustrated with contemporary phototgraphs the book was reprinted several times during and just after the Second World War and then in 1986 with wood-cuts by Christopher Wormell and an Introduction by Richard Williamson.

1941a. Faber and Faber Limited. *First edition.*
'First published in February Mcmxli'. Printed by Westen Printing Sevices. Pp.404. Frontispiece and 10 plates, not reckoned. 208 x 130mm Brown cloth, goldstamped on the spine; top edge stained green or unstained; endpaper maps of the environs of the farm, in green and black, signed 'C.F. Tunnicliffe'. Dust jacket white, printed in brown and green, with a blurb but no quotes from reviews. Price 10/6. Published

January 1941 (D 1995). [4000] copies.

Contents:
- quotations from British Everyman and Sir Oswald Mosley on title-page;
- dedication 'To all who have worked and suffered for the land and the people of Greater Britain';
- 'Author's Note' (p.7) dated 11 November 1940, concerning omissions from the book that probably relate to his political views: 'The publishers have told me that certain passages, including an entire chapter, "are not essential to the story of the farming venture, and they are likely to excite a controversial interest at odds with the main theme of the book". I have therefore decided to remove them: hoping that they may be restored to the text in the happier and healthier age following the end of the War'; (see also letter in *Aylesford Review* Spring 1959);
- illustrations: 11 photographic plates, captioned and unattributed but probably by the author, relating to life on the farm; a small decoration, possibly by Tunnicliffe, is used as a head and tailpiece throughout;
- text (pp.15–403) in 4 Parts and 50 Chapters with headings, dated June 1937 - August 1939, followed by an 'Epigraph' dated 13 June 1940, with owl device:

Part	I	Aspiration	chaps.	1–8
	II	Anticipation		9–18
	III	Preparation		19–36
	IV	Realization		37–50
Epigraph				

1941b. Faber and Faber Limited. *Reprint of the first edition (? revised).*
'Second impression March Mcmxli'. Pp.404 but on thinner paper. Brown cloth, goldstamped; top edge green; endpaper maps. Dust jacket design as 1941a but with quotes from reviews on the front flap. Price 10/6.
Details of text not known (see next item).

1941c. Faber and Faber Limited. *Reprint of the first edition, with a revision; the second text.*
'Third impression November Mcmxli'. Brown cloth, goldstamped; endpaper maps.
Chapter 36 ends 'over the undrained meadows. I could not bear to

hear them' instead of 'over the sodden meadows', p.302.

1942. Readers' Union Limited ... Faber and Faber Limited. *Reprint of 1941c; the second text, with alterations; not illustrated.*
'Made 1942 in Great Britain'. Pp.344 (pagination is incorrect). 190 x 123mm. Reddish brown cloth, whitestamped on spine.

This appears to have been printed from the previous type but with the spacing closed-up to require fewer pages. Alterations, which may not have been by Williamson, are noted on p.84 line 20 with 'old' instead of 'odd', p.182 line 18 with 'jobs' not 'job', and 'plough' instead of 'plow' throughout.

1943. Faber and Faber Limited. *Reprint of 1941c; the second text.*
'Fourth impression February Mcmxliii'. Brown cloth, goldstamped; endpaper maps.

1944. Faber.
'Fifth impression January Mcmxliv' in the bib note of 1948; not seen.

1945. Faber.
'Sixth impression March Mcmxlv' in the bib note of 1948; not seen.

1946. Faber.
'Seventh impression January Mcmxlvi' in the bib note of 1948; not seen.

1948. Faber and Faber Limited. *Reprint of 1941c; the second text.*
'Eighth impression February Mcmxlviii'. Green cloth, blackstamped; endpaper maps. Dust jacket white, printed in red and green. Price 12/6.

1986. Clive Holloway Books. *Reprint of 1941c; the second text, with an Introduction; illustrated by Wormell.*
'This new edition ... published in 1986'. ISBN 0 907745 05 9. Pp.406. Frontispiece and illustrations, not reckoned. 222 x 135mm. Black linson, goldstamped on the spine. Dust jacket white, printed in black and yellow with an additional illustration by Wormell on the front panel and from p.324 on the back panel. Price £9.95.

A photo-reprint of 1941c with print size enlarged and some lines repositioned to compensate for the absence of photograph captions and the footnote on p.289; endpaper maps as previously by Tunnicliffe but printed in black. Includes an 'Introduction' (pp.5–7) by Richard

Williamson dated 'Keepers 1986' that provides background to the book, and illustrations by Christopher Wormell comprising a frontispiece, 16 other full-page woodcuts and 6 vignettes used as tailpieces (all also repeated).

A28 AS THE SUN SHINES

From 1942–1948 the only books that Williamson produced were based on material from the past and four of these were small undistinguished volumes subject to wartime restrictions on paper and printing.

As the Sun Shines (the same title as LL 1933) is the first of these and amounts to a personal mid-life 'retrospective' with a selection of passages up to 15 pp. in length from 18 of the major works he had published to date, excluding only *The Star-Born, On Foot in Devon* and *Devon Holiday.* In an unpublished note he wrote that it was done 'to advertise HW' and that the notes that precede most of the titles were also written by him.

1941. Faber and Faber Limited. *First edition.*
'First published in August Mcmxli'. Printed by Western Printing Services. A 'Sesame' Book. Pp.160. 190 x 120mm. Yellow cloth, redstamped on the front and spine. Dust jacket pink, printed in green, with a list of Sesame Books (21 titles, with series prices) on the back panel; all corners clipped. Price 3/6. Published September 1941 (letter from Faber 1966).

Contents:
- 'Select Bibliography' listing 7 Williamson titles;
- text (pp.9–160) consisting of extracts from 18 books, most with subtitles and brief introductory notes by HW:

	Subtitle:
The Beautiful Years	An Old Farmhouse
The Lone Swallows	Ernie
Dandelion Days	The Longpond
The Peregrine's Saga	The Soldier's Skull
The Dream of Fair Women	April 1919
The Old Stag	Redeye
Tarka the Otter	The Great Winter

The Pathway	Dutchman's Wreck
The Wet Flanders Plain	The Labyrinthe, etc.
The Patriot's Progress	Marching to the Somme
The Village Book	The Way Home
The Labouring Life	note from LL 1933; 'Devonshire cider'
The Gold Falcon	
The Linhay on the Downs	The Pullman
Salar the Salmon	Sisters
Good-bye, West Country	The Mayfly
The Children of Shallowford	
The Story of a Norfolk Farm	Rats

1944. Faber and Faber Limited. *Reprint of the first edition.*
'Second impression March Mcmxliv'. Light orange cloth, redstamped.
Dust jacket grey sugar-paper, printed in green, with a list of Sesame
Books (29 titles, with series prices) on the back panel. Price 3/6.

1945. Faber and Faber Limited. *Reprint of the first edition.*
'Third impression March Mcmxlv'. Orange cloth, redstamped.

1947. Faber and Faber Limited. *Reprint of the first edition.*
'Fourth impression July Mcmxlvii'. Brownish cloth. Dust jacket off-
white, printed in green, with a list of Sesame Books (29 titles, with no
series prices) on the back panel, and HW books on the back flap,
including *A Classic of English Farming* (B 1946a). Price 4/6.

A29 GENIUS OF FRIENDSHIP 'T. E. Lawrence'

Williamson's first contact with T.E. Lawrence was in 1928 after Edward
Garnett had sent Lawrence a copy of *Tarka* for review and critical
comment. Subsequently their acquaintance grew and in *Genius of
Friendship* Williamson gives an account of its development from the
summer of 1929 to Lawrence's sudden death in May 1935, in the form
of a single essay that is part narrative and part eulogy, interspersed
with quotations from Lawrence's letters and references to his own
books. Written at Shallowford in 1936 it could not be published until
permission for the use of the letters had been obtained from the trustees
of Lawrence's literary estate.

1941a. Faber and Faber Limited. *First edition.*
'First published in November Mcmxli'. Printed by R. MacLehose, and
Company. Pp.80. 259 x 164mm. Yellow-brown cloth, goldstamped on
the spine; fore and lower edge untrimmed. Dust jacket pale blue,
printed in black and red, with 'Faber & Faber Ltd' at the foot of the back
panel. Price 10/6. Published [December] 1941. [2000] copies.
    A variant in brown buckram has the same dust jacket and price.

Contents: text (pp.9–78) continuous, without headings, but with a
symbol denoting quotations from Lawrence, ending 'Shallonford [sic],
1936', with owl device.

1941b. Faber and Faber Limited. *Reprint of the first edition.*
'Second impression December Mcmxli'. Orange-brown cloth. Dust
jacket as 1941a but with 'Published by Faber & Faber Ltd' at the foot of
back panel. Price 10/6.
    'Shallonford' remains uncorrected.

1988. The Henry Williamson Society. 1988. *Reprint of the first edition,
with a facsimile.*
'Reprinted by The Henry Williamson Society to celebrate the centenary
of the birth of T.E. Lawrence 16 August 1988'. ISBN 0 9508652 6 5. Pp.78.
208 x 147mm. Card wrappers, beige, printed in black; perfect-bound.
Price £5. 500 copies.
    A photo-reprint of the original, including the error, with a facsimile
of Lawrence's telegram to Williamson of 15 May 1935.

A30 THE SUN IN THE SANDS

The *Sun in the Sands* begins as autobiography with a seemingly
authentic account of the dispute that led to Williamson leaving home in
1921, and the early years in Georgeham, but ends in 1924 as fiction with
a climax that is so obviously contrived that it damages the credibility of
much that has gone before.
    Written mostly in America in 1934 it was offered to Harrison Smith
who had published *The Gold Falcon*, but rejected on the grounds that it
should be either all biography or all novel, an observation that remains
as valid now as it was then. Subsequently it was held by Faber as a
guarantee against possible losses on *Salar* (see A22) until it was

retrieved during the Second World War for publication. In 1961 it was incorporated into *The Innocent Moon* with a new ending that contradicted the original one, prompting one critic (who had obviously been lulled into thinking he was reading autobiography) to describe the author as 'a congenital liar'.

1945a. Faber & Faber Limited. *First edition.*
'First published in Mcmxlv'. Printed by Purnell and Sons. Pp.252. Frontispiece, not reckoned. 190 x 122mm. Red cloth, goldstamped on the spine. Dust jacket white, printed in red and black, with a sunray design on the front panel and a blurb on the front flap with the full text of the untitled note on p.7 (but with 'plough' instead of 'plow'); list of 'New Fiction' on the back panel, ending 'The Unready Heart'; 'Also by Henry Williamson' with 10 titles on the back flap. Price 8/6. Published March 1945 (letter from Faber 1966).

Contents:
- quotation from Julian Grenfell on title-page, Algernon Charles Swinburne p. 9, Richard Lovelace p.113, Francis Thompson p.208;
- untitled note (p.7) by the author giving background to the work (also used as the blurb);
- frontispiece photograph of the author in March 1921;
- text (pp.9–250) in 3 Parts, headed, and 40 sections numbered in the text, ending with owl device:

Part	I	Julian	Sections 1–14
	II	Annabelle	15–26
	III	Barleybrigh	27–40

1945b. Faber & Faber Limited. *Reprint of the first edition.*
'Second impression December Mcmxlv'. Pp.250 (no blank at the end) on thicker paper, making a slightly bulkier book. Red cloth of varying shades, goldstamped. Dust jacket design as 1945a but with 'Faber & Faber' printed lower at the foot of the spine panel. Price 8/6.

Also in a dust jacket with a quote from *The Field* added after the blurb on the front flap and a list of 'New Fiction' ending with 'The Wind and the Rain' on the back panel, price 8/6.

1946. The Right Book Club. *Reprint of the first edition.*
'This edition 1946'. Frontispiece, not reckoned. Red cloth, black-

stamped. Dust jacket white, printed in red. Price to members 2/6.

1948. Faber & Faber Limited. *Reprint of the first edition, with a revision; the second text.*
'Third impression May Mcmxlviii'. Pp.252 (blank at the end). No frontispiece. Red cloth of varying shades, goldstamped. Dust jacket design as 1945a, but with the blurb shortened and a quote from *John O'London's Weekly* on the front flap, 'Books by Henry Williamson' on the back panel and three titles by HW on the back flap including *A Classic of English Farming* (B 1946a). Price 8/6.

Page 115 line 9 has 'I had met him once' in place of 'I never saw him'.

1961. In ***The Innocent Moon*** (A50) pp.135–391. *New edition; rewritten; the third text.*
With the exception of the last section (40) the whole of *The Sun in the Sands* is used to form chapters 7–20 of *The Innocent Moon*. Some passages are the same in both books, but most are extensively reworked and the ending is changed.

A31 TALES OF A DEVON VILLAGE

In the opening Note to this volume Williamson writes: ' *Tales of a Devon Village*, with its companion *Life in a Devon Village*, is compiled with material gathered together originally in two books I wrote some years ago and called *The Village Book* and *The Labouring Life* ... I was never fully satisfied with them; they were a collection of varying fragments rather than unified books. Now, after an interval of several years of hard physical work ... I have set about giving each its own unity, based on what spirit of truth accompanies my life'.

Published in quick succession just a few months after VE day they would also have served to let the public know he was still active.

1945. Faber and Faber Limited. *First edition.*
'First published in this edition Mcmxlv'. Printed by Purnell and Sons. Pp.224. 190 x 123mm. Green cloth, goldstamped on the spine. Dust jacket white, printed in green and black with ads for Faber's 'New Fiction' headed by 'Dear Baby' on the back panel. Price 8/6. Published September 1945. ? 10,000 copies (letter from Faber 1966).

Contents:
- note of explanation on half-title signed 'H.W. 1944';
- text (pp.7–224) in 15 Chapters, made up of 6 titles from *The Village Book* and 8 from *The Labouring Life*, all revised, plus 'The Linhay on the Downs' (again) and a few passages of new text, ending with owl device:

	Source of text:
The Badger Dig	VB, new opening paragraphs, and revised
The Darkening of the Doorway	LL, lines rewritten, and revised
The Well	LL, passages rewritten, and revised
The Mystery of a Damp Cottage	LL 'The Mystery of a Dark Cottage', revised
An Old-World Courting	VB 'A Romance of Old-World Courting', minimal revision
A Village David and Goliath	LL, minimal revision
The Old Cob Cottage	VB, light revision
The Ackymals	VB, a few further changes
Billy Goldsworthy's Barn	VB, light revision
P.C. Bullcornworthy	LL, revised
Cemetery or Burial Ground?	LL, revised
Billy Goldsworthy's Cow	LL, revised
The Zeale Brothers	VB, revised
The Linhay on the Downs	LOD 1934, unchanged
The Fox in the Moonlight	LL, new paragraph, and revised

1946. Faber and Faber Limited. *Reprint of the first edition.*
'Reprinted June Mcmxlvi'. Pp.224 but on thinner paper. Green cloth, goldstamped. Dust jacket design as 1945 but with ads on the back panel headed by 'The Lifeline'. Price 8/6, or 3/6 on an octagonal Faber sticker; also a copy stamped 'Price in Canada $2.50' at the top of the front flap.

1984. Breslich & Foss. *Reprint of the first edition.*
Retitled VILLAGE TALES.
'Published by Robinson Publishing 1984'. Country Classics Series. ISBN 1 85004 019 2. 215 x 133mm. Paperback. Cover illustration from a painting 'Ploughing' by Sir George Clausen. Price £3.95.
A photo-reprint with print size enlarged.

A32 LIFE IN A DEVON VILLAGE

The companion to *Tales of a Devon Village* compiled from elements of *The Village Book* and *The Labouring Life* that were not used in that book (see A31).

1945. Faber and Faber Limited. *First edition.*
'First published in Mcmxlv'. Printed by Purnell and Sons. Pp.288. 190 x 123mm. Orange-red cloth, goldstamped on the spine. Dust jacket white, printed in light and dark brown, with ads for Faber's 'New Fiction' on the back panel headed by 'The Lifeline'. Price 8/6. Published November 1945. ? 10,000 copies (letter from Faber 1966).

Contents:
- 'Note' of explanation (p.6) signed 'H.W. 1921–1944';
- text (pp.7–288) in 23 Chapters, made up of 9 titles from *The Village Book*, 12 from *The Labouring Life* and two that have elements from both books, ending with owl device:

	Source of text:
My Neighbour 'Revvy'	LL 'The Labourer and A Labourer's Life', reshaped and revised, incorporating the previous 'Notes' into a continuous narrative
Birds of Skirr Cottage	VB 'My Owls (1 and 2)', and LL 'Star-Flights of Swifts', all revised
The Sawyers	VB, lightly revised; includes the placard
The First Day of Spring	VB, using all of parts 1, 2 and 3 except 'Interlude', with light revision; no ms illustration
'Muggy'	VB, one word changed
On Scandal, Gossip, Hypocrisy or Self-Deception, Roguery, and Senescence	elements of VB: 'Scandal and Gossip', 'Scriddicks', 'A Mason's Week', 'The Donkey'; and LL: 'Consecration of the New Burial Ground', 'Old Men', with varying degrees of revision

Village Inns: The Lower House	VB, with light revision
The Vacant Fields	VB, with light revision
Village Inns: The Higher House	VB, with light revision
A Farmer's Life	VB 'Washing Day', followed by 'A Farmer's Life' parts 1–4, revised; no ms illustration
Village Children	LL, revised
Old Woolacott	VB, revised
The Fair: Morning	LL, revised
What the Doctor Said	LL, revised
The Fair: Afternoon	LL, revised
The Stream	LL 'The Life of the Stream', revised
Summer Afternoon	LL 'Summer Afternoon by the Sea', revised
A Day on Dunkery	LL 'A Summer Day on Dunkery', minimal revision
A Devon Hillside	LL, with minimal revision
The Firing Gatherer	VB, slight further revision
Devonshire Cider	LL, revised
Consecration of the New Burial Ground	LL, parts not used above, revised
Surview and Farewell	LL, rearranged and revised

1947. The Right Book Club. *Reprint of the first edition.*
'Second impression July, Mcmxlvii' and 'This edition 1947'. Pp.288 but on thicker paper. Red cloth, blackstamped. Dust jacket white, printed in light and dark pink, with a sketch of a village reproduced on the front panel, unattributed.

1948. Faber and Faber Limited. *Reprint of the first edition.*
'Third impression Mcmxlviii'. Red cloth, goldstamped. Dust jacket design as 1945 but with 'Books by Henry Williamson' on the back panel. Price 8/6.

1983. Breslich & Foss. *Reprint of the first edition.*
i) 'Published by Breslich and Foss 1983'. Country Classics series. ISBN 1 85004 005 2. Green paper boards. Dust jacket white, printed in pink and black, with an illustration from a watercolour by Charles Earle on the front panel. Price £8.95.

A photo-reprint with print size enlarged and a one-page 'Publisher's Preface'.

ii) as i) except: ISBN 1 85004 004 4. Paperback. Price £3.95.

A33 THE HENRY WILLIAMSON NATURE BOOKS

This is Putnam's marketing title for a uniform 'edition' of five of Williamson's books of natural history stories, illustrated by Charles Tunnicliffe, and issued as a boxed set in 1946.

In fact, four of the volumes are merely reprints of previous Putnam printings with illustrations that are inferior in quality to the originals. Only *Salar*, originally published by Faber, is a new type-setting and even that has fewer illustrations than the previous UK edition and no colour plates. Three of the edition statements are dated 1945 and consistent in style (TA, LS, PS), but the other two are different and dated 1946, which suggests that the books were printed in an irregular sequence rather than in a single co-ordinated exercise.

All are printed on Adelphi laid paper with the owl device on the title-page and uniformly cased in green cloth, with an 'H.W.' monogram goldstamped on the front cover and the title, author, publisher and a small device goldstamped on the spine; top edges gilt, others untrimmed; issued in a brown cardboard slip-case with a white label on the spine, printed in black, as the 'Illustrated Limited Edition' in [500] sets, priced 6 guineas a set. Whether any of the books were available as individual items before or after the set was issued is not yet clear.

Tarka the Otter (A8): 'First published 1927. Limited illustrated edition 1945', with the dates not in italics. This is at least the sixth printing of the 1932 illustrated edition (the fourth text) but with the title used as a running head and chapter headings placed above the text (not in the margins), establishing the format for the rest of the set.

The Lone Swallows (A2): 'First published 1922. Limited illustrated edition 1945', with the dates not in italics. The third printing of the 1933 illustrated edition with the headings adjusted to match the format of *Tarka*, above.

The Peregrine's Saga (A4): 'First published 1923. Limited illustrated edition 1945', with the dates not in italics. The third printing of the 1934 illustrated edition with the headings adjusted to match the above.

The Old Stag (A6): 'First illustrated edition published February 1933. Reprinted June 1942. Limited illustrated edition 1946', all in italics, and the only place in the set where there is any mention of a previous illustrated edition. The third printing of the 1933 illustrated edition, printed from 1942a with the tailpieces restored and headings adjusted to match the above.

Salar the Salmon (A22): 'First published 1935 by Faber & Faber Ltd. This limited edition published 1946. By kind permission of Messrs. Faber & Faber Ltd.', with the dates not in italics. A new type-setting of the original text in smaller print with the second printing of 47 b/w illustrations from 1936c, a new frontispiece (not present in any other issue) and headings arranged to match the rest of the set.

A34 THE PHASIAN BIRD

In his first new book for eight years Williamson sets an extended nature story in the context of rural England during the Second World War. In *The Story of a Norfolk Farm* he had closed the narrative just before the start of war, but he continued to write during it and in *The Phasian Bird* he uses this material as the backcloth to a tale of an oriental pheasant, hatched in the nest of a native British bird and exposed to the hazards of man and the environment. According to Gower (*Books and Bookmen* March 1960) the ending was rewritten five times but it was not subsequently revised even in the American edition where many other changes were made.

1948. Faber and Faber. *First edition.*
i) 'First published in Mcmxlviii'. Printed by Latimer, Trend and Co. Pp.344. 193 x 120mm. Blue cloth, goldstamped on the spine; top edge pink. Dust jacket white, printed in black, with a colour illustration of a pheasant (based on the description in the book) signed 'M.E.E.' (Mildred Eldridge) on the front panel. Price 10/6. Published November 1948 (letter from Faber 1966).

ii) Cheaper issue: as i) but with top edge unstained and the dust jacket price-clipped with 5/-printed on the front flap. In an unpublished note Williamson says that the book was remaindered within a few years as the first printing was unsold.

Contents:
- quotation on title-page 'The letter killeth';
- 'Note' acknowledging an anonymous source;
- text (pp.11–341) in 4 Parts and 29 Chapters, unheaded:

Part	1	chaps.	1–7
	2		8–13
	3		14–21
	4		22–29

1950. Little, Brown and Company. Boston. *American edition, revised; the second text; illustrated by Doskow.*
'Copyright 1948, 1950 ... First edition. Published October 1950'. Printed in the USA. An Atlantic Monthly Press Book. Pp.xii + 276. Illustrations, reckoned. 209 x 125mm. Red cloth, goldstamped on the front and spine. Dust jacket white, printed in black and green, with the Eldridge design from 1948 on the front panel. Price $4.

Contents (compared to 1948):
- no quotation on title-page;
- dedication 'To Holly and Mossy (Mr. and Mrs. P.C. Hollingsworth of Langham) in gratitude for steady friendship during the dark days';
- definition of 'Pheasant' from an Old Dictionary p.ix;
- 'contained' omitted from the 'Note';
- illustrations: title-page vignette and 25 line drawings as head-pieces, by Israel Doskow;
- text (pp.3–276) in 4 Parts but reduced to 25 chapters, with significant revisions: Parts 1–3 have whole pages, paragraphs and lines omitted with some rewriting and short passages of new text, while Part 4 is condensed from eight chapters to four with the original chapter 23 omitted and the new chapters made up as follows: chapter 22: from the original chap. 22; chapter 23: from parts of original chaps. 24 and 25; chapter 24: from part of original chap. 26, the whole of chap. 27 and part of chap. 28; chapter 25: from parts of the original chap. 29.

1984. The Boydell Press. *Reprint of the first edition.*

'First published in Country Library 1984'. Country Library series. ISBN 0 85115 238 4. Pp.344. Paperback. Cover illustration of a native pheasant by Maurice Pledger. Price £3.95.

The title-page quotation is omitted.

A35 SCRIBBLING LARK

'Scribbling Lark' is the name under which an old cart-horse called Prince is disguised and entered as a runner in the Derby, ridden by two monkeys dressed up as a jockey. Occasionally funny, but mostly just daft, the book was interpreted by one critic as having profound allegorical significance. To Williamson, however, it was just 'my cigarette-card storyette' (Farson, D 1982).

It is the only book that he wrote specifically for children and the last of the 'one-off' experiments that are a feature of the middle phase of his career. In the final phase he would concentrate almost exclusively on the massive work he had been contemplating for thirty years. After the birth of another daughter (Sarah) in 1945, divorce from Loetitia in 1947, and marriage to Christine Duffield in 1949, he was back at Ox's Cross and ready to begin.

1949. Faber and Faber Limited. *First edition.*
'First published in Mcmxlix'. Printed by Purnell and Sons. Pp.160. 206 x 131mm. Orange cloth, goldstamped on the spine. Dust jacket grey, printed in brown and black, with a design of monkeys and a horse on the front panel, unattributed. Price 7/6. Published November 1949 (letter from Faber 1966). [5000 copies].

Contents: text (pp.9–158) in 35 chapters with headings; no dedication, date or owl device.

A36 A CHRONICLE OF ANCIENT SUNLIGHT

A Chronicle of Ancient Sunlight is the overall title that Williamson gave to a series of fifteen books that form a continuous narrative of the fortunes of one dysfunctional family (the Maddisons) during the first half of the twentieth century. From the time of its conception it was at least twenty years before Williamson felt able to begin it and another twenty, including the birth of another son (Michael) and divorce from Christine, before it was finished. Amounting to over 6000 pages and some three million words the books were structured as individual novels but are best read in the order of their publication.

Central to the whole drama is the figure of Phillip Maddison (cousin of Willie in *The Flax of Dream*) who is born in London, serves in the First World War, becomes a writer, and at the time of the Second World War is farming in Devon. In a neat conclusion to the saga, on the penultimate page Williamson has Phillip (as his fictional author) poised to embark on the very 'chronicle' that Williamson has just completed - 'Yes! he cried. I shall start my chronicle in the mid-nineties, on a spring night, with that reserved, shy young man walking up the hill at Wakenham. He was carrying his dark lantern ...'

Clearly this is a reflection of Williamson's own life, but the *Chronicle* is fiction, not autobiography. Events that happened and people that existed are merged seamlessly with others that are pure invention, and it is a measure of the author's craftsmanship that the reader is often unable to determine which is which. As a general rule with Williamson, if there is a conflict between art and reality, art wins.

In a postscript to the final volume, headed 'L'Envoi', he indicates that the origins of this approach lay in a conversation he had with Edward Garnett in 1928 concerning *The Flax of Dream*, in which Garnett had told him: 'A written page may be life; but the test must be, Is it art? A writer may transcribe an actual happening with what is called "realism", yet his work remain comparatively unconvincing. Whereas what is transmuted by the Imagination will convey the spirit of reality, and read as life itself ... "True but imaginary", in Conrad's words.' (see also A2). In the *Chronicle* this is what Williamson set out to achieve, and did.

At the end of 'L'Envoi', with an allusion to Proust, he says 'A thousand scenes from Time regained! Innumerable joys and sorrows, the best and the worst of oneself ... Behind the tears were love and gratitude that one had been born in England, that one had been privileged to experience hardship that had burned away the selfish dross of oneself, and thereby, perhaps, made one worthy of an attempt to speak for those who had not come back from the Western Front.'

Rejected initially by Collins and then Faber, the books were taken up by Macdonald and published as unrelated items until they became 'The Phillip Maddison Novels' on the dust jacket of *A Test to Destruction* (book 8), and finally *A Chronicle of Ancient Sunlight* on the dust jacket and in the list of Williamson's works on the half-title of *The Innocent Moon* (book 9).

Summary of Editions:

1. **Macdonald 1951–69.** 15 volumes of matching size (ten in cloth, five in linson) in varied, colourful and attractive dust jackets by James Broom Lynne. Four of the titles went to a second impression (DL, HDL, FMC, GV) and one to a third (GV). This is certainly the preferred edition but due to varying print runs and particular demand (eg for the five 'war books') some volumes are less accessible than others.

2. **Panther 1962–69.** 13 volumes, in paperback, with pictorial front covers. Marketed as the 'revised edition' it hardly justifies the description as the last two books (LBS, GOW) are not included and in most of the others the textual changes are slight, insignificant, or even bizarre (eg confined to words in German). On the other hand it does have a list of 'Dramatis Personae' which is not provided in any other edition, though the enthusiasm of its compilers seems to have declined as the series progressed.

3. **Macdonald 1984–85.** 15 volumes in dust jackets that are uniform in style but in different pastel colours with well-chosen illustrations on the front panels. A straightforward reprint of the first edition, without adornment, and the only other hardback issue of the full set.

4. **Alan Sutton 1994–99.** 15 volumes, in paperback, also with well-illustrated covers. A reprint of the first edition, with an Introduction by Anne Williamson repeated in each volume, though the type is sometimes reset.

5. Individual volumes have been reprinted by **Zenith** in paperback (DL, DB, YPM) in a series that was evidently aborted, and by **Chiver**s in hardback (FMC, LOL, TD) in response to demand.

The Main Characters:
Names are listed once only and generally in the order of their first significant appearance, but with some in the early books grouped for ease of reference. References in brackets indicate characters that also feature in *The Flax of Dream* or other books. For a genealogy and

comparison of the fictional families and their real-life counterparts see HWSJ 31.

The Dark Lantern
The Maddisons:
  Richard (Dickie) Edward Maddison, Phillip's father (DD)
  Theodora (Dora) Maddison, RM's youngest sister
  (Captain) Maddison, widower, RM's father
  Hilary Robert Von Fohre Maddison, RM's younger brother
  John William Beare Maddison, RM's elder brother, and wife Jenny (BY)
  Augusta (Ada) Maddison, RM's second sister
  Victoria (Viccy) Maddison (Mrs Lemon), RM's third sister
  Isabelle (Belle) Maddison, RM's eldest sister
  George Lemon, husband of Victoria
  Phillip Sidney Thomas Maddison, 'donkey baby' (DD)
The Turneys:
  Henrietta (Hetty) Turney, friend of Dora Maddison
  Thomas William Turney and Sarah, HT's parents
  Hugh Turney, HT's second brother
  Charley Turney, HT's eldest brother
  Dorothy (Dorrie) Turney (Mrs Cakebread), HT's sister
  Joseph Turney, HT's youngest brother
  Aunt Marian, TT's sister
  Sidney Cakebread, husband of Dorothy
  Nathaniel Turney, TT's father
  Bertie (Hubert), Ralph and Gerry Cakebread, HT's nephews
Others:
  Mrs Birkett, midwife, and Mr Birkett, sewerman
  Mrs Feeney, charwoman, and Mr Feeney, Crimean veteran
  Mrs Cummings, PM's landlady, widow of Captain Cummings
  Matthew Pooley, market gardener and nonagenarian
  Lancelot Mallard, friend of Hugh Turney
  Mr Albert Mallard, chairman of Mallard, Carter and Turney, and Mrs Mallard, LM's parents
  Minnie, the Maddisons' German nurse
  Frank Temperley and Mrs Temperley, friends from RM's boyhood (BY)
  Sir Roger Tofield, landowner and director of Doggett's Bank
  Mr Alfred Carter, partner in Mallard, Carter and Turney

Roland Tofield, son of Sir Roger
Mrs Kendon, gamekeeper's wife
Polly, the Turneys' maid
Rev Ernest Hamilton Pepys Mundy, Vicar of St Simon's, and Mrs Ethelburga Mundy
Journend, clerk at the Moon Fire Office
Miranda MacIntosh, Rev Mundy's secretary and second wife
Dr Cave-Browne
Mr Winner, Richard and Hetty's landlord
The Honourable Legge, Bishop of Lichfield
Mr Crowley, Sunday School teacher
Miss Danks, his assistant

Donkey Boy
Family:
  Mavis and Doris, PM's sisters
  Beatrice Murgatroyd, George Lemon's sister
  Percy and Polly Pickering, PM's cousins
  Eliza Pickering, the Thacker's daughter, and husband James (Jim)
  Mrs Thacker, TT's sister, and husband Theodore
Others:
  Monk, a navvy, and Mrs Monk
  Mr Josiah and Mrs Amelia Bigge, neighbours
  Norah Bigge, their daughter
  Mr Groat, PM's tutor, and Mrs Groat
  Miss Thoroughgood, 'Old Loo'sam', proprietor of a Domestic Servants Agency
  Freddie, publican at The Castle
  Mona Monk, Hetty's maid
  Flora Gould (later Mrs Rolls), and Gerard Rolls, neighbours
  Sir Alfred and Lady Catt, the Lemons' neighbours
  Jessie, the Lemons' maid
  The Misses Fanny and May Whitaker, of St Catherine's School
  Rechenda Baggot, Theodora Maddison's friend
  Mr Muggeridge, Richard Maddison's friend
  Mr Harcourt Newman, Thomas Turney's friend
  Helena Rolls, the Rolls's daughter
  Miss Norton, Mrs Wilkins, Mr 'Twiney' Twine, schoolteachers
  Mildenhall, schoolboy
  Mr Alfred 'Gussy' Garstang, Headmaster of Wakenham Road

School
Mrs Robartes, friend of Hetty's, and husband Dr Robartes
Horace Cranmer, schoolboy
Mr Sprunt, pawnbroker
Sir Park Gomme, London County Councillor

Young Phillip Maddison
Family:
Adele, the Lemons' daughter
Willie, John Maddison's son
Tommy and Petal, children of Charles and Florence Turney
Willie Maddison, John's son and PM's cousin (BY)
Beatrice Maddison (previously Murgatroyd), Hilary's wife
Others:
Milton, choirboy
Mr and Mrs Ching and son Tom
Mr and Mrs Wallace and sons Peter, David and Nimmo
Mr and Mrs Pye, neighbours
Mr Graham, local historian and President of Heath School Old Boys
  Club
Mr 'Sailor' Jenkins and Mrs Jenkins, neighbours
Mr and Mrs Todd, neighbours
The 'Higher' Lows, neighbours
Mr and Mrs 'Lower' Low and son Lennie, neighbours
Mr Hawkins, a barber, and son Alfred
Desmond Worsley Whickham Neville, son of Mr and Mrs Neville
Freddy Payne, scout
Mr and Mrs Jones and son Basil
Rupert Purley-Prout, scoutmaster
Allen, scout
Watty Holdwich, Patrol Leader
Captain Blois, St Anselm's Troop
Mr Swinerd, assistant scoutmaster
Lady Mersea, Dowager Countess
Lieutenant Oakfall, the Kent Guides
Oscar Blackman, 'Dick Turpin', scoutmaster
Jack Hart, cadet
Garrott, a policeman (Keechey in the Panther edition)
Mr and Mrs Krebs, friends of Thomas Turney
Mr Bolton, friend of Thomas Turney

Kimberley, Charles Turney's black boy
Sir Wilfred Castleton, owner of *The Daily Trident*
Mr Hemming, general manager of M.C.T.
Miss Rooney, Thomas Turney's housekeeper
Bob, Hugh Turney's man
Mère Ambroisine, Mother Superior
Mr Howlett, manager of Wine Vaults Lane Branch
Cundall, Greenall, Pett and Pype, 'Bagmen' at Heath School

How Dear Is Life
The Moon Fire Office:
    Downham, senior clerk
    Edgar, Branch Messenger
    Mr Hollis, Head clerk
    Mr L Dicks and Mr J Konigswinter, agents
    Cohen and Thistlethwaite, brokers
Others:
    Costello, Old Heathian
    Fitcheyson, President of Old Heathians' F.C.
    'Little Freddy' Fanlight, Inspector for Moon Life Assurance Co.
    Great Aunt Hepzibiah, Thomas Turney's sister
    Furrow, from Moon Fire Head Office
    Billy Bolton, son of Thomas Turney's friend
    Sylvia, friend of Theodora Maddison
    Eugene, Brazilian friend of Desmond Neville
    Jack Temperley, WM's friend, son of Frank (BY)
    Elsie Norman, Willie's girl (BY)
    Grannie Nobbs
London Highlanders:
    Lance-corporal 'Morty' Mortimore
    Captain 'Fiery' Forbes
    Baldwin, and Church, of 'B' Company
    The Earl of Findhorn, Commanding Officer
    Colonel 'Oscar' Hatton, 'the Iron Colonel', Second in Command
    Lieutenant Bruce Ogilby
    Kirk, Blunden, Collins, Kerry, Martin, the Church brothers, Elliott,
      Douglas, and Tommy Atkins, of 'B' Company
    Captain MacTaggart, Medical Officer
    Sergeant 'Grannie' Henshaw
    Captain 'Oats' McQuaker

A Fox Under My Cloak

'Mrs Freddy', wife of Freddy the publican.

'Lieutenant' Wilkins (later Devereux-Wilkins), friend of Mavis Maddison

Monty, garage manager

Fairy, husband Basil, and sister Estelle

The Military:

Glass, London Highlander

Lieutenant Thorverton, ditto

Colonel 'Strawballs' Haycock, 1st Battalion, the Gaultshires

Captain 'Jonah' Whale, ditto

Brigadier-General 'Crasher' Joliffe-Howard, General Staff

Lieutenant Baldersby, ditto

Lieutenant O'Connor, ditto

Major 'Hairy Harry' Fridkin, ditto

Lieutenant Brendon, ditto

Lieutenat Dimmock, ditto

Colonel Broad, Navvie's Battalion

Lieutenant Merrit, ditto

Captain Harold 'Spectre' West, 2nd Battalion

'Twinkle' Nobbs, a deserter

Colonel Mowbray, 2nd Battalion

Sergeant Jones

Captain 'Nosey' Orlebar, General Staff

The Golden Virgin

Nina, Mavis' friend

Dr Dashwood, local doctor and acquaintance of PM

Dr Toogood, R.A.M.C.

Captain Jasper Kingsman, Prince Regent's Own Regiment

Milman, ditto

Captain Bruce Bason, ditto

Wigg, ditto

Cox, ditto

Father Aloysius, priest and friend of the Kingsmans

Frances and Alice

Lily Cornford, and Mrs Cornford

Det. Sergeant Keechey, Randiswell Police (see Garrott in YPM)

Georgiana, Lady Stafford

Piston, Somme veteran

Love and the Loveless
    Captain Teddy Pinnegar, Machine Gun Corps
    Lieutenant Montfort, ditto
    Lieutenant 'Darky' Fenwick, ditto
    Captain 'All Weather' Jack Hobart, ditto
    'Ropey' Griggs, riding master
    Lieutenant 'Darky' Fenwick, ditto
    Sergeant Rivett, ditto
    2nd Lieutenant Clewlee, ditto
    Miss Flora 'Flossie' Flowers, proprietress of Flowers' Hotel
    Sasha, and son Alex
    Major Pickles, Asst. Director Veterinary Services
    Sergeant Nolan
    Barrow, batman
    Drivers Cutts, Morris, Tallis, M'Kinnell
    Sergeant Butler
    'Broncho Bill', Australian deserter
    Lieutenant-Colonel Wilmott
    Quartermaster-Sergeant Bowles
    Lieutenant Bright
    Elizabeth - Mavis Maddison's now preferred (second) name
    Major Traill, Etaples Base Depot
    Lieutenant Dixon, Lancashire Fusiliers
    Colonel Firling, Staff
    Brigadier-General Ludlow, Staff
    2nd Lieutenant Allen, the Gaultshires
    2nd Lieutenant Sisley, ditto
    Mr and Mrs West, 'Spectre's' parents

A Test to Destruction
    Lord Satchville, Commanding Officer, the Gaultshires
    Captain Henniker-Sudley, adjutant
    Maude, Dorothy Cakebread's daughter
    Mr Robert (Bill or Bob) Willoughby, friend of Doris
    Docherty, Tabor, and Hedges, subalterns
    Julian Warbeck, the Admiralty (DFW)
    Major 'Pluggy' Marsden
    Lance-corporal Tonks
    Colonel Moggerhanger
    Captain Bill Kidd

Private O'Gorman
Mr Kerr, Gents' Outfitter
Miss Shore, and Nurse Goonhilly, Tregaskis House
Major Wetley, Swayne, and Coupar, fellow-convalescents
Stella, a casual acquaintance
Mrs d'Arcy Fairfax, husband Lionel, and daughter 'Quillie' (DFW)

The Innocent Moon
Mrs Portal-Welch, hostess of the Parnassus Club
Tabitha 'Spica' Trevelian, and parents
Jack O'Donovan, part-time journalist
Mrs Crang, and husband Walter, neighbours
Bernard Bloom, editor of *The Trident*
'Ownsworth' (Houndsworth), news editor
'Naps' Spreycombe, Eve Fairfax's intended (DFW)
Anders Norse, literary agent
Poppett, an Art acquaintance
J.D. Woodford, publisher's reader
'Porky' Tanberry, and wife Brenda (SIS)
Irene Lushington, and daughter Teresa Jane 'Barley' (SIS)
Annabelle and Queenie, daughters of Mrs 'Sophy' Selby-Lloyd (SIS)
Dr MacNab (SIS)
Wigfull, Thistlethwaite, and Charley Mutton, Solicitors (SIS)
Rowley Meek, Bevan Swann, and Archie Meek, Pyrenean companions (SIS)

It Was the Nightingale
Mr 'Georgie' Pole-Cripps, and wife 'Boo'
Arthur Turney, son of Joseph, PM's cousin
May (Mae) and Topsy, Arthur's sisters
Billy, Phillip's son
Mr Mules, postman, Mrs Mules, and daughter Zillah (PW)
Mary Ogilvie, Lucy's cousin (BY)
Mr Sufford Chychester, and wife, Lucy's grandmother (PW)
Lucy Copleston, daughter of Adrian
Martin Beausire, writer and critic
Mr Adrian Copleston, and sons Tim, Fiennes and Ernest
Mrs à Court Smith, and 'Mister', friends of the Coplestons
Teddy Dock, editor
Dikran Michaelis, writer

MacCourage, American publisher

The Power of the Dead
Lucy, PM's second wife
Piers Tofield, with the BBC
Archie Plugge, ditto
Tony Cruft, novelist, and wife Virginia
'Peter' (Hilary Copleston Maddison), Lucy's son
Jasper Driver, publisher
Thomas Morland, O.M., writer
Edward Cornelian, writer
Channerson, artist (GF)
Felicity Ancroft, writer for the BBC
A.B. Cabton, a young writer
Rosamund, Lucy's daughter

The Phoenix Generation
Lady Abeline, Duchess of Gaultshire, and husband Lord George
Lady Georgiana Birkin
Sir Hereward Birkin, leader of the Imperial Socialist Party
Captain 'Boy' Runnymeade
Stefania Rozwitz, a Polish dancer
Rippingall, an old soldier
Rev. Becket Scrimgeour
Mrs Ancroft, Felicity's mother
Mr Fitzwarren, Felicity's guardian
Brother Laurence
Melissa Watt-Wilby, daughter of Lady Abeline and Lucy's cousin
David, Lucy's second son
Laura Wissilcraft
Hurst, a hanger-on
Horatio Bugg
Luke, and Matt, his father, farmhands
Lady Penelope Carnoy
Jonathan, PM's youngest
Fred Riversmill, a painter

A Solitary War
Mrs 'Yipps' Carfax, a colleague of Teddy Pinnegar
Chettwood, features editor

'Pinwheel'
Mrs Valiant, and husband Tom, tenants
Mrs Hammett, and Charley
Arrowsmith
Steve, and Billy the Nelson, farmhands
Mr Arrowsmith, publicity agent
Mr Poluski, publisher
Mr Bacon, agent
Wallington Christie, editor of the N.Q.M.
P.C. Bunnied

Lucifer Before Sunrise

Albert Close, lorry driver (IW)
Poppy, Bert Close's girlfriend (IW)
Major Charles Box, neighbour
Jack the Jackdaw, and Powerful Dick, farmhands
James Valiant, the Valiants' son
Josiah Harn, smallholder
Sarah, Melissa's cousin
Gladstone Gogney, agricultural contractor, and father Walpole
The Inquiline, a nuisance
Bannock MacWhippet, writer
Major 'Buster' Cloudesley
'Ginger', ex bomber pilot
Edward, Felicity's son
Humphrey Mariner, painter
Elias Quaxter, valuer

The Gale of the World

Molly, and Peregrine Bucentaur
Miranda, Roger, and Imogen, their children
Aaron Kedd, smallholder and local preacher
Osgood Nilsson, roving correspondent for a N.Y. paper, and his wife
    Rosalie
Globe-Mornington, night-porter at the Barbarians' (later at
    Cloudesley's)
Mr Strangeways, Barrister
Caspar Schwenkfelder, founder of the College of Diaphany
Major 'Mad' Piston, and his wife
Hugh Cloudesley, 23rd Baron, cousin of 'Buster'

Beth, wife of Piers Tofield
Manfred Cloudesley, 22nd Baron, father of 'Buster'
Mr Corney, pub landlord

A37 THE DARK LANTERN

The first volume of the *Chronicle* is essentially a prologue in which
Williamson sets the scene for the entrance of the figure that will domi-
nate the whole work - Phillip Sidney Thomas Maddison. When the
book opens it is 1893 and Richard Maddison is out with his 'dark
lantern', a contraption for collecting butterflies and moths which is his
only escape from a dead-end job in the City of London, but like any
young man in his twenties he has his aspirations, and union with Hetty
Turney is one of them. By the end of the book it is 1895 (the year in
which Williamson himself was born) and 'donkey boy' has arrived.

1951. Macdonald & Co., (Publishers) Ltd. *First edition.*
'First published in 1951 ...' Printed by Purnell and Sons. Pp.432. 202 x
129mm. Red cloth, goldstamped on the spine. Dust jacket white,
printed in yellow, brown, green and black, with a design of geese in
flight by Broom Lynne on the front and spine panels; ads for
Macdonald's 'Leading Novels' on the back panel. Price 12/6. Published
November 1951 (letter from Macdonald, 1970). 10,000 copies.
    A variant in green cloth has minor differences in the goldstamping
on the spine but the same dust jacket and price.

Contents:
- dedication 'To Malcolm Elwin' (author and friend; see B 1947);
- text (pp.11–432) in 5 Parts and 31 Chapters with headings, ending with
owl device:

Part	1	Camberwell Beauty	chaps.	1–8
	2	Hetty's Birthday Party		9–13
	3	New Home		14–18
	4	Winter of 1894–95		19–23
	5	Death and Resurrection		24–31

1962. A Panther Book. *New edition, revised; the second text.*
'Panther edition published 1962'. Published by Hamilton and Co.

Printed by Petty and Sons. Panther 1386. Pp.352. 177 x 110mm. Paperback. Cover illustration of a young man and woman, signed 'Richards'. Price 5/-

'Dramatis Personae' with 56 names. Revisions noted on pp.23, 24 with 'Jenny' instead of 'Hetty', pp.25–6 where two new paragraphs are added and one rewritten, and pp.276, 280, 338; no owl device.

1966. Macdonald. *Reprint of the first edition.*
'Second impression 1966'. Green cloth, goldstamped. Dust jacket design as 1951 but with new blurb on the flaps and a list of titles in the *Chronicle* up to *The Phoenix Generation* on the back panel. Price 18s on flap, £2 on sticker.

1970. A Panther Book. *Reprint of 1962; the second text.*
'Reprinted 1970'. Published by Panther Books. Panther 586 01386 5/2. Paperback. Cover illustration from a painting 'The Bayswater Omnibus' (London Museum). Price 7/-.

1984a. Macdonald & Co. *Reprint of the first edition.*
'This edition published in 1984 ...' ISBN 0 356 01803 3. Blue linson, goldstamped. Dust jacket white, printed in light blue and black, with detail from a painting 'The Crystal Palace' by Pissaro on the front panel. Price £9.95 on flap, £12.95 on sticker.

1984b. Zenith. *Reprint of the first edition.*
'This paperback edition 1984.' Published by Arrow Books. ISBN 0 09 933930 7. Paperback. Cover illustration from a painting of a city street by Christopher Sharples. Price £3.50.

1994. Alan Sutton Publishing Limited. *Reprint of the first edition, with an Introduction.*
'First published in this edition in the United Kingdom in 1994'. Pocket Classics series. ISBN 0 7509 0819 X. Paperback. Cover illustration from a painting 'An English Autumn' by Ford Madox Brown. Price £5.99.

Includes a six-page Introduction by Anne Williamson, mostly biographical, dated Summer 1994; repeated throughout the series.

A38 DONKEY BOY

When Phillip Maddison was born he was 'donkey baby' to the local children, on the grounds that he was thought to be covered in donkey hair and have very long ears; he might even have to be taken away 'because such a thing would not be allowed to grow up'. Some months later, when he was christened, he was seen to be normal, but in order to thrive he had had to be fed on ass's milk, so the name stuck. *Donkey Boy* covers his progress from the age of two to the age of ten, when he will have to go to secondary school. It is a period marked by exasperation in roughly equal measure for the father, mother and child.

1952. Macdonald & Co., (Publishers) Ltd. *First edition.*
i) 'First published in 1952 ...' Printed by Purnell and Sons. Pp.400. 203 x 129mm. Green cloth, goldstamped on the spine. Dust jacket white, printed in green, yellow, brown and black, with a design of children in a wood, fishing, by Broom Lynne, on the front and spine panels. Price 12/6. Published October 1952 (letter from Macdonald 1970). 10,000 copies.

ii) Reissue: as i) except: maroon linson. 200 x 126mm. Dust jacket white, printed in beige, brown and black, with a portrait of a figure in a cap designed by Berry, Fleming and Asssociates on the front panel and a full list of titles in the Chronicle on the back panel (as GV 1966ii). ISBN 0 356 10809 1 on the back flap. Price £2.75.
Sheets of the first edition in a new casing and dust jacket that cannot have been issued earlier than the 1970s when the ISBN system was introduced.

Contents:
- quotation from Pestalozzi on title-page;
- dedication 'To John Middleton Murry' (see D 1986a);
- 'Acknowledgment' for permission to quote from Kipling;
- text (pp.11–400) in 3 Parts and 30 Chapters with headings, ending 'November 1951 - March 1952, Devon', with owl device:

Part	1	Joy	chaps.	1–9
	2	Courage		10–19
	3	The Way		20–30

1962. A Panther Book. *New edition, revised, the second text.*

'Panther edition published 1962'. Published by Hamilton and Co. Printed by Petty and Sons. Panther 1410. Pp.352. 177 x 110mm. Paperback. Cover illustration of four figures, unattributed. Price 5/-.

'Dramatis Personae' with 70 names (many repeated from DL). Revisions noted on pp.37, 47, 137, 143, 244, 293, mostly minor, but p.47 has 'which led to the red flag of socialism and communism being unfurled' in place of 'which led to Socialism, and so to the terrors of class-warfare and Communism'; no date, place or owl device.

1970. A Panther Book. *Reprint of 1962; the second text.*
'Reprinted 1970'. Published by Panther Books. Panther 586 01410 1/2. Paperback. All-round cover illustration from a painting of a pastoral scene, unattributed. Price 7/-.

1984a. Macdonald & Co. *Reprint of the first edition.*
'This edition published in 1984 ...'. ISBN 0 356 01809 1. Purplish linson, goldstamped. Dust jacket white, printed in yellow and black, with detail from a painting 'Mornington Crescent 1911' by Spencer F. Gore on the front panel. Price £9.95.

1984b. Zenith. *Reprint of the first edition.*
'This paperback edition 1984'. Published by Arrow Books. ISBN 0 09 936820 X. Paperback. Cover illustration from a painting of St Paul's Cathedral, unattributed. Price £3.50.

1994. Alan Sutton Publishing Limited. *Reprint of the first edition.*
'First published in this edition in the United Kingdom in 1994'. Pocket Classics series. ISBN 0 7509 0818 1. Paperback. Cover illustration from a painting 'Too Old to Play' by Harry Brooker. Price £5.99.

Includes the Introduction by Anne Williamson as in DL 1994.

A39 TALES OF MOORLAND & ESTUARY

Tales of Moorland and Estuary is Williamson's fourth collection of short stories from his early years, in the style of *The Peregrine's Saga* and *The Old Stag*, and including 'The Crake' (said to have been 'filleted' by an alcoholic re-write man when it was published in *Esquire*, CNS p.305), the five stories incorporated in *Devon Holiday*, 'A Crown of Life' which had already appeared in several magazines, and some new material. When the pieces were collected again in *Collected Nature Stories* (A58) 'A

Winter's Tale' was put with *The Peregrine's Saga*, where it appears to have been overlooked for the 1981 edition of this title.

1953. Macdonald. *First edition; illustrated by Broom Lynne.*
'Published in 1953 by ...' Printed by Purnell and Sons. Pp.256. Illustrations, reckoned. 203 x 130mm. Green cloth, goldstamped on the spine. Dust jacket white, printed in grey-green, yellow and black, with illustrations by Broom Lynne (repeated from the book) on the front panel and an additional owl vignette on the spine panel. Price 12/6. Published March 1953 (letter from Macdonald 1970). 5000 copies.

Contents:
- dedication 'To Miss Imogen Mais' with a three-page letter of explanation and reminiscence headed 'Dear God-Daughter' and ending 'Always your devoted friend from the chimney corner. The Author. Windwhistle. Candlemas 1953';
- illustrations: 12 line drawings by Broom Lynne as headpieces to each story (two repeated on title-page and/or dust jacket) and the owl vignette;
- text (pp.7–256) with 12 titled stories, ending with owl device:

	Notes:
A Winter's Tale	
The Crake	begun in 1922, completed in 1951; (see *Esquire* 1952)
A Hero of the Sands	
Incidents of an Afternoon Walk	
The Heller	from DH, with minimal revision
The Yellow Boots	from DH 'The Story of the Poisoned Hounds', with minor revision
The White Stoat	from DH 'Swagdagger Crosses a Field', revised
The Dog who ate His Punishment	from DH, revised
The Maiden Salmon	from DH, with minor revisions
Trout	'added to' (in dedication); ? source
A Crown of Life	previously in *Nash's* 1935, and others

Where the Bright Waters Meet

1970a. A Panther Book. *New edition; illustrated.*
'Panther edition published 1970'. Published by Panther Books. Printed by Hunt Barnard and Co. Panther 586 13280 0. Pp.208. 178 x 111mm. Paperback. All-round cover photograph by Kenneth Scowen. Price 6/- (30p).

1970b. In *Collected Nature Stories* (A58, pp.17–31, 303–472). *New edition; revised; illustrated.*
The dedication and accompanying letter are omitted and replaced by a three-page 'Preface' giving a brief history of HW's early publications. All 12 titles are included (most lightly revised), with their headpieces, but for some reason 'A Winter's Tale' is placed with *The Peregrine's Saga*.

1981. Macdonald Futura Publishers. *New edition of the 1970b text; 11 titles; not illustrated.*
'First Futura edition 1981'. Photoset by Rowland Phototypesetting Ltd. ISBN 0 7088 2107 3. Pp.viii + 216. 177 x 107mm. Paperback. All-round cover illustration from a painting 'A Dell in Devonshire' by Miles Birket Foster. Price £1.75.

This has the Preface and 11 titles as in CNS, but without 'A Winter's Tale' (see above) or the illustrations.

A40 YOUNG PHILLIP MADDISON

The third book of the *Chronicle* is the story of Phillip's adolescence from the age of 11 to the time when he leaves school and faces the world of work. In *Dandelion Days* Williamson had already written at length on his experiences of the educational system and its defects as he saw them, so here the focus is on Phillip's extra-curricular life with its excitements, calamities, hormonal stirrings and disappointments, all magnified by an undercurrent of tension within the family.

1953. Macdonald & Co., (Publishers) Ltd. *First edition.*
'First Published in 1953 ...' Printed by Purnell and Sons. Pp.416. 203 x 128mm. Red linson, goldstamped on the spine. Dust jacket white, printed in blue, red, black and yellow with a design of kite-flying by Broom Lynne on the front and spine panels. Price 12/6. Published

November 1953 (letter from Macdonald 1970). 7500 copies.

Contents:
- quotations from Traditional Saying and Thomas Turney on title-page, Scout Law p.159, D.H. Lawrence p.224;
- dedication 'To John Heygate' (author and long-time friend; see B 1931a);
- text (pp.9–416) in 4 Parts and 30 Chapters with headings, ending 'October 1952 - August 1953, Devon', with owl device:

Part	1	An Edwardian Boyhood	chaps.	1–12
	2	Some Scouting for Boys		13–17
	3	The Wind's Will		18–24
	4	Wonderful to be Alive		25–30

1962. A Panther Book. *New edition, revised; the second text.*
'Panther edition published December 1962'. Published by Hamilton and Co. Printed by Petty and Sons. Panther 1455. Pp.352. 177 x 112mm. Paperback. Cover illustration of a female figure, unattributed. Price 5/-
.
'Dramatis Personae' with 95 names (including repeats from previously) grouped under headings ('Maddisons', 'Local Boys', etc). Revisions are confined to a few individual words, eg the quotation on p.241 line 36 where 'victims' becomes 'bastards'; no date, place, or owl device.

1984. Macdonald & Co. *Reprint of the first edition.*
'This edition published in 1984 ...' ISBN 0 356 01810 5. Purple linson, goldstamped on the spine. Dust jacket white, printed in lavender and black, with detail from a painting 'In a Garden' by Henry Tonks on the front panel. Price £9.95.

1985. Zenith. *Reprint of the first edition.*
'This paperback edition 1985'. Published by Arrow Books. ISBN 0 09 939540 1. Paperback. Cover illustration from a painting of crowds at the seaside, unattributed. Price £3.95.

1995. Alan Sutton Publishing Limited. *Reprint of the first edition.*
'First published in this edition in the United Kingdom in 1995'. Pocket Classics series. ISBN 0 7509 0956 0. Paperback. Cover illustration from

a painting 'One Man and His Dog' by Evariste Carpentier. Price £5.99. Includes the Introduction by Anne Williamson as in DL 1994.

A41 HOW DEAR IS LIFE

How Dear is Life is the first of five highly-rated and consecutive 'war books' that form a separate entity within the sequence of the *Chronicle*, with each book covering roughly one year of the 1914–18 war. When Williamson wrote *The Flax of Dream* he already knew that he wanted to write about the war at greater length than could be fitted into that work, and these volumes effectively fill the gap between the end of *Dandelion Days* and the start of *The Dream of Fair Women*.

For the young Phillip Maddison 1914 is not a good year. Trapped in his mundane job and tempted by the offer of a £4 grant and the prospect of summer camps paid for by the Army he joins the Territorials, only to find that this year they are going to be camping in Flanders.

1954. Macdonald: London. *First edition.*
'First published in 1954 ...' Printed by Purnell and Sons. Pp.336. 202 x 129mm. Blue cloth, goldstamped on the spine. Dust jacket white, printed in blue, black, yellow and red, with a design of flowers and a rifle by Broom Lynne on the front and spine panels; ads for three *Chronicle* titles and *Tales of Moorland and Estuary* on the back flap. Price 12/6. Published October 1954 (publication slip). 7500 copies.

Contents:
- quotation from Admiral Nelson on half-title, Shakespeare p. 9, Viscount French pp.143, 223, von Kluck p.223;
- dedication 'To C.M.D.W.' without whose help these novels might have remained unwritten' (the second Mrs Williamson);
- note concerning characters and events in the book and acknowledgement of sources;
- text (pp.11–335) in 3 Parts and 31 Chapters, with headings, ending 'August 1953 February 1954, Devon', with owl device:

Part	1	Wine Vaults Lane	chaps.	1–10
	2	The Great Adventure		11–18
	3	The Red Little, Dead Little Army		19–31

1963. A Panther Book. *New edition, revised; the second text.*

'Panther edition published March 1963'. Published by Hamilton and Co. Printed by Petty and Sons. Panther 1488. Pp.320. 177 x 110mm. Paperback. Cover illustration of a wounded soldier, unattributed. Price 5/-.

'Dramatis Personae' with 80 names (including repeats) grouped under headings, but with the first edition note concerning the characters omitted. On p.233 line 8 'beyond' is added to the end of the sentence; no date, place, or owl device.

1966. Macdonald: London. *Reprint of the first edition.*
'Second impression April 1966'. Green cloth, goldstamped. Dust jacket design as 1954 but with new blurb on the front flap and a list of titles in the *Chronicle* up to *The Phoenix Generation* on the back flap. Price 18s on flap, £2 on sticker.

1984. Macdonald. *Reprint of the first edition.*
'This edition published in 1984 ...' ISBN 0 356 01811 3. Peach linson, goldstamped. Dust jacket pink, printed in black, with illustration from a painting 'Thou Shalt Not Steal' by John S. Sargent on the front panel. Price £9.95.

A photo-reprint with print size reduced.

1985. Zenith. *Reprint of the first edition.*
'This paperback edition 1985'. Published by Arrow Books. ISBN 0 09 943820 8. Paperback. Cover illustration from a painting of a shell-hole and dead soldier, unattributed. Price £3.95.

A photo-reprint with print size reduced.

1995. Alan Sutton Publishing Limited. *Reprint of the first edition.*
'First published in this edition in the United Kingdom in 1995'. Pocket Classics series. ISBN 0 7509 0955 2. Paperback. Cover illustration from a painting 'A Letter' by Frank Dadd. Price £5.99.

A photo-reprint with print size reduced. Includes the Introduction by Anne Williamson as DL 1994.

A42 A FOX UNDER MY CLOAK

In *A Fox Under My Cloak* the narrative starts with the Christmas Day truce of 1914 (the event that permanently shaped Williamson's view of war) and ends in October 1915, after the Battle of Loos. In the preliminary Note and Dedication he says 'Many of the scenes in this novel are authentic, including those which are based on incidents recorded in the Official History of the Great War ... Each of the characters in this novel had an existence in the 1914–18 war, though not all necessarily acted or played their parts in the times and places mentioned in the story'. In the blurb on the dust jacket he adds 'There are no villains in the story - only human beings'.

1955. Macdonald: London. *First edition.*
'First published in 1955 ...' Printed by Purnell and Sons. Pp.416. 202 x 129mm. Fawn cloth, redstamped on the spine. Dust jacket white, printed in red, grey, black and brown, with a design of a war landscape by Broom Lynne on the front and spine panels; ads for preceding titles in the Chronicle on the back panel. Price 15/-, or with no price printed. Published November 1955 (bib note in 1962). 6000 copies.

Contents:
- quotation from *The Daily Trident* p.253;
- 'Author's Note and Dedication' acknowledging sources, with the dedication to 'Captain Douglas Bell, M.C.... old school-fellow and comrade-in-arms, wounded at Lone Tree during the battle of Loos, 1915' (see B 1929);
- text (pp.11–415) in 3 Parts and 30 Chapters with headings, ending 'February 1954 - May 1955, Devon', with owl device:

Part	I	Leytonstone Louts	chaps.	1–8
	2	Temporary Gentleman		9–16
	3	The Battle of Loos		17–30

1962. Macdonald: London. *Reprint of the first edition.*
'Second impression March 1962'. Red cloth, goldstamped. Dust jacket as 1955. Price 15/-, or with no price printed.

1963. A Panther Book. *New edition, revised, the second text.*
'Panther edition published August 1963'. Published by Hamilton and Co. Printed by Petty and Sons. Panther 1552. Pp.352. 178 x 110mm. Paperback. Cover illustration from a painting 'No-man's Land' by Chevalier Fortunino Matania. Price 5/-.

An Australian issue, cut to 172 x 108mm, has '7/6 Aust.' on the front cover.

'Dramatis Personae' with 52 names (including repeats) grouped under headings. Revisions are present on at least 28 pages with words or lines added, changed or omitted; on p.125 'The Prince Regent's Own Regiment' replaces 'The Middlesex Regiment', on p.136 'Commanding Officer' replaces 'Colonel' and on p.140 'Quarters' replaces 'Sergeant-major'; no date, place, or owl device.

1983. Chivers Press. *Reprint of the first edition.*
'This edition published by Chivers Press ... 1983'. A New Portway Book. ISBN 0 86220 522 0. Red linson. Dust jacket white, printed in red and black, with a note on the back panel 'This book has been produced and published on behalf of the London and Home Counties Branch of the Library Association. The title was selected from suggestions submitted by Librarians throughout the United Kingdom ...'

1985. Macdonald. *Reprint of the first edition.*
'This edition published in 1985 ...' ISBN 0 356 01812 1. Grey linson, goldstamped. Dust jacket pale grey, printed in black, with illustration from a painting 'A Street in Arras' by John Singer Sargent on the front panel. Price £12.95.

1996. Alan Sutton Publishing Limited. *Reprint of the first edition.*
'First published in this edition in the United Kingdom in 1996'. Pocket Classics series. ISBN 0 7509 1214 6. Paperback. Cover illustration from a painting 'The Triumph of Death' by Pieter Brueghel the Elder. Price £6.99.

Includes the Introduction by Anne Williamson as in DL 1994.

A43 THE GOLDEN VIRGIN

It is now the second year of the war and Phillip Maddison is in England recovering from the effects of the first year, when his leave is interrupted by preparations for the battle of the Somme. In the town of Albert a prominent statue of the Madonna and Child (the 'Golden Virgin' of the title) has been damaged by artillery and is leaning precariously, but has not actually collapsed. For the troops and the population it has become a symbol of the uncertainty and suspense of the war and the legend grows that not until it finally falls will the war end.

1957. Macdonald: London. *First edition.*
'First published in 1957 ...' Printed by Purnell and Sons. Pp.448. 202 x
129mm. Red cloth, goldstamped on the spine. Dust jacket white,
printed in red, black, blue and yellow, with a design of a leaning statue
by Broom Lynne on the front and spine panels; ads for preceding titles
in the Chronicle on the back panel; some with a 'Daily Mail Book of the
Month' wraparound. Price 16/-, or with no price printed. Published
September 1957 (review slip). 6500 copies.

Contents:
- quotation from Father Aloysius on title-page, Margot Asquith and
Shakespeare p.10;
- dedication 'To Richard Aldington' (see *Aylesford Review* 1963);
- 'Acknowledgement' of permission to quote from 'Into Battle' by Capt.
Julian Grenfell;
- text (pp.11–448) in 3 Parts and 28 Chapters with headings, followed by
'L'Envoi', and ending 'Devon - Suffolk. January 1956 - January 1957',
with owl device:

Part	1	The Wild Boy	chaps.	1–12
	2	The Somme		13–19
	3	The Quiet Boy		20–28

1961. Macdonald: London. *Reprint of the first edition; revised; the second
text.*
'Second impression May 1961'. Red cloth, goldstamped. Dust jacket
design as 1957, but with press reviews on the back flap. Price 16/-.
    A passage of 16 lines on p.296 relating to the Ulster Division is
rewritten.

1963. A Panther Book. *New edition, with a further revision; the third text.*
'Panther edition published October 1963'. Published by Hamilton and
Co. Printed by Petty and Sons. Panther 1586. Pp.384. 177 x 110mm.
Paperback. All-round cover illustration of a trench with wounded men
by Chevalier Fortunino Matania. Price 5/-.
    'Dramatis Personae' with 38 names (including repeats) grouped
under headings. The only change noted from the 1961 text is on p.225
where the response of the German prisoner is given as 'Ich verweigere

die Aussage!' instead of 'Bitte! Nicht sprechen!'; no date, place, or owl device.

1966. Macdonald: London. *Reprint of 1961; the second text.*
i) 'Third impression January 1966'. Red cloth. Dust jacket as 1957, but with new blurb on the flaps and a list of titles in the *Chronicle* up to *The Phoenix Generation* on the back panel. Price 18/- on flap, £2 on sticker.

ii) Reissue: as i) except: light green linson. Dust jacket white, printed in green, yellow and black, with a portrait of a soldier designed by Berry Fleming and Associates on the front panel and a full list of titles in the *Chronicle* on the back panel (as DB 1952ii); ISBN 0 356 01813 X on the back flap. Price £2.75 on flap, £4.95 on sticker.
   Sheets of the third impression in a new casing and dust jacket that cannot have been issued earlier than the 1970s when the ISBN system was introduced.

1984. Macdonald. *Reprint of 1961; the second text.*
'This edition published in 1984 ...' ISBN 0-356-01813-X. Pale purplish linson. Dust jacket white, printed in yellow and black, with illustration from a painting 'The Household Brigade Passing to the Ypres Salient' by William Orpen on the front panel. Price £9.95.

1996. Alan Sutton Publishing Limited. *Reprint of 1961, the second text.*
'First published in this edition in the United Kingdom in 1996'. Pocket Classics series. ISBN 0 7509 1215 4. Paperback. Cover illustration from a painting 'The Battle of the Somme' by Richard Caton Woodville. Price £6.99.
   Includes the Introduction by Anne Williamson as in DL 1994.

A44 A CLEAR WATER STREAM

When Williamson moved to Shallowford Cottage in 1929 the lease included the rights to a good stretch of fishing on a Devon stream, the River Bray. Nearly 30 years later, in *A Clear Water Stream*, he recalls the pleasures he had from exploring, stocking and learning about the river, along with memories of fishing in Canada in 1930, the Hebrides in 1931, and Georgia (USA) in 1934 - the latter including some of the material he had already published in *The Linhay on the Downs* (A20).

In content and style the book belongs with *The Children of Shallowford* and *Goodbye West Country* and the reminiscence would have provided a welcome relief from the intensity of writing the war books. It was the only new, full-length book that he wrote while engaged on the *Chronicle* and the last of his books to be published by Faber.

1958. Faber and Faber. *First edition.*
'First published in Mcmlviii'. Printed by Western Printing Services. Pp.232. 206 x 131mm. Blue cloth, whitestamped on the spine. Dust jacket blue-green, printed in dark green, black and red (with the same general design as COS 1959). Price 15/-. Published June 1958 (letter from Faber 1966). 5000 copies.

Contents:
- dedication 'To Harry and Mollie Stevenson Balfour';
- text (pp.11–229) in 17 sections, numbered and titled, ending 'April - September 1957, Devon.', with owl device:

1   Fishing Cottage
2   The Boy Who Loved Fishing
3   I Survey the River
4   I Visit a Fish Farm, and Meet Poachers
5   Dark Months
6   The Judge's Warning
7   I Make a Hatchery
8   At Last, a Dry-fly Purist!
9   Canadian Backwoodsman
10 I Stare at Water and Make Dams
11 Water Play
12 Spate
13 I Behold the Hebrides
14 Nog & Co.
15 Migration
16 In the Deep South — consists largely of passages from 'Southern Sun' (LOD pp.279–99) rearranged and rewritten
17 'All Things Linked are' — includes passages from 'Southern Sun' and 'To England' (LOD pp.299–302, 314–5)

1959a. The Country Book Club. *Reprint of the first edition.*
'This Country Book Club edition was produced in 1959 for sale to its members only ...' Blue linson. Dust jacket white, printed in blue-green.

1959b. Ives Washburn, Inc. New York. *American reprint of the first edition.*
'First published in the United States in 1959'. LCCCN 59–9366. Pp.232. 209 x 134mm. Blue cloth, blackstamped on the spine. Dust jacket white, printed in blue, green and black. Price $3.50.
   No date, place, or owl device.

1975. Macdonald and Jane's. *Reprint of the first edition, with revisions; illustrated.*
'This new revised, illustrated edition published in 1975 ...' ISBN 0 356 08202 4. Pp.232. Illustrations, reckoned. Green linson, goldstamped on the spine. Dust jacket white, printed in black and green, with a colour illustration by Peter Cross.
   The dedication is now 'To Loetitia who said "Thank you for giving me such beautiful children"'. Illustrations comprise 17 line drawings as headpieces by Peter Cross. Occasional words are changed or added on pp.30, 33, 63 (two new lines), 195, 216.

Foreign-language edition:
1965. *Der Fluss Vor Meinem Haus.* Verlag Paul Parey. Hamburg und Berlin, 1965. Translated from the English by Burkhard W. Julkenback. Includes three photographs taken from GWC and two from COS.

A45 LOVE AND THE LOVELESS A Soldier's Tale

At the beginning of *Love and the Loveless* it is the autumn of 1916 and Phillip Maddison is training for a new posting and preparing to return to France for his fourth 'adventure', but the war on the Western Front is bogged down in attacks and counter-attacks on the Hindenberg Line, the Messines Ridge and Passchendaele. At Etaples the troops are discontented, disillusioned and mutinous, but by the end of the year they have dug themselves in for yet another winter.

1958. Macdonald: London. *First edition.*
'First published in 1958'. Printed by Purnell and Sons. Pp.384. 204 x

129mm. Green cloth, goldstamped on the spine. Dust jacket white, printed in red, green and black, with a design of a handshake over no-man's-land by Broom Lynne on the front and spine panels; ads for preceding titles in the *Chronicle* on the back panel. Price 16/- on flap, 18/- on a label. Published October 1958 (letter from Macdonald 1970). 7000 copies.

Contents:
- explanatory note (2 paragraphs) on half-title;
- quotation from 'Sir Orfeo' on title-page;
- dedication to 'Sir John Squire, J.C. Squire & Jack Squire ...';
- text (pp.11–384) in 4 Parts and 21 Chapters with headings, ending 'Devon. May 1957 - May 1958', with owl device:

Part	1	The Black Prince	chaps.	1–5
	2	'All Weather Jack' Hobart		6–8
	3	'Sharpshooter' Downham		9–15
	4	'Spectre' West		16–21

1963. A Panther Book. *New edition, revised; the second text.*
'Panther edition published December 1963'. Published by Hamilton and Co. Printed by Petty and Sons. Panther 1611. Pp.352. 177 x 110mm. Paperback. All-round cover illustration from 'How the three Gunners of 'L' Battery RHA won their V.C.' by Chevalier Fortunino Matania. Price 5/-.

The explanatory note is revised and the dedication reduced 'To J.C. Squire' with no text. 'Dramatis Personae' with 46 names (mostly new) grouped under headings. Revisions noted on p.174 where six words are added to line 39 and 'France' replaces 'Belgium' in the last line, and to some German words on pp.251, 267, 301, 305; no date, place, or owl device.

1974. Cedric Chivers. *Reprint of the first edition.*
'This edition published ... by arrangement with the copyright holder at the request of the London and Home Counties Branch of the Library Association 1974'. ISBN 0 85594 981 3. Dust jacket with an all-round design from a painting of a barren battlefield, unattributed. Price £2.60 (£1.95 to members).

1984. Macdonald. *Reprint of the first edition.*

'This edition published in 1984 ...' ISBN 0 356 01814 8. Blue linson. Dust jacket white, printed in mauve and black, with illustration from a painting 'Epehy' by Haydn R. Mackey on the front panel. Price £9.95. The explanatory note is omitted.

1997. Sutton Publishing. *Reprint of the first edition.*
'First published in this edition in the United Kingdom in 1997'. Pocket Classics series. ISBN 0 7509 1471 8. Paperback. Cover illustrations from a painting 'The Triumph of Death' by Pieter Brueghel the Elder. Price £6.99.

No explanatory note, but includes the Introduction by Anne Williamson as in DL 1994.

A46 THE HENRY WILLIAMSON ANIMAL SAGA

The HW Animal Saga is a more significant volume than its conventional omnibus format might suggest as it includes a new text of *Tarka* (the fifth), a new text of *Salar* (the second), two extended short stories ('The Epic of Brock the Badger' and 'Chakchek the Peregrine') both with some revisions, and new elements written to introduce the book as a whole and each individual title. In the general Foreword Williamson says that these works represent 'the four chief epics of the natural world of the first half of my life ... for which four special pieces have been written, whereby the reader is led into the author's realm of river, sea, earth and air.'

1960a. Macdonald. *First edition.*
'This edition first published in 1960 by ...' Printed by Purnell and Sons. Pp.480. 223 x 138mm. Fawn cloth, with green panel, goldstamped, on the spine. Dust jacket white, printed in green, black and brown, with decorations from the title-page repeated on the front panel and all four titles listed on the front and spine panels; photograph of Williamson outside Skirr Cottage, unattributed, on the back panel; ads for the *Chronicle* up to LOL on the back flap. Price 21/-. Published February 1960 (letter from Macdonald 1970). 5000 copies.

Contents:
- title-page decorations and drawings of fauna by Stein;
- 'Foreword' signed 'H.W. Devon, 1959', introducing the four titles:

	Notes:
Tarka the Otter	(pp.11–199), the fifth text, with additional elements
dedication	now 'To the Memory of William Henry Rogers
The Gentleman's River	new text, on the genesis and writing of the book (linked to *Modern Man* 1952; differs from *Country Life* 1952)
The First Year	
The Last Year	
Apologia pro verba mea	a response to criticism of his use of dialect terms (see 'Provincialisms' in LL and *London Mercury* 1928)
Salar the Salmon	(pp.201–375), the second text, with additional elements
dedication	as previously
The Sun in Taurus	new text, on river pollution
Tideways	
Spring Spate	
Summer River	
Winter Star-Stream	
Epigraph, A Personal Note	new text, on the writing and publication of the book
The Epic of Brock the Badger	(pp.377–417), from OS 1933, with occasional revision
(introduction)	new text
1	the opening pages and part I of 1933
2–3	parts II–III of 1933
Chakchek the Peregrine	(pp.419–77), 'The Peregrine's Saga' from PS 1934, with occasional revision
(introduction)	new text,
1–5	parts I–V of 1934, with owl device p.478.

1960b. Macdonald. *Reprint of the first edition.*
'Second impression April 1960'. Fawn cloth, green panel, goldstamped,

on the spine.

1963. Macdonald. *Reprint of the first edition.*
'Third impression May 1963'. Fawn cloth, green panel, goldstamped, on the spine. Dust jacket design as 1960a but with ads for the *Chronicle* up to PD on the back flap.

1968. Macdonald. *Reprint of the first edition.*
'Fourth impression 1968'. SBN 256 01736 2. Fawn cloth, green panel, goldstamped, on the spine. Dust jacket now with 'Tarka the Otter and others including Salar the Salmon' on the front and spine panels; list of *Chronicle* titles up to LBS on the back flap. Price 30/-.

1974. Book Club Associates. *Reprint of the first edition.*
'This edition published 1974 ...' Orange linson, goldstamped on the spine. Dust jacket design as 1968 but with 'BCA' at the foot of the spine panel and quotes from reviews of HWAS in place of titles on the back flap.

1975. Book Club Associates. *Reprint of the first edition.*
'This edition published 1975 ...' Brown linson, goldstamped on the spine. Dust jacket as 1974.

1978. Book Club Associates. *Reprint of the first edition.*
'Seventh impression 1978'. ISBN 0 356 10736 2. 240 x 150mm. Light grey paper boards. Dust jacket white, printed in brown and black, designed by David Fordham, with a colour photograph of an otter by Steve Downer (from the film) on the front panel and of the author on the back panel.

A47 SOME NATURE WRITERS AND CIVILIZATION

The text of The Wedmore Memorial Lecture that Williamson had been invited to give as a member of The Royal Society of Literature, in London on 9 October 1958. Reprinted with its 'Postscript' from the Society's transactions *Essays by Divers Hands* (B 1960b).

[1960]. No publisher. *Reprint from the first edition.*
No date. 'Reprinted from Essays by Divers Hands Volume XXX' on the

front cover, with title and author. Printed at the University Press, Oxford. Pp.18. 215 x 140mm. Blue paper wrappers, printed in black; stapled. For distribution by the author [? 100 copies].

Contents:
- note on the Wedmore Memorial Lecture
- text (pp.1–18) mostly concerning Richard Jefferies and W.H. Hudson.

A48 A TEST TO DESTRUCTION

In the last of the 'war books' it is 1918 and for civilians and combatants war fatigue has set in. Phillip Maddison has been declared unfit for the front line but is determined to get back to France for a fifth time, though he does not expect to survive. When he does he is faced with the problem of what to do with the rest of his life ('No-Man's-Land in Civvy Street' as Williamson describes it in Part 5) and wonders whether he might become a writer.

1960. Macdonald: London. *First edition.*
'First published in 1960'. Printed by Purnell and Sons. Pp.464. 203 x 130mm. Red cloth, silverstamped on the spine. Dust jacket white, printed in red and black, with a design of a fox (insignia of the 5th Army) and one pip (? by Broom Lynne) on the spine panel and a reproduction of an etching presented to Williamson by C.R.W. Nevinson on the back panel. Price 18/6. Published November 1960 (letter from Macdonald 1970). 7000 copies.

Contents:
- quotation from Alfred Lord Tennyson on title-page, Lord Moran p.209, Augustus Williamson p.313, G.K. Chesterton p.379;
- dedication 'To George D Painter' (literary critic);
- 'Acknowledgements' for permission to quote;
- text (pp.11–461) in 5 Parts and 23 Chapters with headings, ending 'November 1958 - March 1960, Devon' with owl device:

Part	1	Anticipation	chaps.	1–5
	2	Action		6–11
	3	Tension		12–16
	4	The Lost Kingdom		17–20

5   No-Man's-Land in Civvy Street   21–23

1964. A Panther Book. *New edition, revised; the second text.*
'Panther edition published February 1964'. Published by Hamilton and
Co. Printed by Petty and Sons. Panther 1632. Pp.384. 178 x 110mm.
Paperback. Cover illustration of a trench under gas attack by Chevalier
Fortunino Matania. Price 5/-.
    'Dramatis Personae' with 21 names, grouped under headings.
German words are corrected or changed on pp.7, 47, 59, 81, 83, 93, 95,
107, 116, 155; no date, place, or owl device.

1980. Chivers Press. *Reprint of the first edition.*
'This edition published by ... at the request of the London and Home
Counties Branch of the Library Association 1980'. A New Portway
Book. ISBN 0 86220 503 4. Red linson. Dust jacket white, printed in
orange, green and black, designed by Redwood Burn Limited.
    A photo-reprint with print size enlarged.

1985. Macdonald. *Reprint of the first edition.*
'This edition published in 1985 ...' ISBN 0 356 01816 4. Grey-brown
linson. Dust jacket white, printed in yellow and black, with illustration
from a painting 'Outside Charing Cross Station, Casualties from the
battle of the Somme arriving in London 1916' by J. Hodgson Lobley on
the front panel. Price £12.95.

1997. Sutton Publishing. *Reprint of the first edition.*
'First published in this edition in the United Kingdom in 1997'. Pocket
Classics series. ISBN 0 7509 1470 X. Paperback. Cover illustration from
a painting 'The Reverend Harold Battiscombe at his desk' by Harold
John Wilde Gilman. Price £6.99.
    Includes the Introduction by Anne Williamson as in DL 1994.

A49 IN THE WOODS

In the Woods is a short account of an interlude in 1941 when Williamson
returned to Georgeham under wartime travel restrictions with Bert
Close, 'Poppy', a tractor and a circular saw, to clear some woodland.
    From the late 1950s he had shared a strong personal and literary
friendship with the Reverend Brocard Sewell, who edited *The Aylesford*

Review for the English Carmelites, and when the journal ran into financial difficulties the book was offered to them for publication, with the proceeds going to the Order. Later it was incorporated into *Lucifer Before Sunrise* (A55) as chapters 6–8, 'Woodland Idyll'.

1960. St Albert's Press. *First edition.*
i) 'One thousand copies have been printed at St Albert's Press, Llandeilo, in the Autumn of 1960 and the type distributed. Numbers 1–50, signed by the author, are bound in cloth boards; numbers 50–1000 in paper covers.This copy is number ...' followed by the number in ink on p.56. Pp.viii + 58 (the front 'endpaper' is part of the gathering). 184 x 123mm. Pale blue paper-covered card covers, printed in black on the front; perfect-bound. Dust jacket in the same colour as the covers, printed in black, dated 1961, in two variants which appear to have been matched to the books randomly and prior to publication: a) with a vignette from Thomas Bewick on the front panel and a note concerning the title and number of copies on the back, and b) with different lettering and without the Bewick vignette. Published [January] 1961. Price 10/6. 950 copies.

ii) Signed issue: as i) except: the number on p.56 is followed by the author's signature in ink. 193 x 125. Cream paper-covered boards, backed in green buckram, goldstamped. Price 42/-. 50 copies, plus 10 bound and signed but not numbered, marked 'Out of Series'.

Contents: text (pp.l-54) in 11 sections, numbered but unheaded, ending 'Stiffkey, Norfolk, 1943', with owl device on p.57.

A50 THE INNOCENT MOON

In a fine precis of *The Innocent Moon* quoted on the cover of the Panther edition 1965 Sid Chaplin says: 'The young officer is foraging for a living and looking for the ideal lover, and being ham-fisted at both. He peddles advertising space on commission, works up or invents trivialities for a national newspaper, and finally escapes to a cottage in Devon ...'

This is also, of course, the story of *The Sun in the Sands* (A30) which is used to form the bulk of *The Innocent Moon* but with the text rewritten in the third person so that the story is no longer that of Henry

Williamson but of Phillip Maddison.

1961. Macdonald: London. *First edition.*
'Published in 1961 ...' Printed by Purnell and Sons, Paulton and London. Pp.416. 202 x 129mm. Orange-red cloth, silverstamped on the spine. Dust jacket white, printed in red, blue, purple, yellow and black, with a design of two figures in a landscape [by Broom Lynne] on the front and spine panels. Price 18/-. Published October 1961 (letter from Macdonald 1970). 7500 copies.

Contents:
- quotation from William Blake p.7, Algernon Charles Swinburne p.133, Edgar Allan Poe p.227, Richard Jefferies p.357;
- dedication 'To William Kean Seymour' (who had nominated HW for membership of the Royal Society of Literature);
- text (pp.9–415) in 4 Parts and 21 Chapters with headings, ending 'March 1934 - March 1961, Florida - Devon', with owl device:

Part 1	Spica Virginis	chaps.	1–6
2	Julian		7–11, (from SIS chaps. 1–14)
3	Annabelle		12–18, (from SIS chaps. 15–26)
4	Barley		19–21, (from SIS chaps. 27–39)

1965. A Panther Book. *New edition, revised; the second text.*
'Panther edition published May 1965'. Published by Panther Books. Printed by Petty and Sons. Panther 1844. Pp.384. 177 x 110mm. Paperback. Cover illustrations from the Radio Times Hulton Picture Library. Price 5/-.
    'Dramatis Personae' with 21 names, grouped under headings. In the text occasional words are omitted or changed on pp.81, 214, 329, 342, with 'Daddy overworks all the time' added on p.381 line 29; no owl device.

1985. Macdonald. *Reprint of the first edition.*
'This edition published in 1985'. ISBN 0 356 01817 2. Black linson. Dust jacket white, printed in pale grey and black, with illustration from a painting 'In the Field' by Dame Laura Knight on the front panel. Price £12.95.

1998. Sutton Publishing. *Reprint of the first edition.*

'First published in this edition in the United Kingdom in 1998'. Pocket Classics series. ISBN 0 7509 1977 9. Paperback. Cover illustration from a painting 'Indecision' by Charles Sillem Lidderdale. Price £7.99.

Includes the Introduction by Anne Williamson as in DL 1994.

A51 IT WAS THE NIGHTINGALE

It is the mid-1920s. Phillip Maddison is married and looking to a better future but his fortunes alternate between gain and loss, separation and union, heartache and heartease. He writes bits and pieces about birds and animals for the magazines, is planning a book about an otter and starts a novel (*The Flax of Dream* in Williamson's life) but these will not support a family, so he may have to think about farming.

1962. Macdonald. *First edition.*
'First published in 1962 ...' Printed by Purnell and Sons. Pp.360. 202 x 128mm. Red cloth, goldstamped on the spine. Dust jacket printed in grey, yellow, red and black, with a design of a 'reaping hook severing a rose bud from the stem' (see p.71), probably by Broom Lynne, on the front and spine panels. Price 18/-. Published September 1962 (review slip). [7500] copies.

Contents:
- quotation from Roy Campbell on title-page, Lord Byron p.9, anon p.77, 'Adrian Copleston' p.191, Elizabeth Barrett Browning p.269;
- dedication 'To Eric and Kathleen Watkins';
- text (pp.9–357) in 5 Parts and 21 Chapters with headings, ending 'Journalized: Artois - Somme, 1924–1925. Drafted: Florida, 1934. Recast and rewritten: Devon, March 1961–July 1962', with owl device:

Part	1	Lark and Nightingale	chaps.	1–4
	2	Pilgrimage		5–7
	3	At the Mules'		8–11
	4	Down Close		12– 16
	5	Lucy		17–21

1965. A Panther Book. *New edition, revised; the second text.*
'Panther edition published October 1965'. Published by Panther Books. Printed by Hunt Barnhard and Co. Panther 1932. Pp.320. 177 x 110mm.

Paperback. Cover illustrations from the Radio Times-Hulton Picture Library and *The Old Motor*. Price 5/-.

'Dramatis Personae' with 24 names, grouped under headings. Words are changed or omitted on pp.63, 68, 102, 161, and four lines rewritten on p.313; no date, place, or owl device.

1985. Macdonald. *Reprint of the first edition.*
'This edition published in 1985 ...' ISBN 0 356 01818 0. Black linson. Dust jacket printed in deep mauve, with illustration from a painting 'A Cottage Door' by David Woodlock on the front panel. Price £12.95.

1998. Sutton Publishing. *Reprint of the first edition.*
'First published in this edition in the United Kingdom in 1998'. Pocket Classics series. ISBN 0 7509 1978 7. Paperback. Cover illustration from a painting 'Peeling Vegetables' by Fanny Fildes. Price £7.99.

Includes the Introduction by Anne Williamson as in DL 1994.

A52 THE POWER OF THE DEAD

Phillip Maddison is now in his thirties and working a farm that has a trout stream. On the domestic front his family is expanding, while on the literary side he wins a prize with a book about an otter and gets a generous advance for a book about a trout.

In Williamson's parallel existence that just about covers *The Story of a Norfolk Farm*, *A Clear Water Stream*, *The Children of Shallowford*, *Tarka the Otter* and *Salar the Salmon*.

1963. Macdonald. *First edition.*
'First published in 1963 ...' Printed by Purnell and Sons. Pp.368. 203 x 129mm. Red cloth, goldstamped on the spine. Dust jacket printed in green, yellow and black, with the title designed by 'BL' (Broom Lynne). Price 18/-. Published October 1963 (letter from Macdonald 1970). 7500 copies.

Contents:
- quotation from J.P. Stern on title-page, Algernon Charles Swinburne p.9;
- dedication 'To Maurice Wiggin' (author);
- text (pp.11–365) in 3 Parts and 16 Chapters with headings, ending

'Christmas 1961 - Midsummer 1963, Devon', with owl device:

Part	1	A Drive to Perfection	chaps.	1–5
	2	The Solitary Summer		6–10
	3	Straws in the Wind		11–16

1966. A Panther Book. *New edition, revised; the second text.*
'Panther edition published 1966'. Published by Panther Books. Printed by Cox and Wyman. Panther 2164. Pp.320. 177 x 111mm. Paperback. Cover photograph, unattributed. Price 5/-.

'Dramatis Personae' with 21 names, grouped under headings. Two words on p.69 and one on p.149 are spelt differently but no other changes noted; ends with the date and place but no owl device.

1985. Macdonald. *Reprint of the first edition.*
'This edition published in 1985 ...' ISBN 0 356 01830 X. Brown linson. Dust jacket printed in pale yellow and black, with illustration from a painting 'The Mowers' by Sir George Clausen on the front panel. Price £12.95.

1999. Sutton Publishing. *Reprint of the first edition.*
'First published in this edition in the United Kingdom in 1999'. Pocket Classics series. ISBN 0 7509 2153 6. Paperback. Cover illustration from a painting 'A Devonshire Idyll' by James Clarke Hook. Price £7.99.

Includes the Introduction by Anne Williamson as in DL 1994.

A53 THE PHOENIX GENERATION

In *The Phoenix Generation* Williamson covers the decade from 1929–39, years that saw the election of a Labour Government, economic depression, Oswald Mosley's 'Alternative', and the build-up to another war. Phillip Maddison has given up farming but is fathering children, having affairs, and writing, with enough time to attend one of Hitler's Nuremberg rallies (as in *Goodbye West Country*). Needing somewhere for the family to live he buys a derelict farm, on the coast of the North Sea.

1965. Macdonald: London. *First edition.*
'First published in 1965 ...' Printed by Purnell and Sons. Pp.392. 204 x

129mm. Red linson, goldstamped on the spine. Dust jacket white, printed in red, green and black, with a design of a phoenix (? by Broom Lynne) on the front panel. Price 25/- on flap, £2 on sticker. Published October 1965 (letter from Macdonald 1970). 7500 copies.

Contents:
- quotation from John Donne on title-page;
- text (pp.9–385) in 3 Parts and 20 Chapters with headings, ending with 'Journalised: Devon 1935 - Norfolk 1941. Drafted: Devon 1952–56. Recast and rewritten: Devon-Sussex-London 1964–5', with owl device:

Part	1	Felicity	chaps.	1–4
	2	Melissa		5–10
	3	Waifs and Strays		11–20

1967. A Panther Book. *New edition, revised; the second text.*
'Panther edition published 1967'. Published by Panther Books. Printed by Cox and Wyman. Panther 23437. Pp.384. 177 x 112mm. Paperback. Cover photographs, unattributed. Price 61/-.
'Dramatis Personae' with 25 names in two groups. On p.143 line 14 'in Britain' is omitted, and on p.145 line 30 'St. Luke's' replaces 'St. Martin's'; on p.301 line 1 'Birkin Hereward' is corrected to 'Hereward Birkin'; no date, place or owl device.

1985. Macdonald. *Reprint of the first edition.*
'This edition published in 1985 ...' ISBN 0 356 01743 5. Green linson. Dust jacket printed in green and black, with illustration from a painting 'The Cow Shed' by Jean-Louis Van Kuyck on the front panel. Price £12.95.

1999. Sutton Publishing. *Reprint of the first edition.*
'First published in this edition in the United Kingdom in 1999'. Pocket Classics series. ISBN 0 7509 2152 8. Paperback. Cover illustration from a painting 'Garden Flowers' by Theo van Rysselberghe. Price £7.99.
Includes the Introduction by Anne Williamson as in DL 1994; no owl device.

A54 A SOLITARY WAR

A *Solitary War* starts where *The Story of a Norfolk Farm* ended, in September 1939. War has been declared and within a few months there will be bombers over the coast of East Anglia but this time Phillip Maddison is not fighting the foreign hordes. As he struggles to make his new farm productive his battles are with obduracy, prejudice, officialdom and the elemental forces of Nature.

1966. Macdonald: London. *First edition.*
'First published in 1966 ...' Printed by Purnell and Sons. Pp.384. 203 x 130mm. Red linson, goldstamped on the spine. Dust jacket printed in grey, blue, red and black, with designs of a Union Jack and swastika combined on the front panel and a British roundel and swastika, probably by Broom Lynne, on the spine panel. Price 25/- on flap, £2 on sticker. Published September 1966 (letter from Macdonald 1970). 7500 copies.

Contents:
- quotation from St. Augustine on title-page, Edith Sitwell p.67;
- dedication 'To Oswald and Diana Mosley in friendship';
- text (pp.11–375) in 4 Parts and 25 Chapters with headings, ending 'Journalised: Norfolk - Devon 1941. Novelised: 1949–1957 - Devon. Recast: Devon-London 1965', with owl device:

Part	1	The Bad Lands	chaps.	1-4
	2	Sisyphus & Co.		5–16
	3	Immortal Corn		17–21
	4	Blitzkreig		22–25

1969. A Panther Book. *New edition.*
'Panther edition published 1969'. Published by Panther Books. Printed by Cox and Wyman. No.586 02844 7. Pp.368. 176 x 110mm. Paperback. Cover photograph by Jozef Gross. Price 7/-.
    'Dramatis Personae' with 14 names in two groups. Spelling and hyphenation are altered in places but no textual changes are noted; no date, place or owl device.

1985. Macdonald. *Reprint of the first edition.*
'This edition published in 1985 ...' ISBN 0 356 01926 8. Grey-brown

linson. Dust jacket brownish, printed in black, with illustration from a painting 'The Kitchen Garden' by B.J. de Hoog on the front panel; 'Macdonald' imprint absent from the foot of the spine panel in all copies seen to date. Price £12.95.

A photo-reprint with print size reduced.

1999. Sutton Publishing. *Reprint of the first edition.*
'First published in this edition in the United kingdom in 1999'. Pocket Classics series. ISBN 0 7509 2157 9. Paperback. Cover illustration from a painting 'A Golden Harvest' by George Turner. Price £7.99.

A photo-reprint with print size as 1985. Includes the Introduction by Anne Williamson as in DL 1994; no date, place or owl device.

A55 LUCIFER BEFORE SUNRISE

The penultimate book of the *Chronicle* is the story of Phillip Maddison's farming from the autumn of 1940 to the end of the Second World War. It was originally written during the war for separate publication as a sequel to *The Story of a Norfolk Farm* but was then formed into *Lucifer Before Sunrise*, which was completed out of sequence. Chapters 6–8 ('Woodland Idyll') are a reworked version of *In the Woods* (A49), the fragment of autobiography that Williamson published for the Carmelites in 1960. In chapter 36 (pp.511–12) for the first time in the whole series he writes in the first person.

1967. Macdonald: London. *First edition.*
'First published in 1967 ...' Printed by Purnell and Sons. Pp.520. 203 x 128mm. Black linson, goldstamped on the spine. Dust jacket printed in black, red and green with an arrow design by Broom Lynne. Price 35/- on flap, £2 on sticker. Published October 1967 (letter from Macdonald 1970). 7000 copies.

A variant jacket has both the author's name and arrow in yellow on the spine panel (instead of white and red) but the same price.

Contents:
- quotations from unknown and Thomas Hardy on title-page, Adolph Hitler and Winston Churchill p.11, Richard Jefferies p.80, Jan Smuts p.125, Dag Hammerskjold p.126, Lord Moran p.226, Thomas Callander pp.278, 280, 460, Catullus p.364, Hotspur p.459;

- dedication 'To Father Brocard Sewell of Aylesford Priory, Kent' (see A49, B 1960a);
- 'Acknowledgements' for permission to quote;
- text (pp.15–515) in 2 Books, 7 Parts and 36 Chapters with headings, ending '1941–1967, Norfolk - Devon', with owl device:

Book 1 The Island Fortress
Part	1	Winter - Spring 1941	chaps.	1–5
	2	Woodland Idyll		6–8
	3	The Dark and Abysm of Time		9–14
	4	'A Cad's War'		15–18

Book 2 The Malevolent Glint
Part	1	Crux	chaps.	19–24
	2	'Still Are Thy Pleasant Voices'		25–31
	3	Death of the Doppelganger		32–36

1985. Macdonald. *Reprint of the first edition.*
'This edition published in 1985 ...' ISBN 0 356 01943 8. Turquoise linson. Dust jacket printed in blue and black, with illustration from a painting 'Southern England, Spitfires attacking flying bombs, 1944', unattributed, on the front panel. Price £12.95.
A photo-reprint with print size reduced.

1999. Sutton Publishing. *Reprint of the first edition.*
'First published in this edition in the United Kingdom in 1999'. Pocket Classics series. ISBN 0 7509 2156 0. Paperback. Cover illustration from a painting 'In the Farmyard' by Eugene Joors. Price £7.99.
A photo-reprint with print size as 1985. 'Acknowledgements' omitted; includes the Introduction by Anne Williamson as in DL 1994.

A56 THE GALE OF THE WORLD

For the last volume of the *Chronicle* Williamson creates a dramatic climax based on the actual storm and flood that devastated the North Devon coastal town of Lynmouth on the night of Friday 15th August 1952. But the climax is not an ending: having survived the cataclysm Phillip Maddison feels able to begin the chronicle of his life - the very chronicle that Williamson has just finished. In a brief postscript headed

'L'Envoi' Williamson describes his emotions on completing the work that had been twenty years in the thinking and another twenty in the making.

1969. Macdonald: London. *First edition.*
i) First state (unpublished): 'First published in 1969 ...' Printed by Tonbridge Printers. SBN 356 02456 3. Pp.368. 202 x 128mm. Black linson, goldstamped on the spine. Dust jacket printed in brown, black, red and white, with a design of a glider against an abstract landscape by Broom Lynne on the front and spine panels. Price 30/-.

In a letter dated May 1969 Williamson indicates that publication was due in February 1969 but was delayed, firstly by the need for extensive corrections to the galley-proofs, and then by the finding after 3000 copies had been printed and bound that on one page the lines had been mixed up, leading to the whole batch being scrapped. In 1981 Lionel Dakers wrote that the batch consisted of 1500 copies of which 12 or so were retained, including one that Williamson had given him inscribed and dated 2 July 1969, but at the present time many more copies than this would appear to be in circulation.

In this state p.34 lines 27–9 are misprinted to the point where they make no sense, p.271 line 12 ends 'The sight made him randy.', pp.273–81 have the incorrect running head 'Enter Peregrin', and there is no owl device on p.361.

ii) Second state (published): as i) except for the text. Price 30/-. Published May 1969. 6000 copies.

In this state p.34 line 28 is corrected, p.271 line 12 ends 'ball in her mouth', the running head on pp.273–81 is corrected and p.361 has the owl device, but a new error is introduced on p.123 where lines 26 and 32 are transposed, and other pages have printing, spelling and punctuation errors that remain uncorrected. This is the only first edition in the *Chronicle* that was not printed by Purnell and it seems reasonable to suppose that this may have had something to do with the problems.

Contents:
- quotation from Winston Churchill p. 9, Jung p.103, anon (in French) p.303;
- dedication 'To Kenneth Allsop';
- 'Acknowledgements' for permission to quote;
- text (pp.11–361) in 4 Parts and 25 Chapters with headings, ending

'1964–1968, Devon' with owl device on p.361, followed by 'L'Envoi' (pp.363–4) ending '1949–1968 H.W.':

Part	1	Moon of the Homeless Ghosts	chaps.	1–9
	2	Ladies Observed		10–17
	3	Summer in Another Land		18–22
	4	St. Elmo's Fire		23–25
	L'Envoi			

1985. Macdonald. *Reprint of the first edition, second state.*
'This edition published in 1985 ...' ISBN 0 356 01456 3. Orange linson. Dust jacket printed in orange-brown and black, with illustration from a painting 'The Sandy Margin of the Sea' by B.W. Leader on the front panel. Price £12.95.

A photo-reprint with print size reduced.

1999. Sutton Publishing. *Reprint of the first edition, second state.*
'First published in this edition in the United Kingdom in 1999'. Pocket Classics series. ISBN 0 7509 2155 2. Paperback. Cover illustration from a painting by Erik Dorn Bodom. Price £7.99.

A photo-reprint with print size as 1985. Includes the Introduction by Anne Williamson as in DL1994.

A57 CONTRIBUTIONS TO THE WEEKLY DISPATCH (July, 1920 – January, 1921)

In the period between demobilisation in 1919 and going to Devon in 1921 Williamson was employed for six months on the staff of a Sunday paper, the *Weekly Dispatch,* mainly to write a column of 'light-car' notes under the heading 'On the Road'. At the time his own experience of personal transport was limited to a motorbike, but that was no hindrance: as he explained to the editor, 'I can write about anything'. It was his only spell as a salaried writer and in 'Confessions of a Fake Merchant' (B 1930a) he recalls his time on the paper which is repre-sented as 'The Weekly Courier' in chapters 3 and 4 of *The Innocent Moon* (A50).

Contributions is a collection of everything he wrote for the paper, identified and arranged by John Gregory, with an Introduction when it was reprinted by the HWS. It is the first collection of Williamson's work by another hand and the only such item published during his lifetime. To avoid problems with copyright he insisted that it should be printed in a small edition that was strictly 'not for sale' and issued only by private distribution.

1969. No printer or publisher. *First edition.*
Title on the front cover, dated 1969; no title-page. 'These articles are the copyright of the author, being reproduced here with his permission. This collection must not, under any circumstances, be offered for sale. This edition, privately printed by lithographic process for John Gregory, is limited to seven numbered copies. This is number ...' followed by the number in ink on p.2. Pp.60. 200 x 125mm. Light brown card covers, printed in black on the front; perfect-bound. Issued October 1969, by private distribution. 20 copies: seven numbered as above, and 13 out-of-series, with the edition statement but unnumbered, in a black plastic holding backstrip.

Contents:
- text (pp.7–59) with 38 items, arranged in three groups by John Gregory, with an 'Epigraph' quoting HW's editor, Bernard Falk (from *He Laughed in Fleet Street*, Hutchinson, 1937), and HW (from B 1930a); items marked * were unsigned in the paper but attributed by Gregory and confirmed by HW:

	Date:
The Country Week:	
I	01.08.20
II	08.08.20
III	22.08.20
IV	29.08.20
V	05.09.20
VI	12.09.20
On the Road	
Touring luxury in light cars	18.07.20
How to halve the oil bills	25.07.20
Real value of light car speed trials	01.08.20
Holiday car casualties	08.08.20
Best mixture for light cars	15.08.20
No traps, but police omnipotent	22.08.20
Pitfalls for the light-car owner	29.08.20

How to save fuel on the light car	05.09.20
Angry pedestrian v worried driver	12.09.20
Paraffin as light car fuel	19.09.20
Light car trips on winter days	26.09.20
New strides in light car design	03.10.20
Light cars and the future	10.10.20
Light cars versus cycle outfits	17.10.20
2–stroke light car engines	24.10.20
Drop in prices at Olympia	31.10.20
Motor show crowds London	07.11.20
£5,000,000 from car show	14.11.20
Motor-cycle exhibition	21.11.20
Britain leads the world	28.11.20
Motor shows in retrospect	12.12.20
Car with a sky	02.01.21

Miscellanea

Parkin on bowling	18.07.20
A real thriller *	18.07.20
How I keep fit *	18.07.20
Grannie's flight *	25.07.20
Blouse censor interviewed *	25.07.20
Laying a Kent ghost	25.07.20
7,000 miles to a grave *	25.07.20
Blanket snare *	29.08.20
Falcon's raid on London * (a fake	12.09.20
news item; see 'The Outlaw' in LS 1922)	
In the tiger's den*	17.10.20

Epigraph

1983. The Henry Williamson Society. *Reprint of the first edition, with an Introduction.*

Retitled 'THE WEEKLY DISPATCH. Articles Contributed by Henry Williamson in the years 1920– 1921' .

'Published by the Henry Williamson Society 1983' on the title-page. ISBN 0 9508652 1 4. Pp.viii + 58. 197 x 125mm. Brown card wrappers, printed in black on the front; stapled. Price £3. 500 copies.

Repaginated, with a two-page Introduction by John Gregory dated April 1983 giving an account of the project and his correspondence with HW (see also HWSJ 39).

A58 COLLECTED NATURE STORIES

Collected Nature Stories is made up from 10 of the 15 items in the 1934 edition of *The Peregrine's Saga*, 8 of the 9 items in the 1933 edition of *The Old Stag* and all 12 titles in *Tales of Moorland and Estuary*, revised, rearranged (with 'A Winter's Tale' placed under PS) and sometimes retitled, with a General Introduction to the whole book and a new Preface to each of the three main titles.

In the Introduction Williamson states: 'Within the covers of this book are almost all the short stories about birds, animals and fish I wrote in my youth. With them are a few brief tales ... about old people who lived, or had lived, in some of the villages of North Devon.' The 'almost all' presumably refers to the omission of any material from *The Lone Swallows*, perhaps because he regarded it as less satisfactory than the other work.

1970. Macdonald. *First edition; illustrated.*
'This edition first published in 1970 by ...' Printed by Tonbridge Printers. SBN 356 02945 X. Pp.ii + 478, with errata slip stating 'Page 56, after last line add: the green leaves, hiding the black spines of the hedge,' in most copies, tipped-in, usually on the front free endpaper but sometimes on p.57. Illustrations, reckoned. 222 x 135mm. Black linson, goldstamped on the spine. Dust jacket white, printed in brown, yellow and black, designed by Barrie Carr, with the woodcut from p.137 reproduced on the front panel; photograph of the author on his Norton motorcycle in 1921 by Oswald Jones on the back panel. Price £2. Published May 1970 (letter from Macdonald 1970). 7000 copies.

Contents:
- 'General Introduction' (pp.7–11) with background and reminiscence;
- illustrations: a) 35 full-page woodcuts (one repeated on dust jacket) and two tailpieces by C.F. Tunicliffe from PS and OS, photo-enlarged but of poor quality compared to the originals and not captioned; b) 12 headpieces (one repeated on title-page) by Broom Lynne from TME, photo-reduced;
- texts: ending with owl device and 'Acknowledgements' for the illustrations:

Notes:
The Peregrine's Saga and other wild tales (pp.13–145), from PS

	1934, with minimal revision
Preface	new text
A Winter's Tale	from TME, revised; headpiece by B.L.
The Mouse	
A Weed's Tale	
Air Gipsies	previously 'The Air Gipsies'
Wood Rogue	previously 'The Wood Rogue'
Aliens	
The Chronicle of Halbert and Znarr	previously 'Chronicle of Halbert and Znarr'
Mewliboy	
Bluemantle	
The Meal	
Unknown	
The Old Stag and other hunting stories	(pp.147–301), from OS 1933, all revised
Preface	new text
Stumberleap	
The Trapper's Mates	
Zoe	
The Five Lives of the Isle of Wight Parson	
Redeye	
T'chackamma	
The Rape of the Pale Pink Pyjamas	previously 'The Flight of the Pale Pink Pyjamas'; partly rewritten
My Day with the Beagles	
Tales of Moorland and Estuary	(pp.303–472); most revised
Preface	new text
The Crake	
A Hero of the Sands	
Incidents of an Afternoon's Walk	previously 'Incidents of

	an Afternoon Walk'
Swagdagger Crosses a Field	previously 'The White Stoat'; rewritten
The Yellow Boots	
Crime and Punishment	previously 'The Dog who ate his Punishment'
Trout	
The Heller	
A Crown of Life	no revisions noted
The Maiden Salmon	
Where the Bright Waters Meet	

1976a. Macdonald and Jane's. *Reprint of the first edition; illustrated.*
'Second impression, 1976'. ISBN 0 356 02945 X. 216 x 135mm. Light brown linson, goldstamped. Dust jacket by Ian Fleming and Associates Ltd. with a design by Graham Berry on the front panel and a photograph of the author on the back panel.

The error on p.56 is corrected.

1976b. Book Club Associates. *Reprint or reissue of 1976a.*
'This edition published 1976 by ... Second impression 1976'. 216 x 135mm. Brown linson. Dust jacket as 1976a but with 'BCA' at the foot of the spine panel.

1980. Macdonald General Books. *Reprint of 1976a.*
'This impression 1980'. ISBN 0 356 02945 X. Format as 1976a; front flap price-clipped and with an M and J sticker price £6.95.

1995. Little, Brown and Company. *New edition of 1976a, with an Introduction.*
'This edition published in Great Britain in 1995'. Printed by Clays Ltd. ISBN 0 316 87738 7. Pp.x + 470. 230 x 148mm. Paperback. Cover illustration by David Frankland. Price £12.99.

A bulky book, in larger print, with a four-page Introduction by Richard Williamson dated December 1995.

A59 THE SCANDAROON

At the age of 72 Williamson had finished the *Chronicle* but there was still unfinished business in the form of *The Scandaroon* - a tale of a special pigeon and a young boy that was based on a brief period in the summer of 1924 when he had acted as 'tutor' to Patrick Foulds, the son of a Georgeham resident.

He had started the book in 1955 but then put it aside on the forceful advice of John Middleton Murry that if he allowed anything else to interfere with writing the *Chronicle* he would do 'irreparable injury' to that work and to himself.

In an introduction (printed only on the flaps of the dust jacket) he says that when he resumed in 1971 he found that 'the personal narrative method of telling the story came naturally and happily to me; for I had known the living characters and merely had to observe them; Peter ... the Admiral ...the Doctor ... Sam the publican and his wife Zillah ... finally, it all fell to be a piece of reporting ... well, it's all neatly packaged in the story.'

Neatly packaged it is. Reminiscent of Georgeham fifty years earlier and with a flavour of *Tarka* and *The Phasian Bird*, it is a well-rounded and fitting conclusion to a lifetime of storytelling.

1972a. Macdonald. *First edition, illustrated.*
i) 'First published in Great Britain in 1972 ...' Printed by Hazell Watson and Viney. SBN 356 03963 3. Pp.152. Illustrations, reckoned. 223 x 137mm. Light brown linson, stamped dark brown on the front and spine; endpapers yellow. Dust jacket white, printed in purple and black, with two colour illustrations of pigeons by Ken Lilly on the front panel and a photograph of the author on his motorcycle in 1921 by Oswald Jones on the back panel; blurb on both flaps printed in blue. Price £1.95. Published October 1972. [5000] copies.

ii) Signed, numbered issue: as i) except: edition statement on recto of half-title 'This edition signed by the author is limited to 250 copies of which this in number ...' followed by the number in ink, with the signature of the author under the title. Dark blue rexine, goldstamped on the front and spine with headband, marker tab and light blue endpapers, in a dark blue plain rexine slip-case. 250 copies.

Contents:
- dedication 'To my dear friend of Devon and Irish days, Sir John Heygate, where 'the pigeon' saw its first light in the summer days over Bellarena in Co. Derry';
- illustrations: 19 line drawings by Ken Lilly, one on title-page, one on dedication page (double-spread) and 17 as headpieces (plus dust jacket as above);
- text (pp.13–152) in 4 Parts titled and 17 sections with headings, ending 'Bellarena 1955 - Ox's Cross 1972', with owl device:

Part	1	The Danziger Bird	sections	1–5
	2	The Sun in Aries		6–9
	3	Exciting Preparations		10–14
	4	Midsummer Revel		15–17

1972b. Macdonald. *Reprint of the first edition.*
'Second impression 1972'. As i) above except the blurb on the dust jacket is printed in black, not blue. Price £1.95. [2000] copies.

1973a. Macdonald. *Reprint of the first edition.*
'Third impression 1973'. As 1972 b.

1973b. Saturday Review Press. New York. *American reprint of the first edition.*
'First American edition 1973'. Printed in the U.S.A. ISBN 0 8415 0240 4. Pp.156 (last 4 blank). 214 x 138mm. Yellow paper-covered boards, backed in red cloth, goldstamped on the spine. Dust jacket illustration as 1972a on the front panel, but with no photograph on the back panel. Price $5.95.

A60 DAYS OF WONDER

The Daily Express was the first paper to take Williamson's work on a regular basis and from 1921 to the start of the Second World War he contributed over 100 articles (see Section C) on a variety of subjects including natural history, the First World War and the Norfolk farm venture. In 1966, to commemorate the fiftieth anniversay of 'The Somme', he was asked to contribute again, following which he provided a piece on natural history at roughly monthly intervals up to

March 1971.

Days of Wonder contains all his contributions from this second spell with the paper, in the first of a series of posthumous collections of his more ephemeral work edited by John Gregory for the Henry Williamson Society.

1987. The Henry Williarnson Society. *First edition.*
i) 'This collection first published by The Henry Williamson Society 1987'. ISBN 0 9508652 3 0. Pp.iv + 104. Illustrations, reckoned. 210 x 148mm. Card covers red, printed in black; perfect-bound. Price £9. 475 copies.

ii) Limited issue: as i) except: 'This is a Limited Edition of 25. This is No ...' followed by the number and signature of Richard Williamson in ink, on recto of the third leaf; signed by John Gregory on p.4. ISBN 0 9508652 2 2. Pp.x + 108 (added blanks). 218 x 149mm. Cockerell marbled paper boards, half-bound in brown calf. Price £25. 25 copies.

Contents:
- 'Introduction' by Richard Williamson (2 pp.);
- 'Editor's note and acknowledgements' dated 'J.G. 1987';
- illustrations: 17 drawings or designs by R.A. Richardson and D. Roberts, reproduced from *The Daily Express;*
- text (pp.5–104) with 38 items, in date order:

	Date:
The Somme - just fifty years after	3 parts:
	29.06.66,
	30.06.66,
	01.07.66
'Oil will hang the black drapes of death ...'	29.03.67
The battle of Vimy Ridge	2 parts:
	06.04.67,
	07.04.67
'I fancy that if the generation ...'	22.07.67
Freedom of the house - for a fox	22.12.67
How the hawks lost the war game	01.06.68
The deadly hobby - hunting butterflies	29.06.68
What that lovely little bird told me	27.07.68
Our bonfire revels in the owl's larder	31.08.68

Just before the turn of the year ...	28.09.68
Moment of fear amid the forest shadows	26.10.68
Fifty years ago ...	09.11.68
The noble hunter's back in town!	30.11.68
Reflections in an ancient sunlight	28.12.68
Country commuters flying in the face of danger	01.02.69
Days of wonder that set the night on fire	22.02.69
Rooked - as anarchy reigns in the house	22.03.69
Spring rushes back to my valley	26.04.69
Why otters need friends ...	14.05.69
Mother drops by and it's high speed dinner	24.05.69
The glorious days of bully hunting	28.06.69
High on Exmoor - in search of myself	02.08.69
Salute to seal island!	30.08.69
Heartbreak of a bird so very much in love	27.09.69
In the chill of the night, a killer gladiator strikes	25.10.69
The owls that went bump in the night	29.11.69
The deadly differences of the good companions	07.02.70
As my barn owls await their happy event	28.02.70
Miss Starling insists on a home before marriage	28.03.70
When lovebirds came tapping at my window-pane	25.04.70
The visitor who stalks by night!	30.05.70
When thieves fall out, then the feathers really fly	18.07.70
When a rare beauty comes out of her shell	26.09.70
Wild cry for help on a lonely road	31.10.70
Save the innocents	3 parts:
	16.11.70,
	17.11.70,
	18.11.70
Silent night - when the guns held their peace	19.12.70
Yes, you can sometimes trust an old fox	06.02.71
After the storm, the dance of the phantoms	27.03.71

A61 FROM A COUNTRY HILLTOP

Articles by Williamson from 1958–1964, mostly with a pastoral theme, collected from *The Co-operative Home Magazine*, *Home Magazine*, and *The Sunday Times*, edited and with an Introduction by John Gregory.

1988. The Henry Williamson Society. *First edition.*
i) 'This collection first published by The Henry Williamson Society 1988'. ISBN 0 9508652 5 7. Pp.132. Illustrations, reckoned. 210 x 148mm. Card covers green, printed in black; perfect-bound. Price £8.50. 450 copies.

ii) Limited issue: as i) except: 'This book has been published by ... in a limited edition of 500 copies. 450 copies are bound in paper covers. 50 copies are bound in quarter morocco ... This is copy number ...' followed by the number in ink, on p.133. ISBN 0 9508652 4 9. Pp.ii + 136 (added blanks). 224 x 148mm. Straw-coloured cloth boards, quarter-bound in green morocco. Price £40. 50 copies.

Contents:
- 'Introduction' (2 pp.) dated 'J.G. 1988' and 'Acknowledgements';
- illustrations: frontispiece photograph of HW by Daniel Farson, and one line drawing unsigned;
- text (pp.9–131) with 58 items, arranged in three sections:

	Source:
From a Country Hilltop: nos.I-IX	*Co-op Home Magazine* 1958
nos.X-XLII	*Home Magazine* Jan. 1959–62
Out of Doors	*Sunday Times:*
Return to the fold	14.01.62
Echo of the gale	11.02.62
Timid Wat and Robbie	11.03.62
War and peace at Cranborne	08.04.62
Bird listening	06.05.62
On the Braunton Burrows	10.06.62
Two for a farthing	29.07.62
When the salmon run into the purse	18.11.62
Time out on the Burrows	25.11.62
The caviare-eater	30.12.62
End of the gallypot	03.03.63
Bird of fire	21.04.63
A natural being again	26.05.63
A long day out of the dungeon	14.07.63
Out of doors	25.10.64
The Last Summer	*Sunday Times Magazine* 02.08.64

A62 SOME NOTES ON 'THE FLAX OF DREAM' And Other Essays

Five of Williamson's contributions to *The Aylesford Review*, including a review of his own book *Lucifer Before Sunrise* under the pseudonym 'Green Jacket', reprinted and published as a personal initiative by Colin Stanley.

1988. Paupers' Press. *First edition.*
i) 'First edition 1988'. The 'Aylesford Review' essays, vol. 2. ISBN 0 946650 10 1. Pp.32. Illustration, reckoned. 210 x 147mm. Card covers green, printed in black; stapled. Price £2.75.

ii) Limited issue: as i) except: 'Limited hardback edition of 100 copies. Copy no....' followed by the number in ink, on sticker on recto of the front free endpaper. ISBN 0 946650 19 5. 214 x 150mm. Green and white paper-covered boards, printed in black. 100 copies.

Contents:
- illustration: reproduction of a photograph of HW by Oswald Jones p.9;
- text (pp.5–29) with 5 titles, followed by a list of HW books in print in August 1988:

	Date:
Machen in Fleet Street	winter 1959–60 (also in B 1960a)
Lucifer or Eosphoros?	autumn 1967
Some notes on 'The Flax of Dream' and 'A Chronicle of Ancient Sunlight'	winter 1957–8
Reflections on a theme	summer 1966
A visit to Richard Aldington	autumn 1963

A63 A BREATH OF COUNTRY AIR Part One

Part One of this title is a reprinting of all except one of Williamson's contributions to *The Evening Standard* for the year 1944, edited and introduced by John Gregory, with a Foreword by Richard Williamson. Together with the articles that are reprinted in Part Two (A64), *Green Fields and Pavements* (A68), and *Heart of England* (A73) they form a contemporary chronicle of life on the Norfolk farm during the wartime years.

1990. The Henry Williamson Society. *First edition.*
i) 'This collection first published by The Henry Williamson Society 1990'. ISBN 0 9508652 8 1. Pp.x + 102. Frontispiece and illustrations, reckoned. 210 x 148mm. Card covers blue, printed in black; perfect-bound. Price £7.95. 450 copies.

ii) Limited issue: as i) except: 'This book has been published by ... in a limited edition of 500 copies. 450 copies are bound in paper covers. 50 copies are bound in quarter morocco. This is copy number ...' followed by the number in ink, on p.103. ISBN 0 9508652 7 3. Pp.xii + 106 (added blanks). 228 x 148mm. Light khaki cloth, quarter-bound in brown morocco. Price £40. 50 copies.

Contents:
- 'Foreword' (2 pp.) by Richard Williamson, with recollections of the period;
- 'Introduction' (2 pp.) dated 'J.G. 1990', with acknowledgements;
- illustrations: frontispiece and p.24, photographs of HW; drawing of Old Hall Farm p.68;
- text (pp.1–101) with 45 titles, in date order:

	Date:
So the farmers are making fortunes!	14.02.44
The land is coming into heart again	21.02.44
This bird makes the farmer happy	28.02.44
Can dogs think?	06.03.44
The pollard ash	13.03.44
They take 10,000 mice in a year	20.03.44
Battle of Hilly Piece	27.03.44
Red drogues over the marshes	03.04.44
A few yards of unofficial potatoes	10.04.44
Secret exit of the otter	17.04.44
Death to the moles!	24.04.44
The snipe's nest	01.05.44
The elms are dying	08.05.44
The nightingale	15.05.44
Bird of mystery	22.05.44

The snake bird	29.05.44
The raven and the jackdaw	05.06.44
My very own pines	12.06.44
A young bird in the hand	19.06.44
Hooly the owl in a clash of loyalties	26.06.44
A droning in the night	03.07.44
Strawberries - and hay	10.07.44
Trout under the willow	17.07.44
Nettlebed became a garden of sunflowers	24.07.44
Raspberries - with cream	31.07.44
The culvert	07.08.44
Salmon in the burn	14.08.44
Non-stop harvest	21.08.44
A day of rest on the farm	28.08.44
The moonlight over the pool	04.09.44
The rain came to the farm	11.09.44
He was a tisky bird	18.09.44
A lone robin sang of hope	25.09.44
Just one day on the farm	02.10.44
Tea for two in a tree	09.10.44
It looked like crazy farming	16.10.44
I used to think rabbit-trappers were cruel	23.10.44
The book man shot his biggest bird	30.10.44
We saw the spirit of the wood	06.11.44
Dead river in green valley	13.11.44
I had to run from a stoat	20.11.44
My tide-door worked!	27.11.44
The redpoll bull	04.12.44
The magic of a poor farmer's boy	11.12.44
Lord of the skies	18.12.44

A64 A BREATH OF COUNTRY AIR Part Two

Part Two of this title includes all Williamson's contributions to *The Evening Standard* for 1945, the year in which he left the farm, followed by 'Quest', a series of articles written for *Woman's Illustrated and Eve's Own* in 1946, edited and introduced by John Gregory, with a Foreword by Robert Williamson.

1991. The Henry Williamson Scoiety. *First edition.*

i) 'This collection first published by The Henry Williamson Society 1991'. ISBN 1 873507 00 3. Pp.x + 128, with errata slip for the incomplete text of 'Spring is a little early' on p.22. Frontispiece and illustrations, reckoned. 210 x 147mm. Card covers blue, printed in black; perfect-bound. Price £8.50. 450 copies.

ii) Limited issue: as i) except: 'This book has been published by ... in a limited edition of 500 copies. 450 copies are bound in paper covers. 50 copies are bound in quarter morocco ... This is copy number ...' followed by the number in ink, on p.129. ISBN 0 9508652 9 X. Pp.xii + 134 (due to added blanks). 228 x 148mm. Light khaki cloth, quarter-bound in brown morocco. Price £40. 50 copies.

Contents:
- 'Foreword' (2pp.) by Robert Williamson, with background to the writings;
- 'Introduction' (2 pp.) dated 'J.G. 1991', with acknowledgements;
- illustrations: 3 photographs (one as frontispiece) and one line drawing unsigned;
- text (pp.1–127) with 37 titles, in date order, followed by 'Quest':

	Date:
Reflections of an otter	01.01.45
The glitter on the water has gone	08.01.45
Seascape	15.01.45
Owls in the thatch	22.01.45
White streamline	29.01.45
Footprints tell the tale	05.02.45
Just grew!	12.02.45
Glimpse of spring	19.02.45
Patience and rhythm	26.02.45
Spring is a little early	05.03.45
Pecking and prising	12.03.45
Running in the rain	19.03.45
The spirit of wild places	26.03.45
So we spare the tree	02.04.45
Wingbeats on water	12.04.45
A wall beside the sea	16.04.45
Everything looks brighter now	23.04.45

Revolution on Britain's farms	14.05.45
The bird voice that is fading	23.05.45
So I left them alone	28.05.45
A robin perched on my toe	04.06.45
This sparrow sings and fights	20.06.45
In a village that changed	28.06.45
The robin that stayed up late	04.07.45
What shall I do about harvest?	24.07.45
Knives and weeds	30.07.45
Fishing with a bamboo pole	20.08.45
A miracle on the beach	06.09.45
An hour on the cliff	18.09.45
I have sold my Norfolk farm	10.10.45
A butterfly over the sea	16.10.45
Buying a house in three minutes	25 10 45
Auction on the farm	30.10.45
Moving from a Norfolk farm	07.11.45
Not such a common cat	14.11.45
The lake of silver laughter	20.11.45
Music of the plough	04.12.45
Quest (parts numbered I-XV)	*Women's Illustrated* 1946

A65 SPRING DAYS IN DEVON and Other Broadcasts

Williamson's first transmission for the BBC was on 16 December 1935 and *Spring Days in Devon* is a collection of transcripts of 22 broadcasts, mostly from 1935–1938, obtained from various sources and edited by John Gregory, with an account of Williamson's connection with the BBC by Valerie Belsey as a Foreword.

1992. The Henry Williamson Society. *First edition.*
i) 'This collection first published 1992'. ISBN 1 873507 01 1. Pp.x + 126. Frontispiece, reckoned. 210 x 148mm. Card covers orange, printed in black; perfect-bound. Price £9.25. 450 copies.

ii) Limited issue: as i) except: 'This book has been published by ... in a limited edition of 500 copies. 450 copies are bound in paper covers. 50 copies are bound in quarter morocco ... This is copy number ...' followed by the number in ink, on p.127. ISBN 1 873507 02 X. Pp.x + 128 (added blank). 216 x 151mm. Green cloth, quarter-bound in red morocco. Price £40. 50 copies.

Contents:
- 'Editor's Note and Acknowledgements' dated 'J.G. 1992';
- 'Foreword' (3 pp.) by Valerie R. Belsey dated 'Totnes, January 1992';
- Frontispiece, photograph of HW;
- text (pp.1–124) with 22 titles, in order of transmission (except*):

	Transmitted:	Source of text:
Recipe for country life	16.12.35	*Listener* 24.12.35
Spring days in Devon	21.03.36	25.03.36
The headland	03.04.36	15.04.36
East wind	16.04.36	29.04.36
Our gulf stream spring	01.05.36	13.05.36
The deserted shore	15.05.36	27.05.36
Around Dartmoor	25.05.36	10.06.36
Diversions in a garden	12.06.36	01.07.36
Country mind and town mind	29.06.36	08.07.36
Red deer	28.09.36	GWC chap. 10 (A25)
The otter	28.10.36	*Listener* 04.11.36
The barn owl*	18.12.36	transcript
Tryst at the gibbet*	14.12.36	*Listener* 23.12.36,
The badger: England's oldest inhabitant	05.02.37	24.02.37
Buying a farm	22.08.38	01.09.38
Getting to work	29.08.38	08.09.38
Building a home	05.09.38	15.09.38
The spirit of England	12.09.38	22.09.38
Devon revisited	20.09.38	corrected script
West Country reminiscences	01.06.39	transcript
Atlantic headland	not known	*Listener* 03.08.39
Forty years in wild Devon	11.08.54	transcript

A66 PEN AND PLOUGH Further Broadcasts

A sequel to A65, with transcripts of 21 broadcasts by Williamson from April 1938 to May 1967, taken mostly from his typescripts or mss but with some from BBC transcripts (* below), arranged, edited and introduced by John Gregory with a checklist of all Williamson's known broadcasts.

1993. The Henry Williamson Society. *First edition.*
i) 'This collection first published 1993'. ISBN 1 873507 03 8. Pp.xii + 108. Illustration, reckoned. 210 x 148mm. Card covers purple, printed in black; perfect-bound. Price £9. 450 copies.

ii) Limited issue: as i) except: 'This book has been published by ... in a limited edition of 500 copies. 450 copies are bound in paper covers. 50 copies are bound in quarter morocco ... This is copy number ...' followed by the number in ink, on p.109. ISBN 1 873507 04 6. Pp.xli + 110 (added blank). 218 x 150mm. Blue cloth, quarter-bound in blue morocco. Price £40. 50 copies.

Contents:
- dedicated to John Homan, past secretary of the HWS;
- 'Acknowledgements', and 'Introduction' dated 'J.G. 1993';
- illustration: photograph of HW p.65;
- text (pp.1–100): 21 titles, arranged in two Parts, followed by 'Appendix' (5 pp.):

	Transmitted:
Part One: The Country Reporter	
Norfolk farmer	21.04.38
Field and pavement	28.04.38
The malkin	05.05.38
Rail and fen	12.05.38
The rain comes	19.05.38
Birdsong reflections	26.05.38
Family and farm	13.09.38
The forest of Exmoor	27.09.38
Still close to earth	04.01.39
The reckoning	18.02.39
The gale	11.03.39

Baggy Point	05.07.39
More West Country reminiscences	28.08.39
On seeing Marilyn Monroe *	03.05.61
The river *	20.05.61
Part Two: Books and Writers	
Lorna Doone and the Doone Valley	15.08.36
Arnold Bennett *	15.02.56
On writing a novel series	07.10.61
Book Reviews:	
*The Home Letters of T E Lawrence ...**	24.08.54
Morale *	28.03.67
The Sea Years of Joseph Conrad *	23.05.67

Appendix: Radio Broadcasts by Henry Williamson, from 16 December 1935 to 17 June 1971. NB: since this list was compiled a letter has surfaced from a listener, dated 7 May 1952, indicating that 'Tiger's Teeth' had recently been broadcast to schools and printed in the Radio Times.

A67 THRENOS FOR T.E. LAWRENCE and Other Writings ... together with A Criticism of Henry Williamson's *Tarka the Otter* by T.E. Lawrence

Threnos for T.E.L. is a miscellaneous collection of some of Williamson's more substantial pieces, published originally in magazines, books by other authors, or out-of-print editions of his own books, selected and edited by John Gregory, with an Introduction and commentary on the essays and their literary connections by J.W. Blench.

1994. The Henry Williamson Society. *First edition.*
i) 'This collection first published 1994'. ISBN 1 873507 05 4. Pp.x + 134. Frontispiece, reckoned. 207 x 144mm. Card covers yellow, printed in black; perfect-bound. Price £9.95. 700 copies.
The first copies of this issue had the spine lettered-up (instead of lettered-down) before the mistake was noted; five of these were retained as artefacts and the remainder recut to slightly smaller size (as above) with the mistake corrected.

ii) Limited issue: as i) except: 'This book has been published by ... in a limited edition of 750 copies. 700 copies are bound in paper covers. 50 copies are bound in quarter morocco ... This is copy number ...' followed by the number in ink, on p.135. ISBN 1 873507 06 2. Pp.x + 136 (added blank). 216 x 148mm. Greyish cloth, quarter-bound in black morocco. Price £50. 50 copies.

Contents:
- 'Acknowledgements' signed 'J.G.';
- 'Introduction' (4 pp.) by J.W. Blench, Durham;
- Frontispiece, photograph of HW in 1930;
- text (pp.1–134) with 14 items by HW, and one by T.E. Lawrence:

	Source:
Threnos for T.E. Lawrence	*European*, May-Jun. 1954
Writers and Poets:	
Some nature writers and civilization	A47
In darkest England	B 1967
A visit to Richard Aldington	*Aylesford Review*, Autumn 1963
Roy Campbell: a portrait	*European*, Feb. 1959
Machen in Fleet Street	*Aylesford Review*, Winter 1959–60; B 1960a
Prefaces and Introductions:	
A Soldier's Diary of the Great War	B 1929
Little Peter the Great	B 1931b
Decent Fellows	B 1931a
Winged Victory	B 1934c
The Unreturning Spring	B 1950
Letters from a Soldier	B 1960c
The Pathway	PW 1931b
The Labouring Life	LL 1932ii

A Criticism of Henry Williamson's *Tarka the Otter* ... From *Men in Print* ... by T.E. Lawrence; The Golden Cockerel Press, 1940

A68 GREEN FIELDS AND PAVEMENTS A Norfolk Farmer in Wartime

Green Fields and Pavements is a collection of articles that Williamson wrote for *The Eastern Daily Press* from 1941–1944, edited by John Gregory, with a Foreword by Bill Williamson and illustrated by Michael Loates. Published for the Centenary of Williamson's birth, with both issues in hardback, it is effectively a continuation of the story of the Norfolk farm but in serial form and real-time, not retrospect.

1995. The Henry Williamson Society. *First edition.*
i) 'This collection first published 1995'. ISBN 1 873507 07 0. Pp.x + 166. Frontispiece and illustrations, reckoned. 237 x 150mm. Green linson, goldstamped on the spine. Dust jacket white, printed in green and black. Price £14.50. 700 copies

ii) Limited issue: as i) except: 'This book has been published by ... in a limited edition of 750 copies. 700 copies are bound in cloth covers. 50 copies are bound in quarter morocco ...' followed by the number and six signatures (Loetitia Williamson, Margaret Bream, Bill, John, Richard and Robert Williamson) in ink, on verso of the second blank. ISBN 1 873507 08 9. Pp.xiv + 168 (added blanks). 248 x 160mm. Grey cloth, quarter-bound in red morocco, goldstamped, all edges gilt, in plain grey cloth slip-case. Price £50. 50 copies.

Contents:
- 'Editor's Note and Acknowledgements' by John Gregory;
- 'An Artist's Tribute' to HW by Mick Loates, Kingsbridge 1995;
- 'Foreword' (2 pp.) by Bill Williamson, Canada, January 1995, with farm recollections;
- illustrations: frontispiece photograph by Oswald Jones, and 14 line drawings by Michael Loates mostly as head or tailpieces (9 also repeated);
- text (pp.1–165) with 48 titles, in date order:

	Date:
The seed goes in	12.03.41
Farming in war time	30.03.42
War and peace	19.04.43 (writing as 'Jacob Tonson', see HWSJ 10)

Faith, hope and clarity	26.04.43 (writing as 'Jacob Tonson'),
News of England	03.05.43 (writing as 'Jacob Tonson'),
A cuckoo singing	10.05.43 (writing as 'Jacob Tonson'),
The little ports	17.05.43 (writing as 'Jacob Tonson'),
Topsy-turvydom	24.05.43 (writing as 'Jacob Tonson'),
Along the coast road	31.05.43 (writing as 'Jacob Tonson'),
The falcon's flight	07.06.43 (writing as 'Jacob Tonson'),
The trout stream	14.06.43 (writing as 'Jacob Tonson'),
The story of Cheepy	21.06.43
Peace in war	28.06.43
Hooly	2 parts: 05.07.43, 12.07.43
Of men and books	19.07.43 (writing as 'Jacob Tonson')
The tragic spirit	2 parts: 26.07.43, 02.08.43
Answers to correspondents	09.08.43
On children	16.08.43
Harvest story	23.08.43
Butterfly	30.08.43
A farmer's trials	06.09.43
The corn is threshed	13.09.43
Journey to the west	22.09.43
Love's labour lost	27.09.43
The God gold	04.10.43
The magpie's nest	11.10.43
Little summer: a pause	18.10.43
Pheasants and partridges	25.10.43
Plowman's folly	01.11.43
The writer's trade	2 parts: 08.11.43, 15.11.43
An old tractor	22.11.43
Seven years after	29.11.43
The clodhoppers	3 parts: 06.12.43, 13.12.43, 20.12.43
A hero of humanity	28.12.43
Finance and farming	03.01.44
Local farming profits	10.01.44
Literary diversion	2 parts: 17.01.44, 24.01.44
Herefordshire hops	31.01.44
Ownership of land	07.02.44
The untidiest nation?	14.02.44
Spit and polish	21.02.44
Odds and ends	28.02.44
Journal of a husbandman	06.03.44

Fuel for the cutting	13.03.44
Pleasant and unpleasant	20.03.44
The task of Sisyphus	27.03.44
Wandering spirit	02.04.44
Country life	10.04.44

A69 THE NOTEBOOK OF A NATURE-LOVER

From May 1933 to February 1936 Williamson wrote exactly 100 articles for *The Sunday Referee*, mostly under the heading 'The Notebook of a Nature-lover' (NNL, numbered 1–45), 'Note Book of a Nature-lover' (NBNL) or 'A Nature-lover's Notebook' (NLN) but sometimes with other variations or unheaded, of which exactly 50 were used by Williamson in 1934 to form the bulk of *The Linhay on the Downs* (see A20).

Printed in this collection are the other 50 items (plus one duplicated from LOD) edited by John Gregory, with a Foreword by Loetitia Williamson and illustrations by Michael Loates.

1996. The Henry Williamson Society. *First edition.*
i) 'This collection first published 1996'. ISBN 1 873507 10 0. Pp.x + 118. Frontispiece and illustrations, reckoned. 210 x 147mm. Card covers white, printed in blue and black, with an additional illustration by Michael Loates on the front; perfect-bound. Price £12.99. 700 copies.

ii) Limited issue: as i) except: 'This book has been published by ... in a limited edition of 750 copies. 50 copies are bound in quarter calf ... and signed by the artist. This is copy number ...' followed by the number and signature of the artist in ink and illustration from the front cover of i), on verso of the first leaf. ISBN 1 873507 11 9. Pp.xii + 118 (added blank). Mauve cloth, quarter-bound in light brown calf. Price £50. 50 copies.

Contents:
- 'Editor's Note and Acknowledgements' by John Gregory;
- 'Foreword' (3pp.) by Mrs Loetitia Williamson with background to the articles, dated 'Suffolk, 1996';
- illustrations: frontispiece drawing of HW from the *Sunday Referee*; 17 line drawings by Michael Loates in the text, mostly as head or tailpieces

(4 also repeated);
- text (pp.3–117) with 51 titles, arranged in four groups, undated, followed by the 'HW' salmon device (from *Salar*) instead of the customary owl:

	Date:	Heading:
Spring:		
Spring lures my husband away	24.03.35	NLN (by HW, pretending to be Loetitia)
Secret of the starling's song	31.03.35	NLN
When dawn breaks over Exmoor	07.04.35	NLN
The loneliest corner of Devon	14.04.35	NLN
Strange visitor from the sea	21.04.35	NLN
The romance of a rail journey	28.04.35	NLN
Finding truth in the sun's path	05.05.35	NLN
Tragedy of the shot buzzards	12.05.35	NLN
A night in a farmhouse kitchen	19.05.35	NLN
Memories of twenty years ago	26.05.35	NLN
A summer day on the sands	02.06.35	NLN
When the salmon return	21.05.33	NNL no.1
The angler's paradise	04.06.33	NNL no.3
Down a Devonshire lane	09.06.35	NLN
There was thunder over Exmoor	16.06.35	NLN
Summer:		
Story of a sticky business	23.06.35	NLN
A storm idyll	30.06.35	NLN
My encounter with a mother partridge	07.07.35	NLN
The devil's darning needle	14.07.35	NLN
An Exmoor holiday	21.07.35	A Nature-lover's Bureau
Some secrets of my day's work	08.07.35	A Nature-lover's Diary
The birds vanish from their sanctuary	04.08.35	A Nature-lover's Diary
Gulf Stream brings strange visitors to Devon	11.08.35	A Nature-lover's Dairy

Dawn over Exmoor	09.09.34	unheaded
The lesson of the spider	16.09.34	unheaded
Autumn:		
Summer passes	23.09.34	unheaded
Leaping the weir	30.09.34	unheaded
Bird migrants of the stratosphere	07.10.34	unheaded
The doomed elm tree	14.10.34	NBNL
Just a bridge	28.10.34	unheaded
In praise of Brighton	11.11.34	unheaded
The ducks	25.11.34	NBNL
The Sussex Downs	02.12.34	NBNL
Are animals trained by fear?	09.12.34	unheaded
After the rain	16.12.34	NBNL
Winter:		
The dweller on the hilltop	23.12.34	NLN
Fisherman's paradise	14.01.34	NNL no.35
The bravest of birds	20.01.35	NLN
The silent sentinel at the gate	26.01.36	unheaded
Stark tragedy in bird land	27.1.35	NLN
The salmon-leap	28.1.34	NNL no.37
A Sunday walk on Exmoor	3.2.35	NLN
Peal leaping	4.2.34	NNL no.38
Out of the mouths of babes	10.2.35	NLN
Life is returning to the moor	17.2.35	NLN
Hill-top meditations	18.2.34	NNL no.40; (part 2 of 'High Peak Canal' in LOD)
The mystery of the orange ship	24.2.35	NLN
Pigeons come to breakfast	23.2.36	unheaded
The country awakes from its winter sleep	3.3.35	NLN
The love song of the curlew	17.3.35	NLN
A message of hope from the west	10 3 35	NLN

A70 WORDS ON THE WEST WIND Selected Essays from The Adelphi 1924–1950 ... with Postscripts by Anne and Richard Williamson

Words on the West Wind comprises 11 items reprinted from *The Adelphi*, of which seven are by Williamson (who edited the magazine for the three issues from October 1948 to June 1949) and four by other authors, edited by John Gregory, with two new pieces that provide background to the selection.

2000. The Henry Williamson Society. *First edition.*
The front cover serves as the title-page, with Contents and edition statement on verso: 'This collection first published 2000'. ISBN 1 873507 16 X. Pp.104. 216 x 140mm. Card covers orange-yellow, printed in black; perfect-bound. Price £7.95. 500 copies.

No 'limited issue' was produced.

Contents: text (pp.1-103) with seven titles by HW and six by others, in irregular order (rearranged below):

Items by HW:	Date:
The Doom of the Peregrine Falcon	Sep 1924
Birth of the Phasian Bird	Jul.-Sep 1948
The Lost Legions	Oct.-Dec. 1948
Report on the Richard Jefferies Centenary	Oct.-Dec. 1948
A Note on Tarka the Otter	Apr.-Jun. 1949
Notes of a 'Prentice Hand	Jan.-Mar. 1949
Words on the West Wind (5 parts)	Jan.-Mar, Apr.-Jun, Jul.-Sep, Autumn Book Number 1949, Jan.-Mar. 1950
Items by others:	
Under the News (poem) by Edward Pine	Oct.-Dec. 1948
Hayfield, by James Farrar	Apr.-Jun. 1946
Atlantic Coast, by James Farrar	Jan.-Mar. 1949
Man into Fox, by Charles Causley	Jul.-Sept. 1949
The West Wind Blows Again, by Anne Williamson	
'That Damned Motorcar', by Richard Williamson	

A71 INDIAN SUMMER NOTEBOOK A Writer's Miscellany

A selection of Williamson's work from various sources, including books, magazines and *The Evening Standard*, with an essay on Williamson by Fr Brocard Sewell. In the Editor's Note John Gregory says 'If the selection has a theme, it is one of people, places and events that had a far-reaching effect on Henry's life - his schooldays, the Christmas Truce on the Western Front in 1914, the writer Richard Jefferies and the poet Francis Thompson, his Norfolk Farm and, of course, North Devon'. Dedicated to Brocard Sewell, who died in April 2000.

2001. The Henry Williamson Society. *First edition.*
i) 'This collection first published 2001'. ISBN 1 873507 18 6. Pp.viii + 88, with errata slip correcting the page references loosely inserted. 217 x 140mm. Card covers yellow, printed in black, with a design by Michael Loates on the front; perfect-bound. Price £9.25. 379 copies.

ii) Limited issue: as i) except: 'This book is published by ... in a limited edition of 400 copies twenty-one of which have been bound in quarter morocco ... and signed by the artist. This is copy number ... ' followed by the number and signature of Michael Loates in ink, on recto of the second leaf and cover illustration from i) on verso. ISBN 1 873507 19 4. Pp.xii + 90 (added blanks). 220 x 145mm. Green cloth, quarter-bound in brown morocco. Price £50. 21 copies.

Contents:
- dedication: 'In memory of Brocard Sewell, O. Carm. 1912–2000. Priest, printer, writer and editor of The Aylesford Review, Vice-President of The Henry Williamson Society';
- 'Editor's Note and Acknowledgements' by John Gregory;
- 'Henry Williamson' (5 pp.) by Brocard Sewell, from *John O'London's Weekly* 21 Sept. 1961;
- text (p.6–86) with 8 titles by HW:

	Source:
Out of the prisoning tower	B 1961a
The Christmas truce	*History of the First World War* (see Section C)

When I was demobilised	*Strand Magazine* 1945
Richard Jefferies	B 1937a
A first adventure with Francis Thompson	B 1966b
English farming	B 1941
The winter of 1941	B 1947
Indian summer notebook:	*Evening Standard*:
My spider, my bee	16.11.64
Leaves in the grass	17.11.64
Blue halls of the wind	18.11.64
Robbie: an innocent ...	19.11.64
Now the summer slips away ...	20.11.64

A72 HENRY WILLIAMSON A brief look at his Life and Writings in North Devon in the 1920s and '30s

An illustrated booklet with brief extracts from ten of Williamson's books and a biographical account of his life in Georgeham by Anne Williamson, edited by Tony Evans and intended as a short introduction to the author's life and work.

2001. The Henry Williamson Society. *First edition.*
No date. 'Published by the Henry Williamson Society' on verso of the front cover. ISBN 1 873507 17 8. Pp.52. Illustrations, reckoned. 210 x 148mm. Card covers white, printed in black, with a photograph of HW on the front; stapled. Price £3. 1500 copies to date.

Contents:
- 'Henry Williamson's Life in Georgeham and North Devon' (9 pp.) by Anne Williamson;
- illustrations: 14 photographs of HW, people, and places, 2 maps;
- text (pp.17–52) with 15 extracts from 10 books, and a list of HW's principal works:

	Source:
Reminiscence	*The Labouring Life*
The lone swallows	*The Lone Swallows*
Uncle Joe	*The Village Book*
Muggy	*The Village Book*
The railway bridge	*Tarka the Otter*

Braunton Burrows	*The Pathway*
The estuary of the two rivers	*Salar the Salmon*
Appledore and the revenge	*The Pathway*
The fair	*The Labouring Life*
Winds of heaven	*The Children of Shallowford*
Saunton Sands	*Goodbye West Country*
Willie Maddison's home at Shelley Cove	*The Dream of Fair Women*
The redds	*Salar the Salmon*
A journey on the Lynton Railway	*On Foot in Devon*
Humpy Bridge	*The Children of Shallowford*

A73 HEART OF ENGLAND Contributions to the Evening Standard 1939–1941

A sequel to the two volumes of *A Breath of Country Air* (A63, 64) with Williamson's contributions to *The Evening Standard* from 29 March 1939 to 25 April 1941, edited with an Introduction and Postscript by John Gregory.

2003. The Henry Williamson Society. *First edition.*
i) 'This collection first published 2003'. ISBN 1 873507 20 8. Pp.viii + 96. Frontispiece and one illustration, reckoned; 4 pp. illustrations not reckoned. 217 x 140mm. Card covers light blue, printed in black and grey with owl device on the front; perfect-bound. Price £8.50. 170 copies.

ii) Limited issue: as i) except: 'The first edition of Heart of England is published by The Henry Williamson Society in a limited edition of 200 copies, thirty of these have been bound in quarter Nigerian goatskin by Brignell Bookbinders, Cambridge. This is copy number ...' followed by the number in ink, on verso of the second leaf. ISBN 1 873507 21 6. Pp.xli + 98 (added blanks). 226 x 150mm. Grey cloth, quarter-bound in maroon goatskin, in grey cloth slip-case. Price £50 plus £7 in slip-case. 30 copies.

Contents:
- 'Introduction' (2 pp.) by John Gregory;
- illustrations: frontispiece photograph of HW, 8 photographs of

Williamson locations, one of Norman Jordan;
- text (pp.1–95) with 33 titles in date order, followed by a one-page
'Postscript' on HW's newspaper articles by John Gregory:

	Date:
Wilderness?	29.03.39
Immortal corn	26.04.39
Heart of England	05.06.39
Heart of England, 2	12.06.39
3 Kronk, king of the crows	19.06.39
4 I made a trout stream - by accident	26.06.39
5 Rabbits feed while men go hungry	03.07.39
6 The swallows in my porch are learning to fly	10.07.39
7 A daily banquet at the fish pool	17.07.39
8 The heron goes fishing	24.07.39
Hunt the stag	31.07.39
9 Forest stolen by the sea	07.08.39
10 The wood of wind-dwarfs	14.08.39
Terns from the Arctic	21.08.39
Harvesting the barley crop	28.08.39
11 I listened to the partridges talking	04.09.39
Heart in the land puts mettle in men	11.09.39
Cats in the front line	27.09.39
Pheasants in the mustard	10.10.39
The joys of farming	16.10.39
Shall we shoot the foxes?	24.10.39
The wind and the rain	28.11.39
Plough of content	13.12.39
Cold comfort	17.01.40
No pity for pigeons	01.02.40
Winter tames them all	16.02.40
Night sun	22.02.40
Voice of the turtle	02.04.40
Springtime on the farm	20.05.40
We're growing our own roast beef again	02.12.40
Two girls saved this farm	26.12.40
The army is taking my best farm labourer away	23.01.41
The barley seed goes in	25.03.41

B: BOOKS EDITED OR WITH A CONTRIBUTION BY WILLIAMSON

Items have been included in this section only if they contain material by Williamson that is original, intentional and identifiable. It does not therefore include anthologies with samples or selections of previously published work, books with transcripts from letters that were not meant for publication, or books to which he may have contributed unspecified parts of the text.

1928. Stephen Southwold (Ed.). *The Children's Play-Hour Book.* No.2. Longmans, Green, 1928.'Timbo's Dream' by HW (pp.141–5), illustrated. Reprinted in HWSJ 32.

1929. Anon. [Capt. D.H. Bell]. *A Soldier's Diary of the Great War.* Faber & Gwyer, 1929. Published in the USA as *In Spite of All Rejoicing,* Duffield and Company, 1929. 'Introduction' by HW (pp.vii-xx) who also prepared the text for publication, dated 28 December 1928, Devon; (see the Dedication in A42). Reprinted in A67.

1930a. T. Michael Pope (Ed.). *The Book of Fleet Street.* Cassell, 1930. 'The Confessions of a Fake Merchant' by HW (pp.280–302). Reprinted in HWSJ 8, 9.

1930b. Stephen Southwold (Ed.). *The Children's Play-Hour Book.* No.4. Longmans, Green, 1930. 'Educating the Cuckoo' by HW.

1931a. John Heygate. *Decent Fellows.* Jonathan Cape and Harrison Smith, USA, 1931. First American edition. 'Introduction' by HW (pp.xi-xxii) written in rebuttal of critics of the first UK edition which was published by Mundanus (Gollancz) 1930 with a dedication to HW but no Introduction. Reprinted in A67.

1931b. H.A. Manhood. *Little Peter the Great.* Joiner & Steele (on a slip tipped-in over William Jackson Ltd. 1931). The Furnival Books No.7. 550 copies, numbered and signed by the author. 'Foreword' by HW (pp.7–11) dated New York City, 1st December 1930. Reprinted in A67.

1931c. Izaak Walton. *The Compleat Angler.* George C. Harrap, 1931. New edition. 'Introduction' by HW (pp.9–16) dated Shallowford, 24 March 1931; illustrated by Arthur Rackham. Reprinted 1975, 1984, 1985 etc.

1934a. Richard Jefferies. *The Amateur Poacher.* Jonathan Cape, 1934. The Travellers' Library. 'Introduction' by HW (pp.11–15) dated Shallowford, June 1934. Reprinted in the magazine *Now and Then* (Winter 1934) and the anthology *Then and Now*, Cape, 1935.

1934b. Richard Jefferies. *Wild Life in a Southern County.* Jonathan Cape, 1934. The Travellers' Library. 'Introduction' by HW (pp.7–10); text as 1934a.

1934c. V.M. Yeates. *Winged Victory.* Jonathan Cape, 1934. Second impression, dated November 1934. Following the death of Yeates in December 1934 later copies of this printing have a memorial 'Tribute to V.M. Yeates' by HW (pp.7–11) dated January 1935; (published also in *John O'London's Weekly* 26.01.35). Reprinted by Cape in 1961 with a revised Tribute and a one-page 'Preface to the New edition' by HW dated July 1961, then in paperback by Sphere Books 1969, Mayflower 1974, and in A67.

The book was first published in June 1934 with the dedication 'To Henry Williamson at whose suggestion this book was begun, with whose encouragement and help it was written and ended'.

1935. Richard Jefferies. *The Gamekeeper at Home.* Jonathan Cape, 1935. The Travellers' Library. 'Introduction' by HW (pp.7–11); text as 1934a.

1936a. Henry Williamson (Ed.). *An Anthology of Modern Nature Writing.* Thomas Nelson, 1936. Modern Anthologies No.6: Nature. Selected passages from 27 authors, including his own 'A Summer Afternoon by the Sea (from LL), with editorial 'rearrangements' and an 'Introduction' (pp.ix-xvi) with brief notes on each author. Reprinted with the Introduction slightly revised in The Argosy Books series 1948.

The other authors selected (in text order) are: Thomas Hardy, W.H. Hudson, Richard Jefferies, John Fortescue, Maurice Hewlett, J.C. Tregarthen, John Galsworthy, Joseph Conrad, Edward Thomas, George Bourne, Francis Brett Young, S.P.B. Mais, Siegfried Sassoon, John Masefield, Wilfrid Ewart, V.M. Yeates, H.M. Tomlinson, Edmund Blunden, Compton Mackenzie, H.J. Massingham, D.H. Lawrence, A.G.

Street, Adrian Bell, Miss E. Turner, H.E. Bates, Eric Taverner.

1936b. *Nature in Britain: An Illustrated Survey.* B.T. Batsford, 1936. The Pilgrims' Library. 'Introduction' by HW (pp.1–18) with notes on the contributors.

1937a. Henry Williamson. *Richard Jefferies: Selections of his Work, with details of his Life and Circumstance, his Death and Immortality.* Faber & Faber, 1937. Extended passages from Jefferies' works, with a general introduction in two parts, I: The English Genius (reprinted in A71), II: To the Two Types of Jefferies Readers, introductions to each section, notes in the text and an 'Epigraph' by HW; illustrated with photographs. Reprinted 1940. Second edition, revised and with Jefferies' 'A Pageant of Summer' added, 1947.

1937b. A.W. Lawrence. *T.E. Lawrence by His Friends.* Jonathan Cape, 1937. Recollections of Lawrence by HW (pp.451–5), untitled.

1937c. Richard Jefferies. *Hodge and His Masters.* Revised by Henry Williamson with a Foreword. Methuen, 1937. 'Foreword' (pp.v–x) dated Old Hall Farm, North Norfolk, June 1937, including an explanation of the revisions which involved moving chapters around, leaving some out, cutting and joining others and changing most of the headings.

1941. Sir E. John Russell. *English Farming.* William Collins, 1941. Britain in Pictures. 'Introduction' by HW (pp.7–10). Reprinted in A71.

1943a. Lilias Rider Haggard and Henry Williamson. *Norfolk Life.* Faber and Faber, 1943. Articles published in *The Eastern Daily Press* by Lilias Haggard worked into a book with the assistance of HW who provides Chapter 1 (pp.7–12) as an introduction. Reprinted, with the ninth impression in 1948.

1943b. Richard Harman (Ed.). *Country-Side Mood.* Blandford Press, 1943. 'A Devon Stream' by HW (pp.22–30); a rewritten version of 'The Story of a Devon Stream' in *Strand* June 1943.

1946a. Richard Jefferies. *A Classic of English Farming: Hodge and His Masters.* Edited and with an Introduction by Henry Williamson. Faber and Faber, 1946. The 'Introduction' (pp.7–20) is a combination of new text and passages from the Foreword in 1937c; in the text the chapters are further rearranged and two headings changed. Reprinted in 1948.

1946b. Richard Harman (Ed.). *Countryside Character: An Anthology.* Blandford Press, 1946. 'The Clodhoppers' by HW (pp.18–34); from the Norfolk farm period.

1947. Malcom Elwin (Ed.). *The Pleasure Ground: A Miscellany of English Writing.* Macdonald, 1947. 'The Winter of 1941' by HW (pp.102–20). Reprinted in A71.

1948. *Tribute to Walter De La Mare: on His 75th Birthday.* Faber, 1948. 'Some Pets of Our Farm' by HW (pp.171–7).

1949. Richard Harman (Ed.). *Country Company: An Anthology.* Blandford Press, 1949. 'The Story of a Norfolk Owl' by HW (pp.111–21); a new version of 'We had an Owl in the Family' in *Strand* December 1944.

1950. James Farrar. *The Unreturning Spring:* Being the Poems, Sketches, Stories, and Letters of James Farrar. Williams and Norgate, 1950. Edited with an 'Introduction' by HW (pp.7–11). New edition with the Introduction slightly revised, Chatto and Windus, 1968. Reprinted in A67.

?1950s. *A Souvenir and Guide of Braunton and District.* The Publicity Committee. No date. 'The Burrows, 1938' and 'Baggy Hole, Revisited in May 1945' by HW. Reprinted in HWSJ 19.

1952a. George J. Gill. *A Fight Against Tithes.* Edited by Donald Gill and S.S. Gill, Haslemere, Surrey. Printed by A.A. Tanner, 1952. A note at the front acknowledges Williamson's 'unrestricted help' with the book and Chapter XVII is an 'Epigraph' by HW (pp.85–8) dated Botesdale, June 1949.

1952b. Keidrych Rhys (Ed.). *Angry Prayers:* A Report on the Convention of British Animal Protection Societies. London, Canine Defence, 1952. 'Portrait of a Spaniel' by HW (pp.29–31).

1960a. Father Brocard Sewell (Ed.). *Arthur Machen.* St Albert's Press, 1960. 350 copies, numbered. 'Machen in Fleet Street' by HW (pp.39–40).

Reprinted in A62, A67.

1960b. N. Hardy Wallis (Ed.). *Essays by Divers Hands:* Being the Transactions of The Royal Society of Literature. New series, volume 30. O.U.P. 1960. The Wedmore Memorial Lecture: 'Some Nature Writers and Civilization' by HW (pp.1–18) with a 'Postscript'. See A47.

1960c. Walter Robson. *Letters from a Soldier.* Faber and Faber, 1960. 'Introduction' by HW (pp.9–14) dated Devon, 11 March 1960.

1961a Brian Inglis (Ed). *John Bull's Schooldays.* Hutchinson, 1961. 'Out of the Prisoning Tower' by HW (pp.144–9); previously in the *Spectator* 1958. Reprinted in A71.

1961b. *Edmund Blunden: Sixty-Five.* The English Society. University of Hong Kong, November 1961. A one-page contribution to the birthday celebration 'From Henry Williamson' (p.183) from Georgeham, North Devon.

1963a. Ronald Blythe. *The Age of Illusion.* Hamish Hamilton, 1963. 'The Rector of Stiffkey' by HW (pp.134–54).

1963b. James Turner (Ed.). *A Book of Gardens.* Cassell, 1963. 'Field Garden' by HW (pp.193–204). Reprinted in HWSJ 6.

1965. Alister Kershaw and Frederic-Jacques Temple (Eds.). *Richard Aldington: An Intimate Portrait.* Southern Illinois University Press, USA 1965. A reminiscence of a visit to Aldington in the winter of 1949 by HW, (pp.164–8), untitled. Reprinted in HWSJ 28.

1966a. Henry Williamson (Ed.). *My Favourite Country Stories.* Lutterworth Press, 1966. A selection from 11 authors with an 'Introduction' (pp.9–10) dated August 1966, Devon.
    Authors selected (in text order) are: W.H. Hudson, H.M. Tomlinson, Flora Thompson, Richard Jefferies, Richard Williamson, Ruth Tomalin, H. Plunket Greene, Alison Uttley, James Farrar, the Earl of Bessborogh, Thomas Hardy.

1966b. Francis Thompson. *The Mistress of Vision.* Saint Albert's Press, 1966. 500 copies, numbered.'A First Adventure with Francis Thompson' by HW (pp.vi-xix). Reprinted in A71.

1966c. Richard Jefferies. *Bevis: The Story of a Boy.* Dent, 1966. Everyman's Library No.850. 'Introduction' by HW (pp.vii-x) dated 1966.

1967. Francis Thompson. *The Hound of Heaven.* The Francis Thompson Society, 1967. 500 copies, numbered. The text of HW's Presidential Address 'In Darkest England' (pp.7–15). Reprinted in A67.

1971a. *The Twelfth Man:* A Book of Original Contributions Brought Together by The Lord's Taverners. Cassell, 1971. 'Genesis of Tarka' by HW (pp.71–8).

1971b. *The Richard Jefferies Society: Twenty-First Anniversary 1950–1971.* The Richard Jefferies Society, 1971. An A5 pamphlet. 'Foreword' by HW (pp.1–3) as President of the Society, dated Easter Day 1971, North Devon.

1973. *The Wipers Times:* A Complete Facsimile of the Famous World War One Trench Newspaper ... Peter Davies, 1973. 'Foreword' by HW (pp.viii-x).

C: PERIODICALS WITH CONTRIBUTIONS BY WILLIAMSON

Titles of periodicals are listed alphabetically (omitting 'The' from the title) with the contributions then arranged chronologically under each periodical. Cross-references indicate where the material is known to have been published later in book form (with or without alteration) or in the HWSJ.

Action (see HWSJ 22)

07.05.38	Good neighbours
13.08.38	August 1914
12.11.38	November 11
31.12.38	Christmas of 1914
28.01.39	Am I a crank because I put my country first?
18.02.39	Youth on the threshold
18.03.39	Advice from Henry Williamson
03.06.39–02.09.39	Everyman's war (13 weekly parts, excluding 15.07.39)
15.07.39	My life's purpose

Adelphi

Sept. 1924	The doom of the peregrine falcon (WW)
Jul.-Sept. 1943	Fare thee well, my poesy
Oct.-Dec. 1943	The tragic spirit (GFP)
Jan.-Mar. 1944	Seven years after
Apr.-Ju. 1944	Prospect and retrospect
Jul.-Sept. 1944	The harvest in the corn hall
Oct.-Dec. 1944	Withypool: June 1940 (HWSJ 35)
Apr.-Jun. 1945	A walk in spring
Jul.-Sept. 1945	Village children of the twenties
Oct.-Dec. 1945	A crown of life: for Benjamin Britten (TME)
Jan.-Mar. 1946	The sun that shines on the dead
Apr.-Jun. 1946	The sun that shines on the dead II
Jul.-Sept. 1946	Farming story
Jan.-Mar. 1947	From 'A Wartime Norfolk Journal': Easter 1944 (HWSJ 36)

Jan.-Mar. 1948	From 'A Chronicle Writ in Darkness'
Apr.-Jun. 1948	Oswald Mosley on style (introduction to a letter from O.M.)
Jul.-Sept. 1948	Birth of the phasian bird (WW)
Oct.-Dec. 1948	EDITED by HW and with his own contributions: The lost legions (WW)
	Report on the Richard Jefferies Centenary (WW)
Jan.-Mar. 1949	EDITED by HW and with his own contributions: Notes of a 'prentice hand (WW)
	Words on the west wind (WW)
Apr.-Jun. 1949	EDITED by HW and with his own contributions: A note on Tarka the otter (WW)
	Words on the west wind (WW)
Jul.-Sept. 1949	Words on the west wind (WW)
Autumn 1949	Words on the west wind (WW)
	review of a translation of 'Faust' by von Goethe
Jan.-Mar. 1950	Words on the west wind: crossing the Alps (WW)

Animal Life

Mar. 1951	Words on the west wind: a monthly chronicle.
Apr. 1951	The dog that ate his punishment
May 1951	In memory of Cheepy
	Words on the west wind
Jun. 1951	Words on the west wind

Animals

08.01.63	The ravens of Baggy

Animal World

c.1938–1939	An animal crosses a field

Antigonish Review

Spring 1970	An affirmation (D 1980a)

Argosy

Oct. 1928	The yellow boots (DH 'The Story of the Poisoned Hounds')
Apr. 1935	The heller
Dec. 1935	Stumberleap
Mar. 1936	No eel for Nog

May 1936	The backbreaker's bride
Jun. 1936	A crown of life (TME)
Oct. 1936	The vigil of mousing Keekee
Apr. 1937	Bill Brock's good turn
Jun. 1937	The five lives of the Isle of Wight parson
Oct. 1967	The stags of Stumberleap

Atlantic Monthly (USA)

Aug. 1927	English idylls
Oct. 1927	The linhay on the downs (LD, LOD)
Nov. 1927	'Muggy,' the rabbit agent (VB)
May 1928	The heller (DH)
Jul. 1929	Swagdagger crosses a field (DH)
Dec. 1934	Christmas (CH)
Jan. 1935	Moonlight
Feb. 1935	A night on Salisbury Plain
May 1935	The dear one
Sept. 1935	Salar the salmon I: tideways
Oct. 1935	Salar the salmon II: spring spate
Nov. 1935	Salar the salmon III: winter star-stream (all abridged)
Jan. 1936	A crown of life (TME)
Jun. 1936	The renewal of self
Nov. 1936	My best hour of fishing
May 1937	East wind
Jun. 1937	Richard Jefferies (B 1937a 'The English Genius')
Mar. 1938	Ravens in Devon
Dec. 1939	The children of Shallowford
Jan. 1940	Tales of my children
Jun. 1940	From a Norfolk farm
Jan. 1945	The snipe's nest
May 1946	Clodhopper
Jun. 1946	Plowing the home hills
Jul. 1947	Hooly

Author

Summer 1953	letter: Author's agents and foreign tax

Aylesford Review

Winter 1957–58	Some notes on 'The Flax of Dream' and 'A

	Chronicle of Ancient Sunlight' (SNO, D 1980a)
Spring 1959	letter re unpublished versions of SNF
	review of 'In Flanders Fields' by L. Wolff
Winter 1959–60	Machen in Fleet Street (SNO, TTL, B 1960a)
Autumn 1963	A visit to Richard Aldington (SNO)
Summer-Autumn 1964	review of 'Berg' by Ann Quin
Summer 1966	Reflections on a theme (SNO)
Autumn 1967	Lucifer or Eosphoros? by 'Green Jacket' (a review of LBS under a pseudonym; SNO)

Bermondsey Book
| Mar. 1926 | The old pond (?OS) |
| Aug. 1929 | The drama of a pond (LOD) |

Bookman
| Dec. 1929 | contribution to 'The Mysterious in Real life' |

Books and Bookmen
| Mar. 1963 | Birth of a chronicle |

British Union Quarterly
| Oct.-Dec. 1939 | Autobiography (extracts from COS) |

Brittania
| 02.11.28 | Hunting to kill (WRD: part I) |
| 09.11.28 | The valley |

Cassell's Magazine
| Sept. 1928 | The heller (DH) |

Catholic Herald
| Mar. 1968 | review: A poet beyond derision; 'Strange Harp, Strange Symphony. The life of Francis Thompson' by J. Walsh |

Cavalcade
| 13.05.44 | 'Give us this day' |
| 12.08.44 | Postwar or postpone? |

Chambers's Journal
Jan. 1951   Trout

Colfeian
Jun. 1922   An open letter; dated 5 May 1922

Colfensia
1908   Some feathered thieves; signed HWW
1915   letter: War news; dated 17.03.15

Collier's Weekly (USA)
11.04.25   No eel for Nog (OS)
26.09.25   The flight of the pale pink pyjamas (OS)
17.10.25   Stumberleap (OS)

Contemporary Review
Jun. 1971   Reflections on the death of a Field Marshal (Haig; HWSJ 34)

Co-operative Home Magazine (continues as Home Magazine)
Apr.-Dec. 1958   articles numbered I-IX, collected in *From a Country Hilltop* (A61)

Country Fair
Sept. 1951   letter

Country Life
04.07.52   The gentleman's river (HWSJ 33; see HWAS)
01.12.55   Vanished life of the fields

Countryman
Jan.-Mar. 1933   The difficulties of rural writing (HWSJ 25)
Apr.-Jun. 1941   contribution to 'The Rural School'

Daily Express
04.01.15   letter: Unofficial truce (from the trenches, dated 26.12.14, submitted by HW's father)
22.01.21   In the country I
05.02.21   In the country II
12.02.21   In the country III

23.02.21	In the country IV
12.03.21	In the country V
16.03.21	A terrified passenger
19.03.21	In the country VI
30.03.21	In the country VII (LS 'Vignettes of Nature II')
16.04.21	In the country VIII
23.04.21	In the country IX (LS 'Vignettes of Nature I')
03.05.21	Sport among the rubbish heaps (LS 'Sportsmen of the Rubbish-Heaps')
07.06.21	Honeymoon flight of the nightjars (LS 'Haunt of the Evejar I')
01.07.21	The kingdom of the thirsty (LS 'Invocation')
19.07.21	Bird mystics (LS)
30.07.21	Death at 150 miles an hour.
20.08.21	Samaritans (LS)
06.09.21	Winged prophets (LS 'Prophet Birds')
15.09.21	Proserpine returns (?LS 'Proserpine's Message')
05.10.21	Brock
13.10.21	Buzzards
05.02.23	Reynard run 'stiff'
10.02.23	letter: Why one hunts
03.03.23	The tale of a cad
14.06.23	The salmon fishers
04.06.24	The tame cuckoo
19.03.27	A night symphony
20.07.27	And this was Ypres (WFP, HWSJ 34)
21.07.27	And this was Ypres II (WFP, HWSJ 34)
22.07.27	And this was Ypres III (WFP, HWSJ 34)
23.07.27	And this was Ypres IV (WFP)
05.12.27	A Devonshire donkey
28.12.27	Char-ley
16.06.28	A seaside episode
08.08.28	Fourteen years after
11.08.28	The last 100 days (HWSJ 34)
18.08.28	The last 100 days: with the 4th Army (HWSJ 34)
23.08.28	The last 100 days: tanks in action (HWSJ 34)
01.09.28	The last 100 days: so why fight on? (HWSJ 34)
17.09.28	I believe in the men who died (HWSJ 34)
26.09.28	(Manchester ed.) The last 100 days: breaking through (HWSJ 34)

01.07.38	The lonely couple
26.07.38	They must come back from the cities (SNF, in chap. 33)
13.08.38	All these things are mine (SNF, in chap. 39)
20.08.38	We shall not harm you
31.08.38	Did this horrify you?
03.10.38	I hope you will get a day's fishing soon, Mr Chamberlain
14.11.38	So we poured our barley into the gutter
26.11.38	Do you know why owls fly so silently? (SNF, in chap. 47)
10.12.38	Can a fish jump?
14.12.38	There's a lot of angry talk up here (SNF, in chaps. 43, 45)
19.12.38	We shall miss our 'tarkies' (SNF, in chap. 46)
28.12.38	The snow will soon be all gone (SNF, in chap. 49)
03.01.39	Bang! My first wild duck (SNF, in chap. 47)
18.02.39	Nine o'clock on Monday mornings
25.02.39	The old raven lost his meal
03.04.39	The casebook of P/C Bullcornworthy
04.04.39	My sheep have silver outlines
10.04.39	Taking a country walk today?
29.04.39	On the ramparts of Ypres I can lie at ease
20.05.39	To whom does the egg belong? The great cuckoo mystery
27.05.39	Even farmers take a day off sometimes (SNF, in last chap.)
10.06.39	£1,000,000 couldn't beat nature
28.08.39	Our backs may ache but we won't be beaten (SNF, in chap. 38)
15.09.39	A big bang on the home front
06.10.39	At the point of the ploughshare
14.11.64	This precious England!
29.06.66–27.03.71	38 titles, collected and listed in *Days of Wonder* (A60)

Daily Mail

16.06.28	A fool in the Pyrenees
23.12.33	I mean to have an old-time Christmas
13.06.57	What is happening in this crazy summer of ours?
08.06.60	letter re Gavin Maxwell's 'Mij'

Daily Mirror
12.11.28   on Remembrance Day at the Cenotaph (HWSJ 18)

Daily News
10.08.25   Swallows in the cliffs
27.08.27   A drama of the Needles (LL 'Above the Needles')

Daily Sketch
01.05.44   This is why the farmer can't sleep

Daily Telegraph
13.06.28   With a boy on the headland (VB 'A Boy on the Headland')
16.10.59   letter: Language pitfalls
04.11.59   letter: B.E.F's Vickers guns
22.12.67   Unknown; in 'Haunted Stories for Christmas Firesides'
18.04.69   (Magazine) The green desert

Devon and Cornwall Journal
Apr.-Jun. 1953   A hero of the sands

Eastern Daily Press
10.10.38   letter: Farmers and the barley crisis
17.11.38   letter: The barley price protest
23.03.39   letter: 'Crush-the-others' system
29.03.39   letter: Pacification of Europe has begun
01.04.39   letter: Prague under the Germans
18.03.41   letter: Sunday ploughing
01.04.41   letter: Military damage on the farm
10.04.41   letter: Military damage
18.04.41   letter re military damage
12.03.41–10.04.44   48 titles, collected and listed in *Green Fields and Pavements* (A68)
12.04.43   letter: A Stiffkey corner
12.01.44   letter: Local farming profits
02.05.44   The snipe's nest
20.04.61   letter re a review of 'In the Woods'

Empire News
03.10.43   A fight to the death

English Digest
Jan. 1940   Chalk for English fields

English Review
Nov. 1920   The night (?LS 'Midsummer Night')
May 1921   The passing of the blossom (LS 'London Children
                  and Wild Flowers')

Esquire (USA)
Jun. 1953   The crake (altered without HW's permission)

European
Sept. 1953   From A Chronicle Writ in Darkness I
Oct. 1953   From A Chronicle Writ in Darkness II
May 1954   Threnos for T.E. Lawrence I (TTL)
Jun. 1954   Threnos for T.E. Lawrence II (TTL)
Nov. 1954   review of 'The Home Letters of T.E. Lawrence and
                  His Brothers'
Sept. 1956   The Bernard Shaw Centenary Luncheon at the
                  Savoy
Feb. 1959   Roy Campbell: a portrait (TTL)

Evening Chronicle
24.05.37   The flight of the falcons

Evening News
19.08.20   My owl
?.?.28   The miracle I saw in France

Evening Standard
08.11.30–28.11.30 Patriot's Progress (serialised)
26.09.36   My best hour of fishing
29.12.36   Elijah and the ravens - why not?
17.05.37   The flight of the falcons
18.06.38   The solitary mayfly
29.03.39–25.03.41 33 titles, collected and listed in *Heart of England*
                  (A72)

14.02.44–18.12.44	45 titles, collected and listed in *A Breath of Country Air, part 1* (A63)
23.12.44	Star of the morning
01.01.45-04.12.45	37 titles, collected and listed in *A Breath of Country Air, part 2* (A64)
27.04.55	The shuck dog; in 'Did it Happen'
03.08.61	The love game - the patient old otter wins
29.06.64	Return to hell 1 (WFP 1987)
30.06.64	Return to hell 2 (WFP 1987)
01.07.64	Return to hell 3 (WFP 1987)
02.07.64	Return to hell 4 (WFP 1987)
03.07.64	Return to hell; concludes (WFP 1987)
04.08.64	review: This was the war that began 50 years ago today; 'Her Privates We' by F. Manning
18.08.64	review: 1914–18 The poets have the last word; 'English Poetry of the First World War' and 'Up the Line to Death'
16.11.64–20.11.64	5 articles, collected and listed in Indian Summer Notebook (A71)
02.09.67	Poet of war (Siegfried Sassoon; HWSJ 6)

Everyman

| 10.10.29 | The future (extract from WFP) |
| 12.12.29 | Winter (extract from BY) |

Family

Apr. 1935	The story of my children I
May 1935	Tales of my children II, III
Jun. 1935	Tales of my children IV
Jul. 1935	Tales of my children V

Farmer's Weekly

| 22.09.61 | The prophet of the golden wheat |

Field

16.07.21	Peregrines in love (LS)
05.04.41	1 am a B. farmer
21.06.41	My bit of Britain

Fortnightly

Aug. 1937   A Wiltshire lad (B 1937a 'The English Genius', abridged)

Fortnightly Review (USA)

Jul.-Dec. 1927   The linhay on the downs (LD, LOD)
May 1930   review: Wild life and open country; 3 books

Foylibra

Jun. 1936   The literature of rural life (text of a talk by HW at Foyles on 21 May)

Garvin's Gazette (Totnes)

Summer 1941   The swamp

Golden Book Magazine (USA)

Sept. 1928   Chakcheck's raid on London
Nov. 1928   Bill Brock's good turn
Nov. 1930   The trapper's mates
Apr. 1933   Death of the killer (DH)

Good Housekeeping

Dec. 1940   The farmer comes into his own

Guardian

12.05.61   review: The Somme offensive; 'The Big Push' by B. Gardner

Harper's Monthly Magazine

Dec. 1932   The backbreaker's bride (PS 1934)
May 1937   My otter

History of the First World War (published in parts)

1970   The Christmas truce (ISN)

Home Magazine (continuation of Co-op Home Magazine)

Jan. 1959–Jan. 1962   articles numbered X-XLII, collected in *From a Country Hilltop* (A61)

Hutchinson's Magazine

Apr. 1923	The saga of Chakchek (PS)
May 1923	Wizzle: son of Chakchek
Sept. 1925	No eel for Nog; illustrated by Warwick Reynolds (OS)

John O'London's Weekly (including its supplement 'The Outline')

13.08.27	Bluemantle (PS 1934)
01.09.28	(Outline) A drama of the Needles: when a falcon and a raven fought (LL)
? 1929	letter re Patriot's Progress
16.04.32	Billy Goldsworthy's cow (LL)
22.06.?33 (or 35)	Thatch
01.12.34	Why genius is tragic (B 1934a 'Introduction')
22.12.34	(Outline) Peregrines over the estuary
26.01.35	V.M. Yeates: a personal tribute (B 1934c)
16.03.35	My adventure with a heron
23.11.35	review: Young man about Europe; 'Motor Tramp' by John Heygate
25.04.36	The making of a soldier
20.06.36	The necessity for fishing: with apologies to P.B. Shelley
28.06.40	The fidelity of England
19.07.40	review: From marsh to meadow; 2 books by H.C. Darby
06.09.40	Days on Devon streams
30.11.51	review: A riotous artist; 'The Second Burst' by Sir Alfred Munnings (HWSJ 30)
28.03.52	review: Augustus John's self-portrait; 'Chiaroscuro'
16.05.52	review: The land made to yield; 'Community Farm' by J.M. Murry
19.03.54	review: Gamekeeper's life; 'Memoirs of a Gamekeeper' by T.W. Turner
02.07.54	review: T.E. Lawrence and his brothers; 'The Home Letters of ...'
16.07.54	review: Supreme nature writer; 'W.H. Hudson' by Ruth Tomalin
10.09.54	review: Tamer of otters; 'An Otter's Story' by E.E. Liers
07.04.60	review: The lion and the lamb; 'Born Free' by Joy

Adamson
22.09.60   review: Man the destroyer; 'Wild Life in America' by
P. Matthiessen

Listener

24.12.35–03.08.39   17 articles, collected and listed in *Spring Days in Devon* (A65)
01.07.36   letter re Biting Stone-crop
21.11.68   introduction to 'A Verse Letter by Siegfried Sassoon'

Literary Digest

Summer 1947   Poor Richard Jefferies (B 1934a 'Introduction', condensed)
Autumn 1949   James Farrar, luminous youth (part 2 of 'The Lost Legions' in *Adelphi* Oct.-Dec. 1948)

Living Age (USA)

Feb. 1937   The otter: a story

London Mercury

Jan. 1926   Otters in winter (HWSJ 33)
Jan. 1927   The ackymals (ACK, LOD)
Feb. 1928   letter: Provincialisms (LL, TA 1964a 'Apologia pro verba mea')
Oct. 1928   The sawyers (VB)
Jan. 1929   Reality in war literature (LOD)
Jul. 1929   The Zeale brothers (VB)
Oct. 1929   The spirit of the village (LL)

Lovat Dickson's Magazine

Mar. 1935   Whatever has happened?

Manchester Guardian

04.04.27   The crowstarver (?LS 1928)
08.03.29   The rabbit agent (VB)

Millinery Trades Journal

May 1921   Mating-time millinery of the birds: the plumage of spring

Modern Man
Autumn 1951 The gentleman's river (see HWAS)

Monthly Criterion
Feb. 1928 The village inns (VB)

My Best Novel (Islington Public Libraries)
1950 The Flax of Dream

Nash's and Pall Mall Magazine
Dec. 1934 The maiden salmon; co-illustrated by C.F. Tunnicliffe (DH)
Dec. 1935 A crown of life (TME)
Feb. 1936 A night on Dartmoor (TME)

Nation and Athenaeum
26.11.27 letter: Feeding habits of otters
07.01.28 letter re otters

Nature Magazine (USA)
Jan. 1941 The mystery of the European cuckoo

New London Magazine
Nov. 1930 – Apr. 1931 The country-side month by month (6 monthly parts; LS 1933 'The Country of the Rain')

News Chronicle
02.06.36 contribution to 'I Stand Today': three questions to war authors
17.08.37 The last hunt

News-Letter (National Labour Party Fortnightly)
01.10.32 Village families

Now and Then
Autumn 1928 review of 'Nightseed' by H.A. Manhood
Spring 1929 review: A note on 'Combed Out' by F.A. Voigt
Winter 1932 review of 'Death in the Afternoon' by Ernest Hemingway

Winter 1934	Richard Jefferies: an introduction (B 1934a 'Introduction')

Our Time
Nov. 1944	Gerald Winstanley foresaw a new England

Outsiders (USA)
May 1929	Bill Brock's farewell I, II (OS 1933 in 'The Epic of Brock the Badger')
	A drama of the needles (LL 'Above the Needles')

Pan Fiction Magazine
Nov. 1922	Raskil, the wood rogue; illustrated by Warwick Reynolds (PS)
Nov. 1923	The revenge of the Chakcheks

Panorama
Spring 1950	My friends the crows

Passing Show
14.04.34	Swagdagger crosses a field (DH)

Pearson's Magazine (USA)
pre Feb. 1922	Bill Brock's last hunt (?PS 'Bloody Bill Brock')
Mar. 1923	The man who did not hunt; illustrated by Lionel Edwards (HWSJ 31)
May 1925	Bill Brock's good turn (OS)
Oct. 1925	The stag of Stumberleap (OS)

Pearson's Weekly
20.08.30	What I am teaching my children about God

Pictorial Review (USA)
?1922	a story of peregrine falcons (cited in SIS p.144)

Poetry Quarterly
Summer 1941	The gaping raven of Morte

Poetry Review
Apr.-Jun. 1959	review: A lost poet - James Farrar 1923–44

Poppy Annual
1941   A tale of ravens

Queen's Quarterly (Ontario, Canada)
Summer 1934   Migration, a story

Radio Times
09.11.28   Armistice Day 1928: what we should remember and
                    what forget (HWSJ 27)
19.03.37   (Countryside No.) Wild animals of England

?Apr.-May 1952 Tiger's Teeth (see note in PEP)

07.11.68   Henry Williamson on the western front
?.?.72   letter: Henry Williamson explains

Rake
1963   The Wet Flanders Plain (the Preface)
1963   The Story of a Norfolk Farm (chap. 1)

Reader's Digest
Jul. 1935 (USA)   Moonlight

Oct. 1936 (USA)   Salar the salmon (condensed)
Nov. 1959   Moonlight
Aug. 1968   Salar the salmon (the ending)

Royal Magazine
pre Feb. 1922   Li'l Jearge (PS)

Saturday Evening Post (USA)
05.01.24   Bill Brock's good turn (OS)
?   Stumberleap (cited in CNS p.151)

Saturday Review
May ?1921   The lone swallows (LS)
?   Spring in a Devon village (LS 'Lady Day in Devon')

Saturday Review of Literature (USA)
09.03.35   letter: Wingless victor; re V.M. Yeates

Scottish Daily Mail
13.06.57   Let me tell you of a startlingly new wild world

Scythe (continuation of The Townsman)
Jul. 1944   Herefordshire hops
Mar. 1945   The fair
Jun. 1945   The farmer's life 1
Autumn 1945   The farmer's life 2
Feb. 1946   The farmer's life 3

Spectator
22.08.58   Out of the prisoning tower (B 1961a)
12.09.58   letter: Devon
20.08.65   review: Richard Jefferies; 'Man of the Fields' by S.J.
                       Looker

Storyteller
Jul. 1933   Death to the killer (DH)

Strand
Jun. 1943   The story of a Devon stream
Dec. 1944   We had an owl in the family
Sept. 1945   When I was demobilised

Sunday Chronicle
23.12.34   This Christmas (CH)

Sunday Dispatch
15.07.28   Bill Brock's last battle
09.09.28   The old cob cottage (VB)

Sunday Express
18.12.21   A house of no morals (HWSJ 31)
25.12.21   Scarecrow Cottage (HWSJ 31)
08.01.22   The woman of Scarecrow Cottage (HWSJ 31)
29.01.22   The day's round at Scarecrow Cottage (HWSJ 31)
22.04.23   Elegy (PS 'Nor' in 'Elegies Three')
06.01.24   My owl-ghosts
08.07.28   A bird-blasted wood (LL)
16.09.28   Windwhistle Cross (LL)

Sunday Referee

28.05.33–03.06.34   50 titles, used by HW in *The Linhay on the Downs* (A20)

21.05.33–23.02.36   50 other titles (plus one also in the above), collected and listed in *The Notebook of a Nature-Lover* (A69)

Sunday Times

29.10.33   obituary of Sir John Fortescue and review of his autobiography

09.02.58   letter: Authors and air war

12.04.59   (Magazine) review: A famous fox: 'Hym' by C.H. Percy

07.06.59   (Magazine) review: Deep in the old country: 'An Hour-Glass on the Run' by Allan Jobson

20.04.61   letter

04.06.61   review: On hearing the last cuckoo: 'A Writer's Journal' by H. Thoreau

16.09.61   review: A tribute to the tommies: 'The Donkeys' by A. Clark

14.01.62–25.10.64   16 titles, collected and listed in *From a Country Hilltop* (A61)

04.03.62   review: Northumbrian bright water: 'Grey Seals' by G. Hickling

?.?.62   Bold marauders 1: Brown owls and carrion crows; 2: Foxy and co. (reprinted in the ST book Encore 1963)

15.12.63   review: All over the place; 'Scholars and Gypsies' by W. Starkie

Time and Tide

1927   The firing gatherer (cited by Girvan in D 1931; LD, VB)

30.05.36   letter: The Flax of Dream

11.07.36   letter: The new Germany

02.05.53   review: Exmoor and birds; 2 books

23.10.54   review: The Squire; 'Sportsmen in a Landscape' by A. Noakes

08.01.55   review: Curragh; 3 books

09.06.56   review: Mother soil; 'From My Experience' by L. Bromfield

18.08.56   review: Country matters; 5 books

03.11.56	review: Firm roots; 'The Land called Me' by Sir J. Russell
17.11.56	review: Partridge and falcon; 2 books
02.11.57	review: The life around us; 2 books
21.12.57	review: Loving observation; 2 books
22.03.58	review: An ordered scheme; 'Earth's Company' by L. Reid
15.11.58	review: Tunnels of silk; 'The World of Spiders' by W. Bristowe
06.12.58	review: Feathered legends; 'The Folklore of Birds' by E. Armstrong
21.03.59	review: The rusty track of Ypres; 'In Flanders Fields' by L. Wolff
19.09.59	review: Melancholy bait; 'Hook, Line and Spinner' by C. Gammon
24.10.59	review: The year of the great divide; '1914' by J. Cameron

Times

24.12.34	obituary of V.M. Yeates
30.12.37	letter: Norfolk coast scenery
15.05.59	(TLS) letter re 'To Keep Faith' by Mrs Middleton Murry
19 08.59	letter: From reed to fish
25.03.66	letter: The Forsytes (HWSJ 32)
04.04.66	letter: The Forsytes (HWSJ 32)
03.11.66	(TLS) letter: Time for reflection; re 'A Solitary War'
07.03.67	letter: Birds of property
24.04.67	letter: Book piracy
18.06.67	letter: No grasshoppers (HWSJ 6)
22.11.67	letter: Mr Fred Majdalany
06.04.68	(Saturday Review) review: The compleat otter; 'Otters' by C.J. Harris
18.07.68	letter re BBC language
07.12.68	letter: Ordeal by owl
26.06.69	(TLS) letter re 'The Gale of the World'
17.08.70	(TLS) letter re 'Collected Nature Stories'
13.08.71	letter: Old contemptibles
?	letter: Snow on their boots; dated 13 June, North Devon

Tit-Bits
01.02.41   Two girls saved this farm

Townsman (continued as The Scythe)
Summer 1943   Farming and finance

T.P's and Cassell's Weekly
14.06.24   The falcon's fighting tactics
21.06.24   Mysterious swifts
28.06.24   Buzzard's food
16.08.24   The rock dwellers
23.08.24   Rabbits' graveyard
06.12.24   Wisdom of the raven
24.01.25   Borne on the flood
21.02.25   A shag's daily ration
07.03.25   Signs of spring
04.04.25   Three feathered friends
01.05.26   The badger dig (VB)
18.08.28   Advice on writer's kink: a fragment of
                   autobiography

TV Times
?Dec. 1968   (Christmas Extra) Will it be a hard winter?

Twenty-Story Magazine
Jan. 1925   Tarka's last hunt
Feb. 1925   Mewliboy (OS)

War Illustrated (published in parts)
1928   part 31: My return to Ypres

Weekly Dispatch
18.07.20–02.01.21 38 titles, collected and listed in *Contributions to The
                   Weekly Dispatch* (A57)

West-Country Magazine
Spring 1938   The gaping raven of Morte
Summer 1946   A reverie of Exmoor
                   The yellow boots I
Autumn 1946   The yellow boots II

Western Morning News
25.03.53   'Improvers' on nature learn lessons of the wild the hardest way

Wide World Magazine
Dec. 1921   Tiger's Teeth (LS)
Jun. 1949   Tiger's Teeth

Windsor Magazine
Jun. 1933   The backbreaker's bride; illustrated by C.F. Tunnicliffe (PS 1934)
Dec. 1933   The dog that ate his punishment (DH)

Women's Illustrated and Eve's Own
Feb.-Oct. 1946   Quest, in 15 numbered parts, mostly fortnightly; collected in *A Breath of Country Air, part 2* (A64)

Yale Review (USA)
Summer 1941   Devon streams

Yorkshire Evening Post
23.05.44   Bird of mystery (HWSJ 14, BCAA)
30.05.44   The snake bird (HWSJ 14, BCAA)

Zoo
Dec. 1936   The flight of the pale pink pyjamas; illustrated by C.F. Tunnicliffe
Apr. 1937   The fish that came out of the tap
Apr. 1938   No eel for Nog

Periodical not known:
1957   review of Jefferies' 'Field and Farm' edited by S.J.Looker
?   The brick-pit lagoons
20.04.73   letter: Recollections of Regulation 18b
?   letter re a bust of Shelley
?   letter re Passchendaele, from Georgeham
20.03.69   letter: The guinea passes
?   A crown of life (illustrated by G. Wilkinson)
?   A crown of life (the type setting differs from those already listed)

D: SELECTED WORKS ABOUT WILLIAMSON

This section includes all the books and pamphlets that are concerned wholly with Henry Williamson and two articles on collecting his books, but not reviews, essays in books, or general magazine articles, all of which are beyond the scope of this work.

1931. I. Waveney Girvan: Together with authentic bibliographical annotations by Another Hand. *A Bibliography and A Critical Survey of the Works of Henry Williamson.* The Alcuin Press, 1931. Pp.56. 420 copies.

A description of Williamson's books up to *The Wild Red Deer of Exmoor* (Al5) with a critical Introduction. 'Annotations by Another Hand' refers to notes provided by Williamson that are included in the text but not identified.

1932. Herbert Faulkner West. *The Dreamer of Devon: An Essay on Henry Williamson.* The Ulysses Press Ltd. 1932. Pp.ii + 38. Frontispiece (photograph of HW). 250 copies.

Written with Williamson's assistance by an American literary academic (later bookseller) following a visit to Shallowford in 1932.

1979. Ted Hughes. *Henry Williamson. A Tribute by Ted Hughes* given at the Service of Thanksgiving at the Royal Parish Church of St Martin-in-the-Fields, 1 December 1977. Rainbow Press, 1979. Pp.20. Frontispiece (portrait of HW by Bill Thomson). Wrappers. 200 copies numbered and signed by Hughes.

1980a. A Symposium. *Henry Williamson, the Man, the Writings.* Tabb House, 1980. ISBN 0 907018 00 9. Pp.xviii + 166. Frontispiece (portrait of HW by Rose Duncan) and 4 plates (photographs) .

Foreword by Brocard Sewell; Introduction by Ronald Duncan; essays by Ruth Tomalin, Kerstin Hegarty, Alexandra Burgess, Diana Mosley, Brocard Sewell, Sylvia Bruce, Hugh Cecil, E.W. Martin, David Hoyle, Roger Mortimore, Oswald Jones; two articles by HW from the *Aylesford Review* 1957–8 and *Antigonish Review* 1970, and the Memorial Address by Ted Hughes (as 1979 above).

1980b. *The Henry Williamson Society Journal.* Number 1 (July 1980) - number 39 (September 2003) and continuing, with a separate cumulative Index (64 pp.) to Issues no.1–31. Illustrated with photographs, facsimiles and drawings. ISSN C 144 9338.

Published by The Henry Williamson Society, initially twice a year as an A5 booklet (except for no.16, the 'Tarka Diamond Jubilee Issue', which was A4 in paper wrappers) and then annually in magazine format from September 1995 (no.31). An essential source for much original material by and about HW.

1981. *Antiquarian Book Monthly Review,* Vol. VIII, Number 3, March 1981. 'Collecting Henry Williamson' by J.R. Gretton (pp.84–9), illustrated. Also in Essays in Book-Collecting, Dereham Books, 1985.

1982. Daniel Farson. *Henry: An Appreciation.* Michael Joseph, 1982. ISBN 0 7181 2122 8. Pp.x + 246. 6 plates (mostly photographs). Reprinted as *Henry Williamson: A Portrait* by Robinson Publishing, 1986, in paperback. ISBN 0 948164 27 1.

A personal memoir by the son of Negley Farson, who was the victim of Williamson's pen as 'Osgood Nilsson' in *The Gale of the World.*

1983. Trevor Beer. *Tarka Country.* Badger Books, 1983. ISBN 0 946 290 059. Pp.80. Illustrations (photographs, line drawings and map). Card covers.

A detailed account of the locations mentioned in *Tarka,* with notes on wildlife and the local Hunts.

1986a. John Middleton Murry. *The Novels of Henry Williamson.* With an Introduction by J.W. Blench. The Henry Williamson Society, 1986. ISBN 0 950 8652 0 6. Pp.80. Card covers.

A reprint of the essay in Murry's *Katherine Mansfield and other Literary Studies,* Constable, 1959.

1986b. Sue Caron. *A Glimpse of the Ancient Sunlight.* The Aylesford Press, 1986. Pp.iv + 44. Frontispiece and one plate (photographs). 'Signed edition' in boards: ISBN 1 869955 01 3; 60 copies, signed by the author and Brocard Sewell, numbered or inscribed 'out of series'. 'Standard edition' in card covers: ISBN 1 869955 00 5; 400 copies.

Caron's account of her relationship with HW, reprinted from *A Screw Loose,* B & T Publishers, 1977; sanctified by a Foreword by Brocard Sewell.

1987. P.A.C.L. *HW's Georgeham: A Beginner's Guide.* 1987. Privately printed. Pp.28. Card covers.

An anonymous booklet about Georgeham characters, real or imagined, in HW's books, with a hand-drawn map of 'Ham'.

1990. Lois Lamplugh. *A Shadowed Man: Henry Williamson 1895–1977.* Wellspring, 1990. Pp.vi + 202. Frontispiece and 6 plates (photographs), in card covers. Second edition, revised, The Exmoor Press, 1991, in boards; ISBN 0 900131 70 5.

A literary biography by one who grew up in Georgeham during the Williamson era.

1992. Melvyn David Higginbottom. *Intellectuals and British Fascism: A Study of Henry Williamson.* Janus Publishing Company, 1992. ISBN 1 85756 085 X. Pp.viii + 88. 2 plates (photographs). Card covers.

An examination of HW's links with the contemporary fascist movement, with Notes and a Bibliography of relevant sources.

1995. Anne Williamson. *Henry Williamson; Tarka and the Last Romantic.* Alan Sutton Publishing Limited, 1995. ISBN 0 7509 0639 1. Pp.xvi + 368. Illustrations. Reprinted, with corrections, 1995. Paperback edition, with corrections and additions, 1997.

A comprehensive life of HW by his daughter-in-law, based on archival material, with over 200 illustrations (photographs and facsimiles of mss), a genealogical table, Notes and a Bibliography of HW's major works.

1996. *Book and Magazine Collector.* No.144, March 1996. 'Henry Williamson' by Barbara Richardson pp.4–16, with a bibliographical list. See also previous articles: 'Henry Williamson, Author of Tarka the Otter' by Geoffrey Brown in No.31, October 1986; and 'The Nonfiction Books of Henry Williamson' by Helen Macleod in No.70, January 1990.

1998. Anne Williamson. *A Patriot's Progress: Henry Williamson and the First World War.* Sutton Publishing, 1998. ISBN 0 7509 1339 8. Pp.xvi + 208. 16 plates.

A detailed reconstruction of HW's wartime experiences using material from the archives and his published writings, with over 30 illustrations (photographs and facsimiles), maps of the Western Front, Notes, and a Bibliography of sources; (should not be confused with A13).

INDEX

Names of illustrators, editors and other contributors to Williamson's work:

Finch, Robert	TA 1990
Fleming, Ian	DB 1952, GV 1966, CNS 1976a
Forbes, David Carl	TA 1973b, 1978a
Fordham, David	HWAS 1978
Fortescue, Sir John	TA 1927a
Graham, Eleanor	TA 1949b
Gill, George G.	B 1952a
Girvan, Waveney	D 1931
Gregory, John	CWD 1969, 1983, DW 1987, FCH 1988, BCAA 1990, BCAB 1991, SDD 1992, PEP 1993, TTL 1994, GFP 1995, NNL 1996, WW 2000, ISN 2001, HE 2003
Gretton, J.R.	D 1981
Haggard, Lilias Rider	B 1943a
Harman, Richard	B 1943b, B 1946b, B 1949
Hegarty, Kerstin	B 1980a
Heygate, John	B 1931a
Higginbottom, Melvyn David	D 1992
Hoyle, David	B 1980a
Hughes, Ted	D 1979, D 1980a
Inglis, Brian	B 1961a
Jefferies, Richard	B 1934a, B1934b, B 1935, B 1937a, B 1937c, B 1946a, B 1966c
Jones, Oswald	TA 1965c, SC 1972a, CNS 1970, D 1980a
Kermode, William	PP 1930a, TA 1929a
Kershaw, Alister	B 1965
Lamplugh, Lois	D 1990
Large, Annabel	TA 1995a
Lawrence, A.W.	B 1937b
Lawson, John	COS 1978
'Lendon'	BY 1921
Lilly, Ken	SC 1972a
Loates, Michael	SA 1987, GFP 1995, NNL 1996, ISN 2001
Lynne, James Broom	DL 1951, DB 1952. TME 1953, YPM 1953, HDL 1954, FMC 1955 GV 1957,

LOL 1958, IM 1961, IWN 1962,
PD 1963,PG 1965, SW 1966, LBS 1967,
GOW 1969, CNS 1970

Manhood, H.A.	B 1931b
Martin E.W.	D 1980a
McBride, Simon	TA 1985a
Mitchinson, K.W.	PP 1999
Morse, C.J.	DD 1922, DFW 1924a
Mortimore, Roger	D 1980a
Mosley, Diana	D 1980a
Murry, John Middleton	D 1986a
'P.A.C.L.'	D 1987
Pledger, Maurice	PB 1984
Pope, Allen Jr.	GWC 1938
Pope, T. Michael	B 1930a
Raquepaw, Christine	TA 1990
Reynolds, Warwick	PS 1923, Pan Fiction Mag 1922
Rhys, Keidrych	B 1952b
'Richards'	DL 1962
Richardson, Barbara	D 1996
Riley, Terry	TA 1986b
Robinson, Paul	TA 1985b
Robson, Walter	B 1960c
Russell, Sir E. John	B 1941
Sainsbury, Hester	TA 1927c
Schwabe, Randolph	WFP 1929a
Sewell, Fr Brocard	ISN 2001, B 1960a, D 1980a
Southwold, Stephen	B 1928, 1930d
Stanley, Colin	SNO 1988
'Stein'	HWAS 1960a
Temple, Frederic-Jacques	B 1965
Thompson, Francis	B 1966b, 1967
Tomalin, Ruth	D 1980a
Trimby, Elizabeth	SA 1972
Tunnicliffe, Charles F.	LS 1933, 1946, PS 1934, OS 1933,